# TANK

# TANK

### THE DEFINITIVE
### VISUAL HISTORY OF
### ARMORED VEHICLES

# Penguin Random House

**DORLING KINDERSLEY**
**Project Art Editor** Katie Cavanagh
**Project Editor** Hugo Wilkinson
**Senior Designer** Stephen Bere
**Senior Editor** Andrew Szudek
**US Editors** Shannon Beatty, Jane Perlmutter
**Design Assistance** Steve Crozier, Jane Ewart, Renata Latipova
**Editorial Assistance** Sam Kennedy, Kate Taylor, Zoe Rutland
**Photographer** Gary Ombler
**Illustrator** Phil Gamble
**Picture Research** Sarah Smithies, Nic Dean
**DK Picture Library** Laura Evans, Romaine Werblow
**Jacket Designer** Mark Cavanagh
**Jacket Editor** Claire Gell
**Jacket Design Development Manager** Sophia MTT
**Producer, Pre-production** Nadine King
**Production Controller** Jude Crozier
**Managing Editor** Gareth Jones
**Managing Art Editor** Lee Griffiths
**Art Director** Karen Self
**Publisher** Liz Wheeler
**Publishing Director** Jonathan Metcalf

**DK INDIA**
**Project Editor** Antara Moitra
**Project Art Editor** Vikas Chauhan
**Editor** Nishtha Kapil
**Art Editors** Priyansha Tuli, Meenal Goel
**Assistant Art Editors** Rohit Bhardwaj, Devika Khosla
**DTP Designers** Vijay Kandwal, Bimlesh Tiwary
**Senior DTP Designers** Sachin Singh, Harish Aggarwal
**Jacket Designer** Suhita Dharamjit
**Jackets Editorial Coordinator** Priyanka Sharma
**Managing Jackets Editor** Saloni Singh
**Pre-production Manager** Balwant Singh
**Production Manager** Pankaj Sharma
**Senior Managing Editor** Rohan Sinha
**Senior Managing Art Editor** Arunesh Talapatra

**THE TANK MUSEUM, BOVINGTON, UK**
**Author and Consultant** David Willey, Curator
**Main Contributor** Ian Hudson, Research Assistant
**Photographer** Matt Sampson

## Smithsonian

**Smithsonian Curator** Barton C. Hacker, Curator, Division of Armed Forces History, Ph.D., M.A., B.A

### Smithsonian Enterprises

**Product Development Manager Licensing Manager** Kealy E. Gordon
**Vice President, Education and Consumer Products** Ellen Nanney, Brigid Ferraro
**Senior Vice President, Education and Consumer Products** Carol LeBlanc
**President** Chris Liedel

Established in 1846, the Smithsonian is the world's largest museum and research complex, dedicated to public education, national service, and scholarship in the arts, sciences, and history. It includes 19 museums and galleries and the National Zoological Park. The total number of artifacts, works of art, and specimens in the Smithsonian's collection is estimated at 156 million.

First American Edition, 2017
Published in the United States by DK Publishing
1745 Broadway, 20th Floor, New York, NY 10019

## For the curious
### www.dk.com

MIX
Paper | Supporting responsible forestry
FSC™ C018179

This book was made with Forest Stewardship Council™ certified paper - one small step in DK's commitment to a sustainable future. **For more information go to www.dk.com/our-green-pledge**

# Contents

# THE FIRST TANKS: TO 1918

The tank had a variety of historical forerunners, which led to the first operational models. These were followed by the amazing variety of machines designed for different functions that were developed, or were starting to be manufactured, by the end of World War I.

## BETWEEN THE WARS: 1918-1939

The interwar period was an age characterized by retrenchment and experiment; tanks were developed in a number of different countries, and exercises were carried out on how best they might be used in the world's newly mechanized armies. One of the outcomes of this was the consolidation of modern tank design.

## WORLD WAR II : 1939-1945

World War II was the catalyst for the tank to show its full potential on a huge scale. Armored vehicles were built in their tens of thousands, becoming not only key weapons in land campaigns all around the globe, but also symbols of nations' military prowess.

# THE COLD WAR: 1945–1991

The rival power blocks of East and West built huge fleets of main battle tanks supported by a range of other armored vehicles, but the Cold War never became "hot," and only some of the tanks saw service in smaller conflicts.

## POST-COLD WAR: AFTER 1991

As world politics adjusted to the end of the Cold War, a new generation of lighter vehicles were designed for asymmetric and counterinsurgency warfare. However, Cold War tank fleets were also given a new lease of life with upgrades, and some new tank designs were built, as conflicts around an unstable world showed the continuing utility of the tank.

## REFERENCE

Based on the three key elements of mobility, firepower, and protection, the tank changed the way land wars were fought.

# Foreword

The stalemate of trench warfare in World War I inspired the British invention of the tank. Self-propelled gun-carrying machines that were wrapped in armor and able to traverse broken ground promised to break the static trench deadlock and restore battlefield mobility. This did not quite happen; tanks played an important but not decisive role in the Allied victory. Nonetheless, their future remained bright.

What exactly their role in future war would be, however, became a subject of interwar controversy. At issue was whether tanks would remain the infantry support weapons they had been in the war, or whether they would become the core of new mobile formations capable of decisive victory. Western democracies opted for a mix of the two, while authoritarian regimes in Italy, Germany, and Russia built large numbers of tanks and created independent armored forces.

The opening campaigns of World War II seemed to settle the issue in favor of armored decisiveness. Main battle tanks became bigger and better, their armor thickening and their guns growing ever more powerful; in armored formations they became the arbiters of battle, as well as symbols of military might for civilians and military alike.

Even as tanks grew more formidable during the later 20th century, however, their battlefield supremacy has been challenged by a flood of new, relatively cheap and effective antitank weapons. The changing

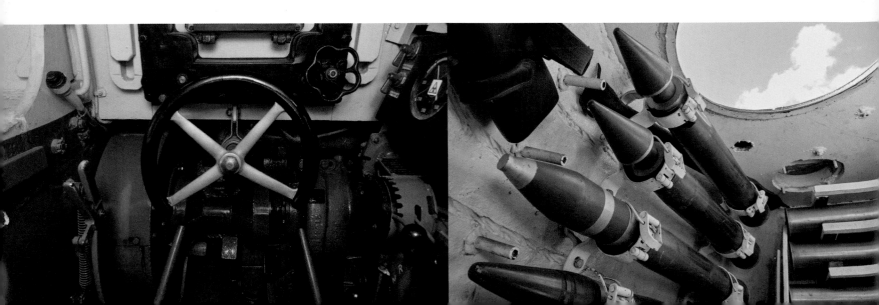

character of war has further undermined tank primacy. As the clash of mass armies in so-called conventional warfare has given way to smaller scale, more irregular warfare, tanks have lost their central role.

Tank formations nonetheless persist as important components of national armed forces everywhere. Further improvements in armor, weaponry, electronics, and general capabilities have continued, with remotely controlled unmanned vehicles high on many nations' wish lists. A century after the tank's 1916 battlefield debut, it remains a potent symbol of military power.

*Barton C Hacker*

BARTON C. HACKER
CURATOR, SMITHSONIAN DIVISION OF ARMED FORCES HISTORY,
PH.D., M.A., B.A

To 1918
# THE FIRST TANKS

Wir schlagen sie — und zeichnen Kriegsanleihe!

# THE FIRST TANKS

**At the beginning of the 20th century** the internal combustion engine and the tracked tractor made the prospect of mobile, armored firepower on the battlefield realistic for the first time. World War I provided the impetus.

The earliest successful tank development took place in Britain. Fosters was contracted to build the first land ship, nicknamed "Little Willie," in July 1915, although a superior design called "Mother" was selected by the Army in February 1916.

The first tank attack took place on September 15, 1916, at Flers-Courcelette. Of the 49 tanks assigned, only nine reached the German lines, but the new weapon created a sensation in Britain. Field Marshal Haig immediately ordered 1,000 more, and work began on improvements.

The first French tanks saw combat in April 1917. They were not as capable at crossing trenches as British vehicles, but they were well armed. The most common French tank, the Renault FT (see pp.24–27), was first used in May 1918. It was the first tank to have a top-mounted turret capable of turning a full 360 degrees. 3,177 were ordered during the war.

The biggest shortcoming of these tanks was their poor reliability. Mechanical breakdowns put more out of action than enemy fire ever did, and availability dropped dramatically over multiple-day attacks. Of the 580 British tanks used at Amiens on August 8, 1918, only 145 were available the next day. Nonetheless, tanks played a greater and greater role as the war continued. During the Allied Hundred Days Offensive of August–November 1918, tanks were a vital part of the combined arms warfare that led to victory.

△ **French tanks on parade**
A battalion of Renault FT-17s leads the victory parade on Bastille Day in Paris, 1919, to celebrate the end of World War I.

> "We heard strange **throbbing** noises, and **lumbering slowly** towards us came three huge **mechanical monsters** such as we had **never seen** before."

BERT CHANEY, BRITISH ARMY SOLDIER, 1916

◁ **A German propaganda poster of World War I announces:** "We're beating them—and investing in War Bonds!"

## Key events

▷ **1902** The Simms Motor War Car, complete with armored hull, pom-pom, and machine guns, is demonstrated.

▷ **1906** Charron, Giradot, et Voigt car with Guye turret and Hotchkiss machine gun is tested in France.

▷ **1912** Two Italian armored cars are used in Libya during the Italo-Turkish War—the first to see action.

▷ **August 1914** The French Minister of War orders 136 armored cars. The first enters service a month later.

▷ **February 1915** The British Admiralty Landships Committee is formed.

▷ **July 1915** "Little Willie" is ordered from Fosters. It moves for the first time on September 9th, just 5 weeks later.

▷ **January 1916** "Mother" is completed, just three months after it was designed.

▷ **February 1916** Mark I tanks are ordered by the British Ministry of Munitions; Schneider CA-1s are ordered by the French Ministry of War.

▷ **September 15, 1916** At the Battle of Flers-Courcelette, tanks first see action.

△ **The Battle of Cambrai**
British Mark IV tanks were the first to penetrate German lines at Cambrai, in 1917. Here, members of the Royal Navy maneuver a tank over a trench.

▷ **April 24, 1918** The first tank-on-tank battle takes place at Villers-Bretonneux, between a German A7V and British Mark IVs.

# Earliest Experiments

For centuries soldiers have wished for machines that could cross a battlefield while remaining impervious to enemy fire. The tank that was developed in the early 20th century was a combination of armor protection, internal combustion engine, and tracks. Attempts to bring all of these to the battlefield were not new. However, what changed in 1915 and 1916 was the way they were combined. Little Willie proved this concept could work, whereas Mother demonstrated the most suitable design.

**Wheels** used for steering

**Huge** front wheels

**Hull**

### △ Hornsby Tractor

| | |
|---|---|
| **Date** 1909 | **Country** UK |
| **Weight** 9.5 tons (8.6 tonnes) | |
| **Engine** 6-cylinder gasoline, 105 hp | |
| **Main armament** None | |

Originally powered by a 60 hp kerosene engine, this was the first tracked vehicle to be used by the British Army. The tracks had replaceable wooden blocks to reduce wear on the metal components. Although the Hornsby was used only for towing artillery, the experience of operating tracked vehicles inspired early work on tanks.

### △ Tsar Tank

| | |
|---|---|
| **Date** 1914 | **Country** Russia |
| **Weight** 44.8 tons (40.6 tonnes) | |
| **Engine** 2 x Sunbeam gasoline, 250 hp each | |
| **Main armament** Unknown | |

The wheels on this vehicle were intended to be large enough to crush battlefield obstacles and prevent the tank from getting bogged down. However, during testing in 1915 the smaller back wheel got stuck in the soft ground. The tank was abandoned at the site and scrapped in 1923.

### ◁ Pedrail Machine

| | |
|---|---|
| **Date** 1915 | **Country** UK |
| **Weight** 28 tons (25.4 tonnes) | |
| **Engine** 2 x Rolls-Royce gasoline, 46 hp each | |
| **Main armament** None | |

Pedrail wheels were an early form of all-terrain track. During 1915, the British produced several designs that made use of these wheels, in the hope they would provide the answer to conditions on the Western Front. However, they were soon superseded by continuous track systems.

**Riveted** chassis

**Rear** light

### ▷ Little Willie

| | |
|---|---|
| **Date** 1915 | **Country** UK |
| **Weight** 17.9 tons (16.3 tonnes) | |
| **Engine** Daimler gasoline, 105hp | |
| **Main armament** None | |

Little Willie was originally equipped with American Bullock tracks. When these proved unsuccessful, the task of replacing them was given to William Tritton, an agricultural machinery expert. The vehicle's design meant it could not cross the widest trenches, but the engine, wheels, and Tritton's tracks were successful and were retained.

**Continuous** tracks

**Rear** wheels

**Elevated** nose

**Engine** exhaust cover

**Canvas** canopy

### △ Mother

**Date** 1916 **Country** UK

**Weight** 31.4 tons (28.4 tonnes)

**Engine** Daimler gasoline, 105 hp

**Main armament** 2 x QF 6-pounder Hotchkiss L/40 guns

This vehicle first demonstrated the iconic rhomboid design that gave British tanks their mobility. The high nose allowed the tank to cross tall obstacles and pull itself out of trenches if it toppled forward. The track design forced the armament into sponsons. Its lack of suspension meant a rough ride for the eight-man crew.

### ▷ Holt 75 Gun Tractor

**Date** 1918 **Country** USA

**Weight** 11.8 tons (10.7 tonnes)

**Engine** Holt 4-cylinder gasoline, 75 hp

**Main armament** None

The Holt 75 was the Allies' standard heavy artillery tractor, with 1,651 delivered between 1915 and 1918. The poor ground conditions were not confined to the battlefield, meaning that tracked vehicles such as this were vital for hauling artillery, supply trains, and other essentials.

**Front** wheel used for steering

**Riveted** armor

# Leonardo da Vinci's "tank"

In 1482, artist and inventor Leonardo da Vinci moved from Florence to Milan and bid for the patronage of Milanese nobleman Ludovico Sforza. He drew out some ideas in his sketchbooks, and his "war car" design—seen here alongside another weapon design—is regarded as one of the precursors of the tank.

## KEY ELEMENTS

Da Vinci wrote to Sforza, "I can make armored cars, safe and unassailable, which will enter the closed ranks of the enemy… behind these our infantry will be able to follow quite unharmed." The idea of an armored battle car dates back to antiquity, and Da Vinci drew inspiration from this, combining three elements—firepower (cannons firing from loopholes), protection (wooden and metal walls), and mobility (four men turning large cranks to power the wheels). The design looks surprisingly modern in shape, with angled surfaces to deflect incoming projectiles. However, the technology of the era would not have supported practical construction, and modern recreations of the design have shown that it could only have moved on a very flat surface, something unlikely to have been found on contemporary battlefields.

**Leonardo da Vinci's sketch** of a "war car" was among the early explorations of the idea of a land weapon combining armor, mobility, and firepower.

# Mark IV

More Mark IVs were made than any other British tank during World War I. Although it looked similar to the earlier Mark I, it featured improvements including an armored fuel tank at the rear, and thicker 0.5 in (12 mm) frontal armor to protect against armor-piercing bullets. The sponsons housing the guns on each side could be pushed inside the tank to allow transportation by train, unlike those on the Mark I, which had to be removed.

**THE MARK IV** made an impact at the Battle of Cambrai in November 1917, the first effective massed tank attack. Over 400 tanks were moved at night by rail to the quiet front line at Cambrai, and launched an assault, cutting deep into the German Hindenburg line.

**REAR VIEW**

The tank was made in "male" and "female" versions: males carried two 6-pounder guns and three machine guns, while females had five machine guns. Female tanks were considered more useful, since machine-gun fire was effective in pinning the enemy while friendly troops advanced; male tanks also had to stop to allow the 6-pounder gunner to aim. After April 1918, "hermaphrodites" with one male and one female sponson were built.

| SPECIFICATIONS | |
|---|---|
| **Name** | Tank, Mark IV |
| **Date** | 1917 |
| **Origin** | UK |
| **Production** | Approx 1,220 |
| **Engine** | Daimler/Knight straight six, 105 hp |
| **Weight** | 31.4 tons (28.4 tonnes) |
| **Armament (male)** | 2 x 6-pounder QF guns; 3 x .303 Lewis machine guns |
| **Armament (female)** | 5 x .303 Lewis machine guns |
| **Crew** | 8 |
| **Armor thickness** | 0.5 in (12 mm) |

Loader — Gunner — Commander
Gearsman
Gearsman
Loader — Gunner — Driver

**Training vehicle**
After World War I, this Mark IV male tank was given to Whale Island, a Royal Navy establishment in Portsmouth, UK. Many gunners for tanks were trained here, since naval personnel were highly experienced at firing weapons from moving platforms.

**Commander** and driver's cab

**Lewis gun**
The Mark IV was equipped with a Lewis machine gun in the front ball mount, and one in each sponson. The Lewis was selected partly for its compact magazine.

**Tactical** number

**THREE-QUARTER VIEW**

**6-pounder** gun in sponson

## 2324

**Vehicle number**
Each tank was given a unique four-digit number—usually painted on the rear side—that stayed with the vehicle throughout its life.

## EXTERIOR

The Mark IV clearly shows the riveted construction of the early tanks—the armor plates were hot-riveted or bolted to a metal framework. The construction meant there were numerous small gaps that allowed bullet "splash" to enter. Crews were issued with masks to protect their faces from hot metal splinters.

**1.** Tactical number  **2.** Driver's vision port (closed)
**3.** Track tensioner  **4.** Male sponson with 6-pounder gun  **5.** Sponson ball machine gun mount (without gun)
**6.** Location of final drive  **7.** Track plates  **8.** Ventilation louvers  **9.** Rear escape hatch  **10.** Towing eye

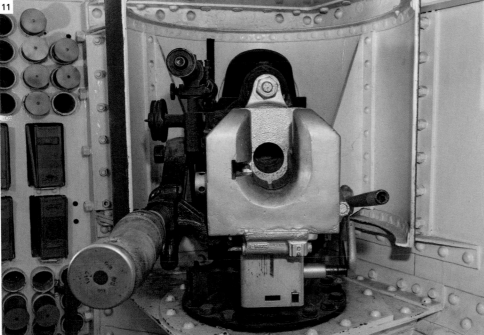

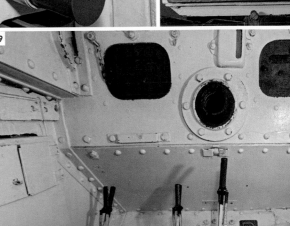

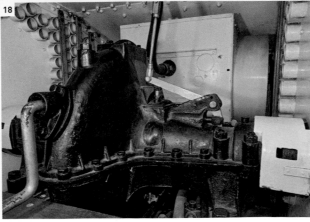

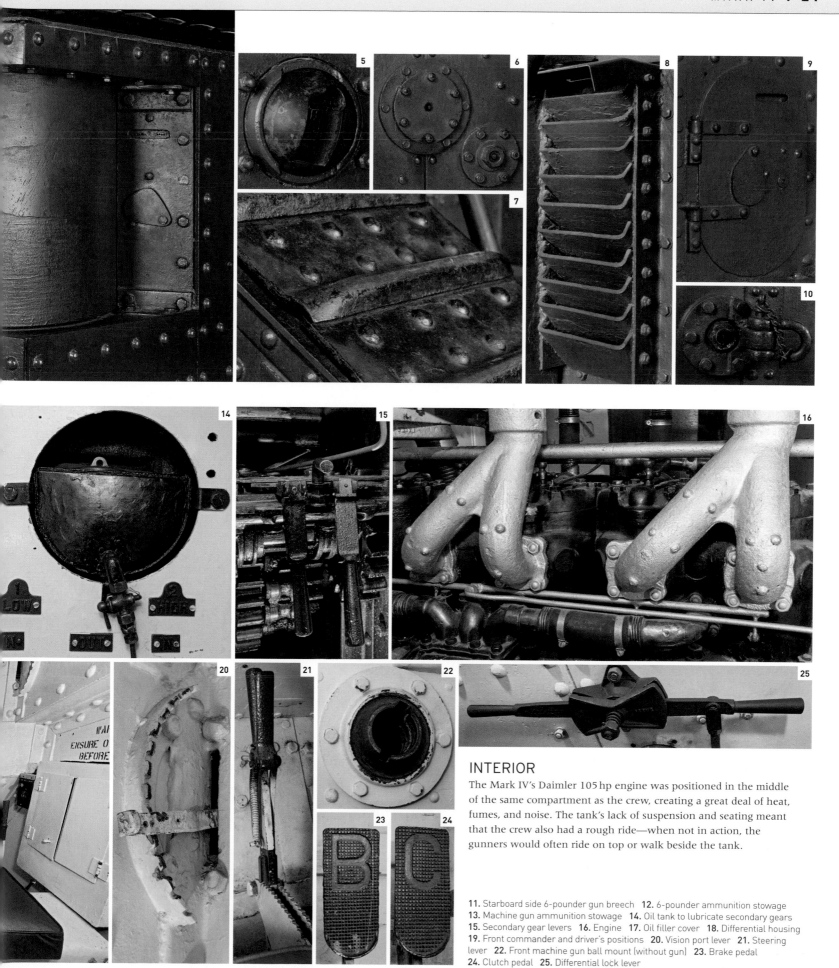

## INTERIOR

The Mark IV's Daimler 105 hp engine was positioned in the middle of the same compartment as the crew, creating a great deal of heat, fumes, and noise. The tank's lack of suspension and seating meant that the crew also had a rough ride—when not in action, the gunners would often ride on top or walk beside the tank.

11. Starboard side 6-pounder gun breech   12. 6-pounder ammunition stowage
13. Machine gun ammunition stowage   14. Oil tank to lubricate secondary gears
15. Secondary gear levers   16. Engine   17. Oil filler cover   18. Differential housing
19. Front commander and driver's positions   20. Vision port lever   21. Steering
lever   22. Front machine gun ball mount (without gun)   23. Brake pedal
24. Clutch pedal   25. Differential lock lever

# Tanks of World War I

Tanks were first used on September 15, 1916. Between then and the Armistice of November 11, 1918, Britain, France, and Germany all developed tanks. Britain's heavy tanks, which had tracks around their entire bodies, were adapted for crossing trenches in support of infantry, and the faster Medium Whippet was developed to support cavalry in more open country. As well as a small number of heavier vehicles, the French used masses of light FT tanks in 1918. Germany built only a small number of A7Vs, relying more on captured British Mark IVs instead.

### △ Mark I

**Date** 1916 **Country** UK

**Weight** 31.4 tons (28.4 tonnes)

**Engine** Daimler gasoline, 105 hp

**Main armament** 2 x QF 6-pounder Hotchkiss L/40 guns

The Mark I was made of armor plate up to 0.5in (12mm) thick. Of the 150 built, half were Male (shown here) and half Female—the latter replacing each of the Male's 6-pounder guns with two .303 Vickers machine guns. The tank had a crew of eight, including four for driving and steering.

### ▷ Schneider CA-1

**Date** 1917 **Country** France

**Weight** 14.9 tons (13.5 tonnes)

**Engine** Schneider 4-cylinder gasoline, 60 hp

**Main armament** 75 mm Schneider Blockhaus gun

The first French tank to see service, the six-man Schneider was based on the Holt tractor. Its 75 mm gun was offset to the right, limiting its field of fire. Four hundred were built, but took heavy losses when they first saw action on April 14, 1917. They struggled to cross trenches, but fared better in the advances of 1918.

**"Sabot"** for crushing barbed wire

**Metal** track links

**Riveted** hull armor

**75 mm** Mle 1897 main gun

**Overhang** for crushing obstacles

### ◁ St. Chamond

**Date** 1917 **Country** France

**Weight** 25.3 tons (23 tonnes)

**Engine** Panhard Levassor 4-cylinder gasoline, 90 hp

**Main armament** 75 mm Mle 1897 gun

The eight-man St. Chamond first saw combat in May 1917. Like the Schneider, it was based on the Holt tractor and had an overhang to crush obstacles—but this also made it prone to getting stuck in trenches. Four hundred were built, and proved useful as assault guns in the open warfare of 1918.

### ▽ Mark IV

**Date** 1917 **Country** UK

**Weight** 31.4 tons (28.4 tonnes)

**Engine** Daimler gasoline, 105 hp

**Main armament** 2 x QF 6-pounder 6 cwt Hotchkiss L/23 guns

The Mark IV was an improvement on Britain's earlier tanks. It was better armored and its guns and sponsons were modified to improve mobility. Also, its gasoline tanks were larger, armored, and were vacuum- rather than gravity-fed. Over 1,200 were built, seeing action from June 1917 until the end of the war.

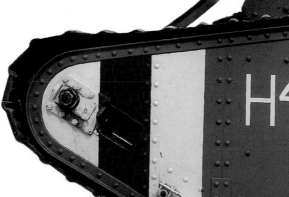

## ▷ A7V Sturmpanzerwagen

**Date** 1918 **Country** Germany

**Weight** 33.6 tons (30.5 tonnes)

**Engine** 2 x Daimler gasoline, 100 hp each

**Main armament** 5.7 cm Maxim-Nordenfelt gun

Germany built just 20 A7Vs, based on the Holt tractor. It had a crew of 18, which operated six machine guns and a 57mm gun. The driver sat at the top and could drive in either direction. It entered service in March 1918, but saw less action than Germany's captured British tanks.

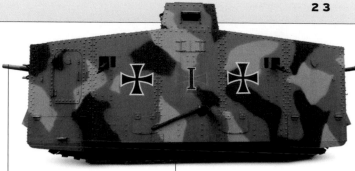

**5.7 cm** Maxim-Nordenfelt gun

**Two** four-cylinder Daimler engines

**Exhaust pipe** and silencer

**Engine compartment** ventilation louver

**Two** Tylor gasoline engines

**White/Red/White** Allied recognition mark

## ◁ Medium Mark A Whippet

**Date** 1918 **Country** UK

**Weight** 15.7 tons (14.2 tonnes)

**Engine** 2 x Tylor gasoline, 45 hp each

**Main armament** 3 x .303 Hotchkiss Mark I machine guns

Intended as a fast tank, the three-man Whippet could reach 8 mph (13 km/h). Each track had its own engine, and steering was controlled by adjusting the two throttles. Whippets were first used in March 1918 and played a significant role in the open warfare of the final months of the war.

**37 mm** main gun

## ▷ Renault FT-17

**Date** 1918 **Country** France

**Weight** 7.2 tons (6.5 tonnes)

**Engine** Renault 4-cylinder gasoline, 35 hp

**Main armament** 37 mm Puteaux SA 18 L/21 gun

The FT was the first tank to have the now-standard layout of engine at the rear, crew at the front, and a fully rotating turret. Armed with either a Hotchkiss machine gun or a 37 mm cannon, it played a major role in the French victories of 1918. It was widely exported, and many were still in use in 1940. Over 3,000 were built.

**Tail** for managing trench crossings

**Rear** drive sprocket

**Vertical** spring suspension

**Length** sufficient for crossing German trenches

**Metal** tracks

## ◁ Mark V

**Date** 1918 **Country** UK

**Weight** 32.5 tons (29.5 tonnes)

**Engine** Ricardo gasoline, 150 hp

**Main armament** 2 x QF 6-pounder 6 cwt Hotchkiss L/23 guns

The Mark Vs were similar in armament and speed to their predecessors, but they had a new epicyclic gearbox that enabled them to be driven by one man. They played a key role in the Allied victory in 1918, and saw postwar service in Ireland, Germany, and Russia. Four hundred were produced.

**Road wheels** contained in hull

# Renault FT-17

The Renault light tank was developed when General Estienne, father of the French tank force in World War I, asked Louis Renault to design a light two-man tank that could support infantry in mass attacks. Renault at first declined since he thought his company lacked experience in such matters, but when asked again in the summer of 1916, he changed his mind and took on the project.

THE RENAULT was essentially a tapered metal box with an engine at the rear and a crew (commander and driver) at the front. It had the very first fully rotating turret, which also had a small dome that could be opened and tilted to ventilate the turret. The armor-plated hull acted as its chassis, and the Renault 35hp engine and gearbox provided five gears (four forward and one reverse). The tank could reach speeds of just under 5mph (8km/h) on the road and had a range of 34km (22 miles). Its small size and weight of just over 7 tons (6 tonnes) meant the tank was easily transportable by truck.

**REAR VIEW**

The tank first saw action in May 1918, and two months later 408 broke through the German front at Soissons, although the French cavalry failed to capitalize on their success. It then evolved into a number of variants, and saw service with the US Army in World War I before being sold to many other nations after the war. France still had ten battalions of Renaults in service in September 1939.

| SPECIFICATIONS | |
| --- | --- |
| **Name** | Renault FT-17 |
| **Date** | 1917 |
| **Origin** | France |
| **Production** | 3,950 |
| **Engine** | Renault 4-cylinder gasoline, 35 hp |
| **Weight** | 7.2 tons (6.5 tonnes) |
| **Main armament** | 37 mm Puteaux SA 18 (shown here) or 8 mm Hotchkiss Mle 1914 |
| **Secondary armament** | None |
| **Crew** | 2 |
| **Armor thickness** | 0.3–0.6 in (8–16 mm) |

Engine

Commander

Driver

**37 mm** Puteaux gun

**Engine** access covers

**Driver's** hatch

**Metal** tracks

**THREE-QUARTER VIEW**

**Leaf spring** fitted to side girder

66724

**The first modern tank**
With its engine in the rear and crew positioned in the front beneath a fully-rotating turret containing the tank's main weapon, the FT-17's configuration was highly influential. It remains the standard layout for tanks today.

**First Company insignia**
The number 1 in the flaming circle indicates that this tank was in the first Company of its unit.

**Ace of spades**
The ace of spades insignia means that this tank belonged to the first Section of its Company—which in this case was the first Company of its unit.

## EXTERIOR

The Renault improved many of the shortcomings of the first French tanks that went into combat. The large front wheel with wooden inserts enabled it to climb in and out of shell holes, and the detachable "tail" extended its trench-crossing ability. Also, the turret had a small dome that served as a cupola and could be opened for ventilation.

**1.** Serial number **2.** Idler wheel **3.** Spring to tension top roller rail **4 .** Driver's hatch **5.** Paired suspension wheels **6.** 37 mm Puteaux gun and recuperator **7.** Engine cover lock **8.** Exhaust silencer **9.** Rear drive sprocket and top roller rail support **10.** Drive sprocket **11.** Front towing eye **12.** Starting handle **13.** Detachable rear tail

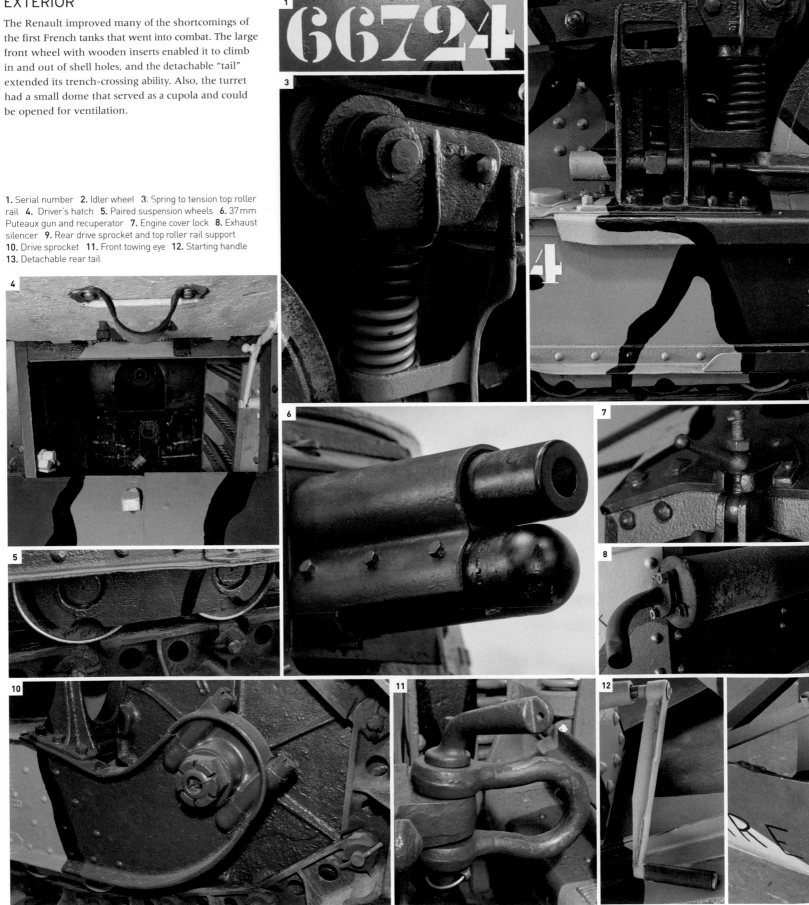

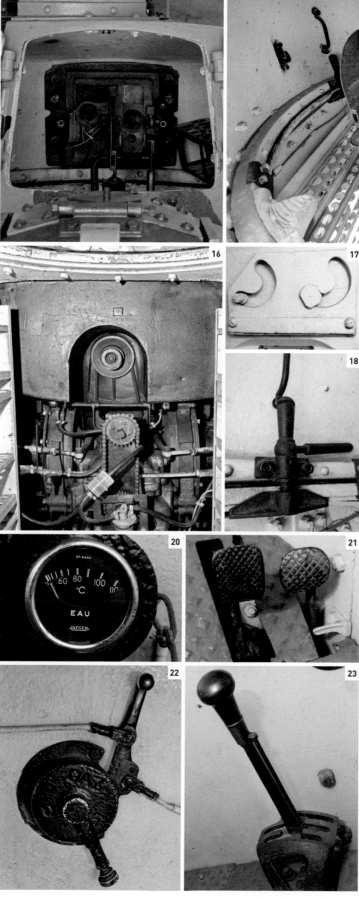

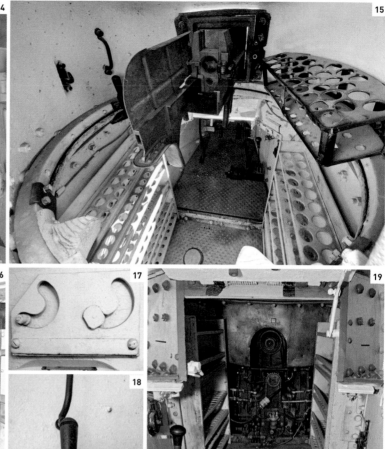

## INTERIOR

As a light tank, the FT-17 had to keep weight down, and it did so partly by being extremely compact. This meant that the crew had to endure unusually cramped conditions; the commander sat on a canvas sling or folding seat, and the driver made do with a floor cushion. The entire crew was surrounded by ammunition stowage and had very poor vision when the hatches were closed; the view ports were simply slits in the armor. The tank's armor was also minimized, being 0.6in (16mm) on the front, but only 0.3in (8mm) on the sides.

**14.** Commander's hatch  **15.** Turret interior, showing ammunition stowage racks  **16.** Engine compartment  **17.** Vision ports  **18.** Turret traverse lock  **19.** Driver's position  **20.** Engine temperature guage  **21.** Engine control pedals  **22.** Carburetor control lever  **23.** Gear shift

Sir William Tritton beside his bridge-carrying tractor

# Great designers
# Tritton and Wilson

After years of stalemate on the Western Front, the Allies finally pierced the German lines in 1917, using an invention that dismayed the enemy—the tank. Designed and constructed in secret, it was the brainchild of two British engineers, William Tritton and Walter Wilson.

WILLIAM TRITTON JOINED the agricultural machinery manufacturers Fosters of Lincoln in 1905 as general manager. He had a background in pump manufacturing and general engineering, and helped Fosters promote its new general purpose agricultural tractor in South America. While at Fosters, he worked with David Roberts in creating a tracked engine to be exported to the Yukon in Canada. Roberts later sold his track patents to the Holt company in the US.

Tritton also promoted the gasoline engine tractor, and just before World War I, both a 40 bhp and a 105 bhp Foster Daimler tractor were marketed. The outbreak of war brought an order for 97 of the huge new tractors to pull naval siege guns. One of the tractors, OHMS No. 44, was adapted to

**Sir William Tritton**
(1875–1946)

**Walter Wilson**
(1874–1957)

carry a 15 ft (4.5 m) bridge, which was slung under its main framework and pushed forward to cross a trench. The experiment was abandoned, but Fosters became known to the authorities for their innovation and speedy vehicles.

In February 1915, Winston Churchill established the Landships Committee to promote mechanical answers to the stalemate on the Western Front. Fosters was approached to start work on one of the early ideas—a big wheel to roll across the fields of barbed wire that protected the German trenches. This project was soon canceled, but in July 1915, following demonstration of a Holt tractor, the Ministry of Munitions placed an order with Fosters for an experimental tracked armored machine. Design work began on August 2, building began on August 11, and the vehicle was first driven on September 8—an extraordinary speed of manufacture by anyone's standards. Only in late August did Tritton hear from the War Office that the machine should be capable of crossing a 5 ft (1.5 m) wide trench and mounting a 4½ ft (1.4 m) parapet, which was beyond its capabilities. As work continued on the No. 1 Lincoln machine (or "Little Willie" as she was later called), Lieutenant Walter Wilson began building a new vehicle with Tritton's assistance. Walter Wilson, a Royal Naval Volunteer Reserve officer, had designed a

**A top-secret design**
Tritton's prototype tank, "Little Willie," was kept under wraps during trials to maintain secrecy. It was the first ever completed tank prototype.

car and a truck before the war. On joining the Royal Naval Air Service team that was working on solutions to trench warfare, he realized that there was a problem with Little Willie's shape. His solution was the new rhomboidal design that is now so familiar—that of the classic World War I tank, complete with tracks looped around its entire body. He also designed the sponsons that housed the tank's guns. On September 26, a wooden model of the tank was approved, and the new prototype, called "Mother," was built in just 99 days.

Wilson was sent to the Metropolitan Carriage and Wagon Company, near Birmingham, to supervise the manufacture of Mark I tanks—125 of which were ordered from Metropolitan and 25 from Fosters, which had a much smaller manufacturing capacity. At Birmingham, Wilson continued designing and was influential in having the Ricardo engine approved for the Mark V tank. This had Wilson's own new gearbox, which enabled the tank to be driven by one man.

Tritton, meanwhile, had started design on a new, faster tank called the Tritton Chaser, which was accepted into service as the Medium Mark A tank, or Whippet. The Chaser had two Tylor engines, one to power each track, and was intended as a

**Mark IV tank at the front**
Canadian troops pose atop a Mark IV tank in 1918. The wooden beam was placed under the vehicle's tracks when it was stuck in mud.

> ## "And **there**, between them, spewing **death**, unearthly monsters."
>
> **2ND LIEUTENANT HERMANN KOHL, 1916**

**World War I posters**
French and Spanish posters praise the might of Tritton and Wilson's invention.

cavalry support weapon. Tritton also created a design for a 100-ton (91-tonne) tank called the Flying Elephant, and designed and built another new tank called the Hornet—6,000 of which were ordered, but only a few of which had been completed by the end of the war. Both Wilson

and Tritton had successful postwar engineering careers and were named by the Royal Commission on Awards to Inventors as the real designers of the first successful tank. It was a weapon that changed the war and the nature of warfare forever.

**Medium Mark C**
Tritton's Medium Mark C tank, or Hornet, was produced at the end of the war—a successful design that was too late to see any action.

**Engineering victory**
Workers assemble a line of Mark IV tanks at Foster's in Lincolnshire, UK, in 1917. An improved version of the Mark I, this was the tank that broke the German lines in 1917.

# The first tank action

The Mark I, seen here in September 1916, was first used at Flers-Courcelette during the Battle of the Somme. Arguments had raged around when to use the first tanks—wait until there were considerable numbers available to make an overwhelming impact, or use what was ready in the pressing circumstances of the time. The British Commander in Chief, Field Marshal Haig, was eager to see some success on the Somme before the winter set in, and he also knew that attacking could relieve the French forces at Verdun. Haig decided to try out the new tanks and assembled two companies to attack; 49 tanks were ready, although the men barely had time to scout the ground before they went into action.

The tanks were spread along a section of the British line—and they were hardly a success. Only nine made it to or across the German frontline, some fired on their own men, some were hit by the British barrage, and many broke down or ditched. Nevertheless, despite the poor performance overall, there were enough successes by certain tanks to allow Haig to claim that "wherever the tanks advanced we took our objectives, and wherever they did not advance we failed." He had seen their potential and ordered 1,000 more.

**A Mark I tank designated C15** at the battle of Flers-Courcelette, the first ever tank action, on September 15, 1916.

# Wartime Experiments

The end of the fighting in November 1918 came as a surprise to Allied commanders. They had been planning to use large numbers of tanks and armored vehicles during 1919, many of which already existed in small numbers and were being prepared for combat. At the end of the war, the British were developing a wide range of specialized armored vehicles, including artillery carriers, bridgelayers, infantry carriers, supply tanks, and repair vehicles. Only a few of these saw service, however.

**Low** tracks

### △ Gun Carrier, Mark I

**Date** 1917 **Country** UK

**Weight** 38.1 tons (34.5 tonnes)

**Engine** Daimler gasoline, 105 hp

**Main armament** None, but carried 60-pounder or 6 in artillery piece

Mechanically based on the Mark I, the Gun Carrier was designed to carry an artillery piece and crew in order to provide fire support to advancing infantry. Fifty were built and saw some action in their intended role, but they were mainly used to carry supplies. In 1918 they were permanently converted for this function.

### ▷ Mark V**

**Date** 1918 **Country** UK

**Weight** 38.1 tons (34.5 tonnes)

**Engine** Ricardo gasoline, 225 hp

**Main armament** 6 x .303 Hotchkiss Mark I* machine guns

To cross wider German trenches, the British used fascines or cribs, and designed new, longer tanks. The Mark V* was essentially a stretched Mark V, while the Mark V** featured a more powerful engine and redesigned track layout.

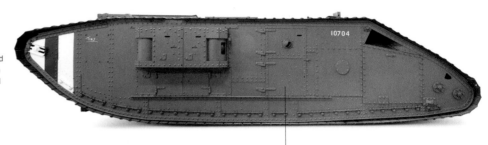

**Side** door

### ▽ Mark VIII

**Date** 1918 **Country** UK, USA

**Weight** 41.4 tons (37.6 tonnes)

**Engine** Ricardo gasoline, 300 hp

**Main armament** 2 x QF 6-pounder 6-cwt Hotchkiss L/23 guns

The Mark VIII "International" was an Anglo-American design intended to be built in France and used by the Allies. It was the first British-designed tank to separate the engine from the crew, improving conditions. After the war, 100 were built in the US, serving until 1930.

12007

MARK VIII

**Riveted** hull armor

**External** frame

**Return** rollers

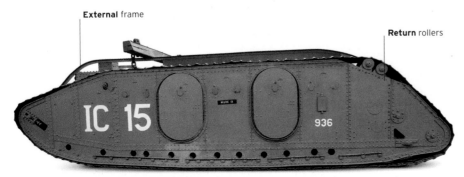

IC 15

936

### ◁ Mark IX

**Date** 1918 **Country** UK

**Weight** 41.4 tons (37.6 tonnes)

**Engine** Ricardo gasoline, 150 hp

**Main armament** 2 x .303 Hotchkiss Mark I* machine guns

Officially called a tank, the Mark IX was in fact the first Armored Personnel Carrier (APC), carrying 30 infantrymen. It was underpowered as it used the same engine as the Mark V, but weighed 10 tons (9 tonnes) more. One Mark IX was used for trials as an amphibious tank, with large floats attached to the side.

### ▷ M1918 3 Ton Tank

**Date** 1918 **Country** USA

**Weight** 3.4 tons (3 tonnes)

**Engine** 2 x Ford Model T gasoline, 45 hp each

**Main armament** .30-caliber machine gun

The M1918 was designed for mass production by the Ford Motor Company using Ford automobile parts, with a two-man crew sitting next to each other between the tracks. However, the US Tank Corps in France did not adopt it, as they considered it to have little value as a combat vehicle. Of a planned 15,000, just 15 were built.

**Large** idler wheel

**Lightweight** frame design

**Axles** securing road wheels

### ◁ Skeleton Tank

**Date** 1918 **Country** USA

**Weight** 10.1 tons (9.1 tonnes)

**Engine** 2 x Beaver 4-cylinder gasoline, 50 hp each

**Main armament** .30-caliber machine gun

This tank's unusual skeleton structure was intended to enable it to cross wide trenches while keeping the vehicle's weight down. The fighting compartment contained the two-man crew and the engine. This design meant sponsons could not be used, so the armament was carried in a roof-mounted turret.

**Rotating** turret

**Front** armor

**Sponson** housing 6-pounder gun

**Allied** insignia

### △ Fiat 2000

**Date** 1917 **Country** Italy

**Weight** 48.4 tons (40.6 tonnes)

**Engine** Fiat Aviazione A.12 6-cylinder gasoline, 240 hp

**Main armament** 65 mm L/17 howitzer

Fiat 2000 was the first Italian tank—its two prototypes were built privately by FIAT in 1917 and donated to the Italian Army in 1918. In 1919, FIAT 2000s were sent to fight in Libya, but its low speed made it ineffective against guerrilla fighters. In addition to the main gun, the tank had six machine guns.

### ▷ Medium Mark C (Hornet)

**Date** 1919 **Country** UK

**Weight** 21.8 tons (19.8 tonnes)

**Engine** Ricardo gasoline, 150 hp

**Main armament** 4 x .303 Hotchkiss Mark I* machine guns

British designers Tritton and Wilson parted ways in 1917 (see pp.28–29). Wilson designed the Medium Mark C in 1918, which was regarded as a superior vehicle to Tritton's Medium Mark B. Fifty were built, and it remained in service until 1923.

# Early Armored Cars

The first armored vehicles to see action in World War I were used by the British and Belgians around Antwerp in 1914. They engaged the German forces as they advanced and acted as rescuers for pilots forced down behind enemy lines. These early cars often had improvised armor and weapons, but specially designed vehicles were soon in service. The stalemate on the Western Front limited the use of armored cars, but they still had value in theaters where the fighting remained mobile.

▷ **Minerva Armored Car**

**Date** 1914 **Country** Belgium

**Weight** 4.5 tons (4.1 tonnes)

**Engine** Minerva 4-cylinder gasoline, 40 hp

**Main armament** 1 x 8 mm Hotchkiss machine gun

The Belgian Army ordered some 30 armored cars from the Belgian car manufacturer Minerva. The first model had no doors or roof, and a top speed of around 25 mph (40 km/h). Later versions were given a roof and enough armor to protect the machine gun.

▷ **Lanchester Armored Car**

**Date** 1915 **Country** UK

**Weight** 5.4 tons (4.9 tonnes)

**Engine** Lanchester 6-cylinder gasoline, 60 hp

**Main armament** .303 Vickers machine gun

The Lanchester began its career with the Royal Naval Air Service. A total of 36 were built, first seeing action in Belgium, where they harassed German forces and rescued downed pilots. In 1916, they were sent to Russia, from where detachments traveled as far as Persia and Turkey.

**Riveted** steel armor

**Spoked** wheels

**Two turrets** with a machine gun in each

**50 hp** engine

▷ **Austin Armored Car**

**Date** 1914 **Country** UK

**Weight** 4.6 tons (4.2 tonnes)

**Engine** Austin gasoline, 50 hp

**Main armament** 2 x .303 Hotchkiss Mark I machine guns

Although the Russian Army was enthusiastic about armored cars, Russia lacked the industrial capacity to build them, forcing it to look overseas. This vehicle was built by the British Austin Company, and Britain subsequently adopted it in 1918. Several Russian versions were captured and used by the new Eastern European nations after the war.

△ **Peugeot modèle 1914 AC**

**Date** 1914 **Country** France

**Weight** 5.5 tons (5 tonnes)

**Engine** Peugeot gasoline, 40 hp

**Main armament** 37 mm Mle 1897 gun

There were two versions of the Peugeot armored car: the AC (autocannon) and the AM (automitrailleuse, or machine gun). Like most armored cars, it was of limited use during the stalemate on the Western Front, and by the time mobile warfare returned in 1918 there were very few left.

▷ **Mgebrov-Renault**

**Date** 1915 **Country** Russia

**Weight** 3.7 tons (3.4 tonnes)

**Engine** Renault 4-cylinder gasoline, 30 hp

**Main armament** 2 x 7.62 mm M1910 machine-guns

The distinctive sloped armor on the Mgebrov-Renault was designed by Captain Vladimir Mgebrov of the Russian Army to improve protection without adding excessive weight. At first, the armament was mounted in an unusual rotating superstructure, but this was replaced in 1916 by two smaller turrets.

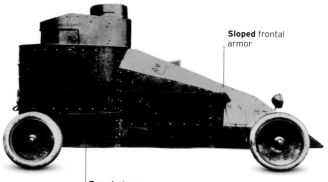

**Sloped** frontal armor

**Turret** at rear

**Double** rear wheels

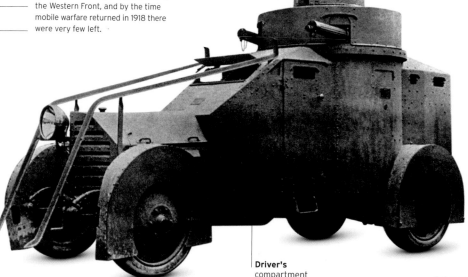

**Driver's** compartment

◁ **Lancia Ansaldo IZ**

**Date** 1916 **Country** Italy

**Weight** 4.1 tons (3.8 tonnes)

**Engine** Lancia V6 gasoline, 40 hp

**Main armament** 3 x 6.5 mm FIAT-Revelli M1914 machine guns

The mountainous Italian Front was not suited to armored cars, but the Lancia Ansaldo played an important role in protecting the Italians retreating after the disaster at Caporetto in 1917. A total of 120 were built, only 10 of which were double-turreted. A few remained in use in Italy's African colonies until World War II.

▷ **Ehrhardt E-V/4**

**Date** 1917 **Country** Germany

**Weight** 8.7 tons (7.9 tonnes)

**Engine** Daimler 6-cylinder gasoline, 80 hp

**Main armament** 3 x 7.92 mm MG 08 machine guns

Unlike most armored cars of World War I, the Erhardt was purpose-built rather than a converted civilian vehicle. It was used on the more mobile Eastern Front until fighting ended. Postwar, as violence engulfed Germany, it was deployed against rioters by the police and by Freikorps (German paramilitary units) against their opponents.

**Driver's** vision ports

**Armored** rear wheels

**Forward left** turret

**Armored** chassis

**Rear** right turret

◁ **Izhorski FIAT**

**Date** 1917 **Country** Russia

**Weight** 5.3 tons (4.8 tonnes)

**Engine** FIAT 6-cylinder gasoline, 60 hp

**Main armament** 2 x 7.62 mm M1910 machine guns

Most Russian armored cars featured two separate turrets, each with a machine gun. The chassis for this model was supplied by FIAT to the Russian Izhorski company, who added the armor. Around 70 were built, each having a crew of five.

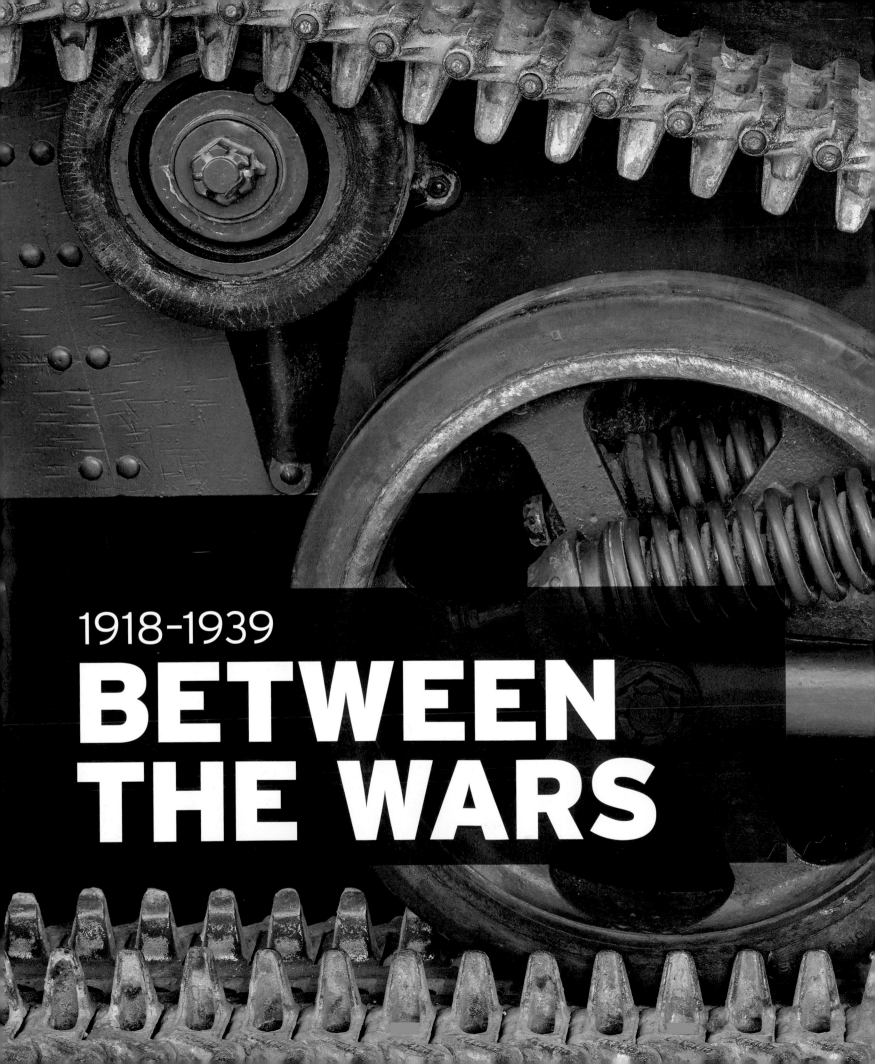

# 1918-1939
# BETWEEN THE WARS

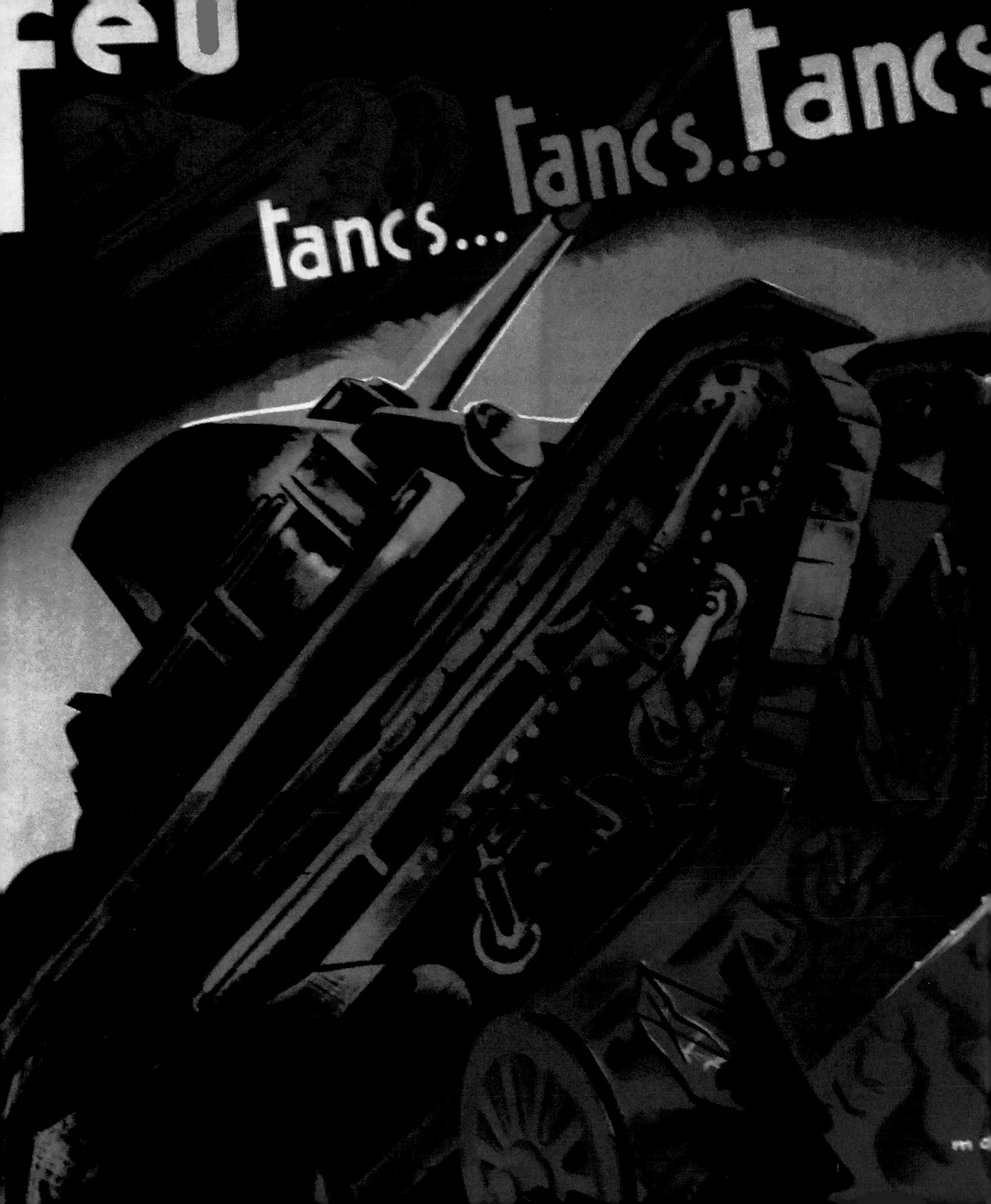
feu
tancs... tancs... tancs

# BETWEEN THE WARS

**Ambitious plans for the production** and use of tanks were dramatically reduced at the end of World War I, but theories for the vehicle's future role proliferated. Some military thinkers believed tanks could and should replace all other types of forces; some felt trench warfare would never be seen again and that the tank was no longer necessary.

The mechanical reliability of tanks improved greatly during this period. This encouraged both theorists and practitioners to consider faster paced and more mobile concepts of operations. Britain led the way at this time, establishing her Experimental Mechanised Force—the first large formation used to test theories of armored warfare—in 1927.

△ **"Spain Resurrected"**
A Spanish nationalist poster celebrates the end of the Spanish Civil War, which saw tanks being used in blitzkrieg fashion for the first time.

Development varied between nations. Britain decided it needed two types of tank—one for infantry support and the other a mobile replacement for cavalry, roles that required very different designs. Germany was forbidden tanks until 1933, so those it built were constructed in secret and tested in the Soviet Union. Armored warfare theories in Germany were based around balanced all-arms mechanized formations operating at high speed. After many years restricted to just the FT, during the 1930s France produced several new tanks for a variety of roles, while the Soviet Union, usually taking foreign designs as a starting point, manufactured thousands of vehicles and developed a doctrine based on high mobility.

During the 1930s, as war began to seem more likely and older tanks reached the end of their lives, a new generation of tanks began to enter service around the world. Many of these vehicles would soon see action.

**"**... the tankers have **destroyed** at Teruel no fewer than 1,000 **fascist troops**... our powerful **tank cannons** have relentlessly forced [them] out of the **trenches.**"
SOVIET COLONEL S. A. KONDRATIEV, DURING THE SPANISH CIVIL WAR, 1937

◁ **A Spanish Republican poster** waxes lyrical about the tank in 1936.

▷ **July 1919** Four Medium Cs take part in the World War I Victory Parade in London, despite not fighting in the war.

▷ **1920** French and American tank units are both placed under the control of their Infantry Branch.

▷ **1923** The British Government's Department of Tank Design is shut down. Tank development becomes the responsibility of private industry.

▷ **1923** The British Royal Tank Corps is formed as a separate branch of service. The first of 166 Vickers Mediums are delivered, the most widely produced tank of the 1920s.

▷ **1929** The Kama Tank School is established at Kazan, in the Soviet Union, allowing Germany to carry out tank development and training.

▷ **1931** The job of developing mechanization within the US Army is assigned to the Cavalry Branch.

▷ **1931** The French Army introduces the D1, its first new tank since 1918.

△ **Japanese tankettes**
The Japanese used thousands of tanks, but most were light vehicles that emphasized mobility over armor.

▷ **October 1935** The first three German Panzer Divisions are formed.

▷ **1935** A Soviet Mechanized Corps of over 1,000 tanks takes part in an exercise at Kiev.

▷ **1936** The Spanish Civil War breaks out; Germany, Italy, and the Soviet Union send their latest tanks to fight.

# Interwar Experiments

As automotive technology improved during the 1920s and '30s, tanks became more reliable and capable. This progress, along with the debate over the future role of tanks on the battlefield, encouraged designers to be innovative. As a result, a wide range of experimental vehicles were developed. Some were designed to provide individual soldiers with armored protection, while others were intended as "land battleships" that could operate unsupported by other arms. Some proved to be harbingers of the future, while others were dead ends.

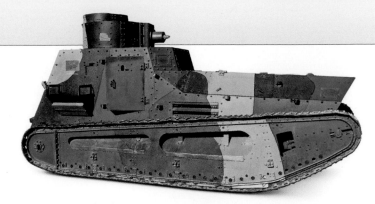

### △ Stridsvagn m/21

**Date** 1921 **Country** Sweden

**Weight** 9.8 tons (8.9 tonnes)

**Engine** Daimler-Benz gasoline, 60 hp

**Main armament** 6.5 mm Ksp m/1914 machine gun

Sweden's very first tank, the four-man m/21 was based on the German LK II prototype. Due to the ban on tanks imposed on Germany by the Treaty of Versailles, the LK II was illegally and secretly exported to Sweden in pieces labeled as tractor parts. The m/21 was used for training purposes, and in the early 1930s five were upgraded to m/21-29 standard.

Riveted turret armor

.303 Lewis machine gun

Reinforced rubber tracks

### ◁ Morris-Martel Tankette

**Date** 1926 **Country** UK

**Weight** 2.5 tons (2.2 tonnes)

**Engine** Morris 4 cylinder gasoline 16 hp

**Main armament** .303 Lewis machine gun

In 1925, British officer Major Gifford Martel designed a one-man tracked vehicle, which soon attracted official attention. When it was demonstrated that it was impossible for one man to both drive the tank and operate the machine gun, a two-man version (shown here) was developed. Used in the Experimental Mechanised Force, the Morris-Martel pioneered the tankette concept.

### ▷ A1E1 Independent

**Date** 1926 **Country** UK

**Weight** 35.8 tons (32.5 tonnes)

**Engine** Armstrong Siddeley V12 gasoline, 270 hp

**Main armament** QF 3-pounder gun

In addition to its main gun, the Independent had four machine guns in four separate turrets, plus a cupola for the commander of its eight-man crew. Only one was ever built, but its design was influential; the Soviet T-35 owes it a debt, as does the German Neubaufahrzeug series and possibly the British triple-turret Cruiser Mark I.

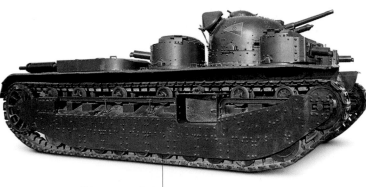

37 mm Bofors m/38 gun

Side armor protects suspension

### ◁ Leichttraktor Vs.Kfz.31

**Date** 1930 **Country** Germany

**Weight** 10.6 tons (9.7 tonnes)

**Engine** Daimler-Benz gasoline, 100 hp

**Main armament** 3.7 cm KwK 36 L/45 gun

By secretly and illegally working with the Soviet Union at the Kama Tank School, Germany was able to build and operate a small number of tanks. Known as "tractors" for cover, they provided both soldiers and industry with experience of designing, building and operating tanks.

Wheels in raised position

### ▷ Christie M1931

| | |
|---|---|
| **Date** 1931 | **Country** USA |

**Weight** 11.8 tons (10.7 tonnes)

**Engine** Liberty V12 gasoline, 338 hp

**Main armament** .50 Browning M2 machine gun

Designed by J. Walter Christie, the M1931 was a follow-up to the turretless M1928. Unlike its predecessor, it was purchased by the US Army, but more influential were the two bought by the Soviets: these evolved into the BT series and the T-34. The tank's suspension and light armor allowed for very high speed, even on rough ground.

**Tracks removed** for increased speed

**Rear** secondary turret

**Front** secondary turret

### ▽ Amphibious Light Tank

**Date** 1939 **Country** UK

**Weight** 4.8 tons (4.4 tonnes)

**Engine** Meadows 6-cylinder EST gasoline, 89 hp

**Main armament** .303 Vickers machine gun

This vehicle was designed for British requirements and was based mechanically on the Vickers Light Tank, rather than the company's earlier amphibious vehicle. Its hull was surrounded by kapok-filled aluminium floats, and it was driven in water by two propellers.

**Boat-shaped** aluminium hull

**Hollow wheels** assist buoyancy

### △ Panzerkampfwagen Neubaufahrzeug

**Date** 1934 **Country** Germany

**Weight** 40.3 tons (36.6 tonnes)

**Engine** BMV Va gasoline, 290 hp

**Main armament** 7.5 cm KwK 37 L/24 gun and 3.7 cm KwK 36 L/45 gun

Intended as the standard German heavy tank to complement the Panzer I-IV vehicles, just five Neubaufahrzeugs were built, including two prototypes. The two main guns were mounted in the same turret, with two smaller machine-gun turrets firing forward and backward. The three combat vehicles saw limited service in Norway in 1940.

### ▽ Stridsvagn fm/31

**Date** 1935 **Country** Sweden

**Weight** 12.9 tons (11.7 tonnes)

**Engine** Maybach DSO 8 gasoline, 150 hp

**Main armament** 37 mm Bofors m/38 gun

One weakness of early tanks was their tracks, which wore out quickly. To overcome this, many countries experimented with tanks that could carry their own wheels. This unique Swedish vehicle could raise or lower its wheels in 30 seconds. However, as tracks became more reliable during the 1930s, convertible vehicles were rendered unneccessary.

# A new kind of cavalry

The mechanization of the cavalry took place at different times across the world. Britain led the way in mechanization after a series of exercises on Salisbury Plain in the late 1920s, which showed the overwhelming advantages of a fully mechanized force—infantry in trucks, artillery towed by tracked or wheeled vehicles, tanks, and tracked scouting carriers.

In 1928, the first British cavalry regiments were mechanized. The Great Depression and the consequent reduced budgets for the military—rather than the innate conservatism of the cavalry regiments—meant it took another 10 years before the remaining cavalry regiments in Britain were mechanized. The British War Office tried to transfer the élan of the cavalry into the new

mechanized roles, with cavalry regiments being used for scouting, reconnaissance, intelligence gathering, and screening advances and retreats.

Memoirs, magazines, and newspapers of the time were full of the sense of loss many in the cavalry felt—for centuries of tradition, for their horses, and for sharp uniforms being replaced with drab coveralls. Lt. Col. C. E. Morgan wrote in a poem: "I've spent my life with 'orses and I loved the work and toil/But I can't stand these new fledged beasts that live on gas and oil."

**British troopers of the Queen's Bays cavalry regiment** are shown a Vickers Light Tank in trials in Dorset, UK in the 1930s.

# Armored Cars

Early tanks were unreliable: their tracks were prone to breaking on rough ground or when handled poorly, and they wore out relatively quickly. Wheeled vehicles, on the other hand, were much more durable, often carried similar firepower and armor protection, and were quieter, and usually faster, except over the roughest terrain. These qualities made armored cars ideal as patrol vehicles, as the British used them in India. Other countries used them for reconnoitering ahead of their tank forces.

**Step** up to driver's cabin

◁ **Peerless Armored Car**

**Date** 1919 **Country** UK

**Weight** 7.7 tons (7 tonnes)

**Engine** Peerless 4-cylinder gasoline, 40 hp

**Main armament** 2 x .303 Hotchkiss Mark I machine-guns

This vehicle paired an armored body supplied by Austin with a Peerless truck chassis. Service in Ireland revealed it to be big and slow, and its solid rubber tires uncomfortable. It was passed on to the Territorial Army, where it was kept by some units until the late 1930s.

▷ **Rolls-Royce Armored Car**

**Date** 1920 **Country** UK

**Weight** 4.8 tons (4.3 tonnes)

**Engine** Rolls-Royce 6-cylinder gasoline, 80 hp

**Main armament** .303 Vickers machine gun

The 1920 Pattern Rolls-Royce was very similar to the Royal Navy's 1914 Pattern. It was used by the British Army and Royal Air Force around the world, including in Ireland, Iraq, Shanghai, and Egypt. Some upgraded 1920 and 1924 Pattern vehicles were used in the North African Desert Campaign in 1940 and 1941.

**Storage space** for equipment

▽ **Lanchester Armored Car**

**Date** 1931 **Country** UK

**Weight** 7.8 tons (7.1 tonnes)

**Engine** Lanchester 6-cylinder gasoline, 90 hp

**Main armament** .50 Vickers machine gun

This vehicle was very different to its wartime namesake (see p.34). Larger and heavier, it had four driven wheels at the rear, a second, rear-facing driver's space at the back, and two additional .303 Vickers machine guns. Thirty-nine were built, 10 carrying a radio instead of the hull Vickers gun. Some survived to fight the Japanese in Malaya in 1941–42.

**Sloped bodywork** deflects projectiles

▷ **Sd Kfz 231 6 rad Armored Car**

**Date** 1932 **Country** Germany

**Weight** 6 tons (5.4 tonnes)

**Engine** Magirus M206 gasoline, 70 hp

**Main armament** 2 cm KwK 30 L/55 cannon

Based on various 6x4 truck chassis, the Sd Kfz 231 began development in 1929. Its crew of four included a second, rear-facing driver. A total of 151 were built. It was used in Austria, Poland, Czechoslovakia, and France, but was withdrawn in 1940 due to poor off-road mobility. This example is a replica.

▽ **Automitrailleuse de Découverte (AMD) Panhard modèle 1935**

| | |
|---|---|
| **Date** 1937 | **Country** France |

**Weight** 8.2 tonnes (9.1 tons)

**Engine** Panhard ISK 4-cylinder gasoline, 105 hp

**Main armament** 25 mm Hotchkiss SA 35 cannon

Intended for reconnaissance, over 1,100 AMD 35s were built. It had a second, rear-facing driver, who also acted as a radio operator. Although it suffered from poor off-road mobility, it was quiet, fast, and popular. Production continued after the French surrender in 1940, and after the war ended in 1945.

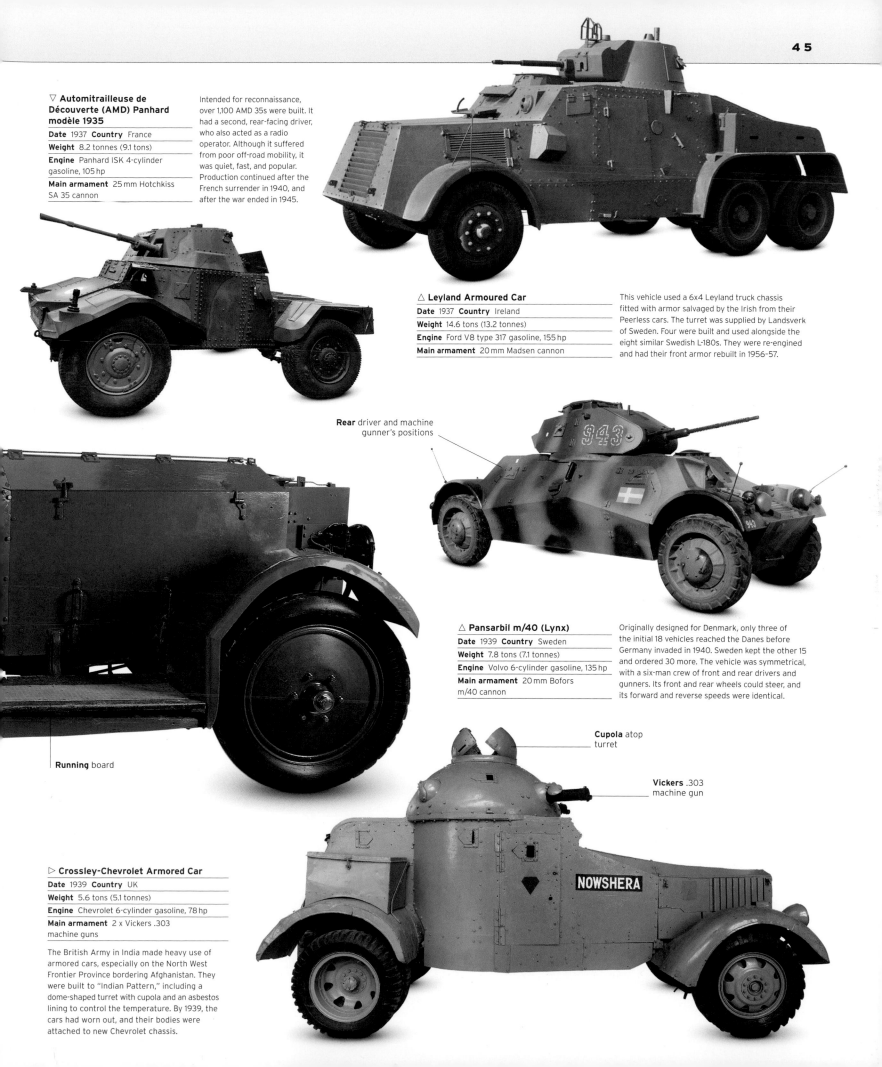

△ **Leyland Armoured Car**

| | |
|---|---|
| **Date** 1937 | **Country** Ireland |

**Weight** 14.6 tons (13.2 tonnes)

**Engine** Ford V8 type 317 gasoline, 155 hp

**Main armament** 20 mm Madsen cannon

This vehicle used a 6x4 Leyland truck chassis fitted with armor salvaged by the Irish from their Peerless cars. The turret was supplied by Landsverk of Sweden. Four were built and used alongside the eight similar Swedish L-180s. They were re-engined and had their front armor rebuilt in 1956-57.

**Rear** driver and machine gunner's positions

△ **Pansarbil m/40 (Lynx)**

| | |
|---|---|
| **Date** 1939 | **Country** Sweden |

**Weight** 7.8 tons (7.1 tonnes)

**Engine** Volvo 6-cylinder gasoline, 135 hp

**Main armament** 20 mm Bofors m/40 cannon

Originally designed for Denmark, only three of the initial 18 vehicles reached the Danes before Germany invaded in 1940. Sweden kept the other 15 and ordered 30 more. The vehicle was symmetrical, with a six-man crew of front and rear drivers and gunners. Its front and rear wheels could steer, and its forward and reverse speeds were identical.

**Running** board

**Cupola** atop turret

**Vickers** .303 machine gun

NOWSHERA

▷ **Crossley-Chevrolet Armored Car**

| | |
|---|---|
| **Date** 1939 | **Country** UK |

**Weight** 5.6 tons (5.1 tonnes)

**Engine** Chevrolet 6-cylinder gasoline, 78 hp

**Main armament** 2 x Vickers .303 machine guns

The British Army in India made heavy use of armored cars, especially on the North West Frontier Province bordering Afghanistan. They were built to "Indian Pattern," including a dome-shaped turret with cupola and an asbestos lining to control the temperature. By 1939, the cars had worn out, and their bodies were attached to new Chevrolet chassis.

# Light Tanks and Tankettes

Military budgets became increasingly stretched as the Great Depression continued throughout the 1930s. Tankettes, a concept that stemmed from the Morris-Martel vehicle, were a relatively cheap way to put a lot of armored firepower onto the battlefield. They were generally used for infantry support and as such became increasingly popular. Light tanks, on the other hand, were larger and better protected, and their role was to take advantage of breakthroughs made by heavier tanks. During this period, most light tanks carried machine guns, antitank guns only appearing toward the end of the 1930s.

.303 Vickers
machine gun

### ▷ Carden-Loyd Carrier
  Mark VI

**Date** 1928 **Country** UK

**Weight** 1.7 tons (1.5 tonnes)

**Engine** Ford Model T gasoline, 22.5 hp

**Main armament** .303 Vickers machine gun

The Carden-Loyd Company built a series of one- and two-man tankettes during the mid 1920s. The Mark VI was the most successful (450 were built by 1935) and it was the last before the company was bought by Vickers. The design was sold around the world, where it influenced the development of many vehicles.

Face-hardened
armor

### ◁ Vickers Light Tank Mark IIA

**Date** 1931 **Country** UK

**Weight** 4.8 tons (4.3 tonnes)

**Engine** Rolls-Royce 6-cylinder gasoline, 66 hp

**Main armament** .303 Vickers machine gun

Descended from the Carden-Loyd, the Vickers Light Tank series was intended to replace armored cars for reconnaissance. The very similar Mark II, IIA, and IIB were the first to enter service. They had a two-man crew, an improved Horstmann suspension system, and new, more effective armor plating. Sixty Mark IIs were built, plus around 50 Indian Pattern variants.

Horstmann
suspension system

Open hatch

Light armor aids
buouyancy

### ◁ T-37A

**Date** 1933 **Country** Soviet Union

**Weight** 3.5 tons (3.2 tonnes)

**Engine** GAZ-AA gasoline, 40 hp

**Main armament** 7.62 mm DT machine gun

The T-37A amphibious tank was developed from the Vickers A4E11, which was sold to the Soviets in 1931. Because of its mobility, it was used for reconnaissance and for infantry support. In order to float it could only be lightly armored, which led to heavy losses when Germany invaded Russia. Around 1,200 were built.

### △ Marmon-Herrington CTL-3

**Date** 1936 **Country** USA

**Weight** 5 tons (4.6 tonnes)

**Engine** Lincoln V-12 petrol, 110 hp

**Main armament** 2 x .30 Browning M1919 machine guns

The CTL-3 was produced for the US Marine Corps, which imposed a 5-ton weight limit due to shipboard handling limitations. This proved to be a major drawback, and by 1939 it was clear that the US Army's light tanks were superior and that their greater weight was manageable.

Twin turrets for
machine guns

### △ Light Tank M2A3

**Date** 1936 **Country** USA

**Weight** 10.6 tons (9.7 tonnes)

**Engine** Continental R-670-9A gasoline, 250 hp

**Main armament** .50 Browning M2 machine gun

The M2 series was designed for infantry support, so
machine guns were all it received for firepower; the
M2A3 had twin turrets, with a .50 machine gun in one
and a .30 in the other. However, lessons from the war
in Europe showed that more weaponry was needed,
so the M2A4 was fitted with a 37 mm gun.

Vertical volute
suspension

Armored "calottes"
for the crew's heads

Sloping glacis
plate amor

Stowage
container

### △ Combat Car M1

**Date** 1937 **Country** USA

**Weight** 10.9 tons (9.9 tonnes)

**Engine** Continental R-670-9A gasoline, 250 hp

**Main armament** .50 Browning M2 machine gun

Between 1920 and 1940, according to US law, only the
US Army's Infantry branch could operate tanks—which
is why this vehicle used by the Cavalry branch had to be
called a "Combat Car." The M1 and M2 introduced many
features that were reused in US tanks throughout World
War II, including the Vertical Volute Suspension System
(VVSS) and the Continental R-670 engine.

### △ UE Tankette

**Date** 1937 **Country** France

**Weight** 3.6 tons (3.3 tonnes)

**Engine** Renault 4-cylinder gasoline, 38 hp

**Main armament** None

Another development of the Carden-Loyd Carrier, the
UE was designed as a lightly armored supply carrier for
infantry. It had a stowage container behind the crew that
could be tipped automatically, and it could tow a range of
gear, such as mortars, antitank guns, and a tracked trailer.
Some 5,000 were built, most of which were unarmed.

Driver's space
front left

### ▷ Vickers Light Tank Mark VIB

**Date** 1937 **Country** UK

**Weight** 5.8 tons (5.3 tonnes)

**Engine** Meadows ESTB 6-cylinder gasoline, 88 hp

**Main armament** .50 Vickers machine gun

The two-man turret, armed with .50 and .303 machine
guns, was introduced on the Mark V version of the Vickers
Light Tank, and the Mark VI added a radio to the bustle.
The Mark VIB was the most common variant, with almost
1,000 built. Combat experience in France, North Africa,
and Greece showed that these tanks were inadequate.

# Light Tank Mark VIB

The Light Tank Mark VI was part of a series developed by Vickers-Armstrongs for the British Army. It was ordered in large numbers from 1936 since it was considered well suited to policing the empire and performing reconnaissance—as well as being relatively cheap. When war broke out in September 1939, over 1,000 of these light tanks were in British Army service, compared to just 150 heavier tanks.

**USED FOR SCOUTING** and securing the flanks of armored forces, the Light Tank Mark VIB was a fast tank for its time, reaching up to 35 mph/(56 km/h) on its Horstmann suspension. Armed with a double machine-gun housing, the turret had two Vickers machine guns—a .50 and a .303. The tank's armor was just over .511 in (13 mm) at its thickest—enough to stop bullets, but nothing heavier.

The three crewmen consisted of the driver, who sat at the front to the left of the engine, and the gunner and commander, who sat in the turret. The commander also acted as the radio operator. Due to its minimal length, the tank could pitch and rock when traveling over rough ground, forcing the gunner and commander in the turret to hang on to avoid being thrown around. The VIB equipped seven cavalry regiments of the British Army's newly formed Royal Armoured Corps in 1940, alongside VIB vehicles in a number of the Royal Tank Regiments. It saw action in many of the early campaigns of World War II, including France and Libya in 1940, and Greece and Crete in 1941.

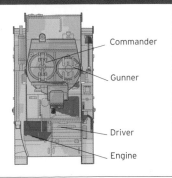

**REAR VIEW**

## SPECIFICATIONS

| Name | Light Tank Mark VIB |
| --- | --- |
| Date | 1936 |
| Origin | UK |
| Production | 1,682 |
| Engine | Meadows 6-cylinder gasoline, 88 hp |
| Weight | 5 tons (4.85 tonnes) |
| Main armament | .50-cal Vickers |
| Secondary armament | .30-cal Vickers |
| Crew | 3 |
| Armor thickness | .511 in (13 mm) |

Commander

Gunner

Driver

Engine

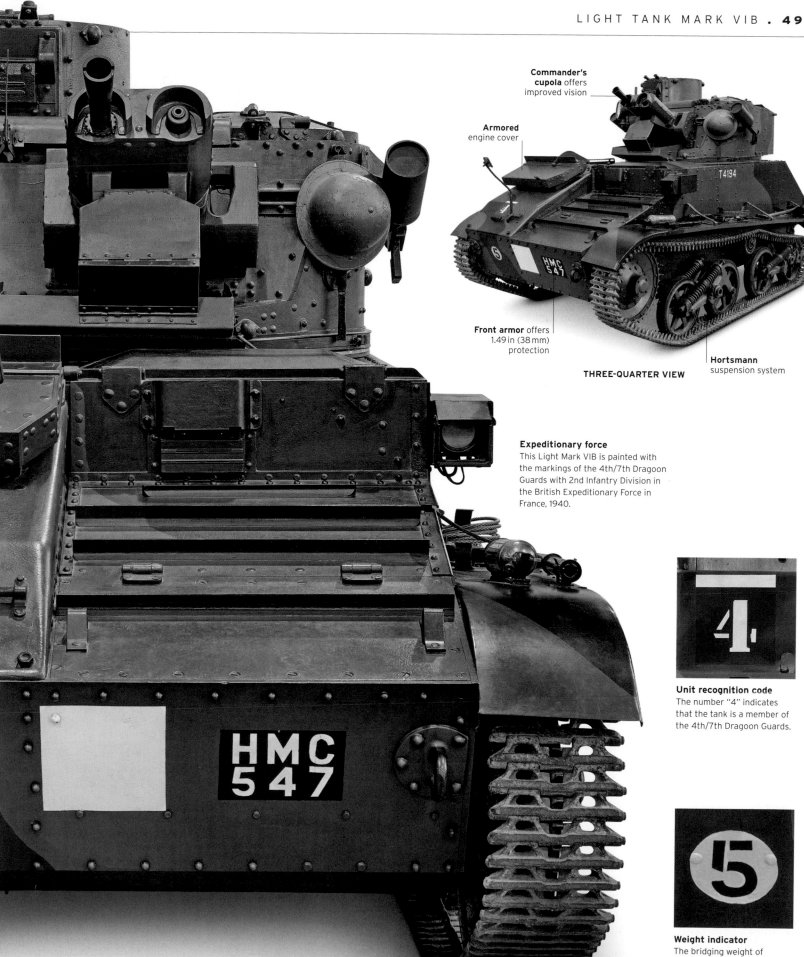

Commander's **cupola** offers improved vision

**Armored** engine cover

**Front armor** offers 1.49 in (38 mm) protection

**Hortsmann** suspension system

**THREE-QUARTER VIEW**

T4194

**Expeditionary force**
This Light Mark VIB is painted with the markings of the 4th/7th Dragoon Guards with 2nd Infantry Division in the British Expeditionary Force in France, 1940.

HMC 547

**Unit recognition code**
The number "4" indicates that the tank is a member of the 4th/7th Dragoon Guards.

**Weight indicator**
The bridging weight of the tank is painted onto its hull, rounded up to the nearest metric ton.

## EXTERIOR

Because the Light Tank Mark VIB was made before the use of periscopes, the crew had to look directly out of armored vision ports, increasing the risk of injury from bullets or shrapnel. Its external maker's plate has had the manufacturer's details chiseled off the brass—this was to stop a captured tank from revealing the manufacturer's address, which would have been a prime target for a German bomber.

**1.** Battalion insignia  **2.** Headlight  **3.** Spotlight  **4.** Driver's vision port  **5.** Fire extinguisher  **6.** Main machine gun and coaxial machine gun  **7.** Smoke grenade launcher  **8.** Commander's vision port  **9.** Manufacturer's plaque with information removed  **10.** Exhaust  **11.** Towing cable  **12.** Aerial mount  **13.** Road wheels in paired suspension unit

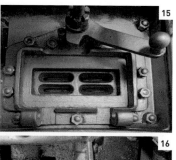

## INTERIOR

Although this tank was constructed in the age of modern production-line manufacturing techniques, it was not mass-produced in the true sense. The fit and finish of the armor plates reveals the level of skill and craftsmanship required to complete them.

**14.** Commander's hatch (open)   **15.** Commander's vision port
**16.** Turret traverse mechanism   **17.** Main machine gun and coaxial machine gun   **18.** Gunner's vision port   **19.** Driver's seat
**20.** Driver's position looking through into tank   **21.** Driver's controls
**22.** Instrument panel

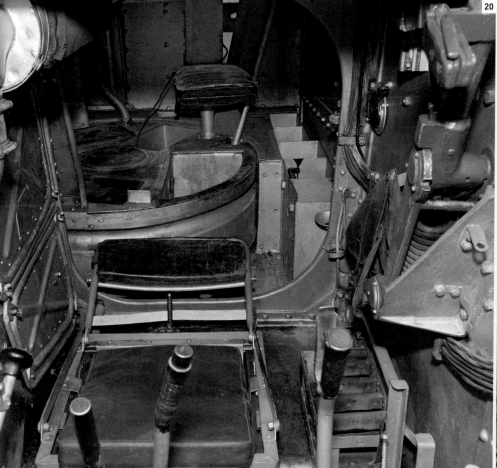

Christie in the M1931 tank he designed for the US Army

# Great designers
# J. Walter Christie

J. Walter Christie is often recorded as being a maverick inventor—irascible, argumentative, and hard to deal with— and it may be that his personality got in the way of his tank designs seeing series production. However, some of his inventions had a great influence on tank development.

**CHRISTIE, AN AMERICAN**, worked as a consulting engineer for a number of steamship lines before turning his attention to car racing. He designed and drove a front-wheel-drive car in the 1907 French Grand Prix, and later the same year was involved in a serious car accident at a racetrack in Pittsburgh while attempting to set a track record. A car he designed—the Christie Racer—later became the first car to lap the Indianapolis speedway at over 100 mph (161 km/h).

Christie also designed taxicabs and fire engines. During World War I, he designed a gun carriage for the US Ordnance Board, but refused to listen to his client's specific requirements.

**J. Walter Christie**
(1865–1944)

His stubbornness in arguing his case and his rudeness before authority became a pattern that did not endear him to the military authorities. However, he did have some success with an amphibious light tank that the US Marine Corps thought had potential, even though it initially had trouble reaching shore during a test. He developed his interest in tanks, and after years of experimentation and large financial investment he displayed a radical new tank chassis to the US military in October 1928. Christie wanted to call his tank Model 1940, because he considered it a dozen years ahead of its time, but it was designated Model 1928.

The new vehicle had large road wheels, which it could run on with the tracks removed. Uniquely, each wheel had its own independent suspension—

**Passing the test**
A T3E2 tank with Christie suspension crosses an obstacle course in 1936. Each wheel had its own suspension, enabling the tank to cross difficult ground with ease.

a "helicoil" spring mounted inside the hull— which gave the tank an extraordinary agility when crossing rough ground, each wheel bumping up and down as it passed over an obstacle. This enabled the tank to travel much faster than conventional tanks, which used the relatively cumbersome "leaf spring" suspension system. To keep weight down and speed up, the tank had thin armor, which was also sloped at the front to deflect projectiles. Christie envisaged his tank being used to penetrate enemy positions and travel at speed far into enemy territory. It weighed only 9 tons (8 tonnes) and had a Liberty engine that gave it a top speed of 42 mph (68 km/h) on tracks—and an extraordinary 70 mph (112 km/h) on its wheels.

The US Army Infantry Tank Board was unimpressed by the tank's thin armor—they saw tanks as infantry support weapons—so they passed Christie onto the Cavalry, who were more interested in armored cars at the time. To add to Christie's frustration, the US military refused to pay the development costs he had incurred.

Christie became more argumentative and embittered, and decided to sell his designs to the highest bidder. This led him to having dealings with a number of foreign countries:

**Experimental design**
Christie's experimental T3E2 tank could move fast, but only had room for a crew of two. The US Army deemed it inadequate as an infantry support weapon.

# "Mr. Christie we don't want them and we won't care who you sell them to."

**MAJOR CHRISTMAS, US ORDNANCE BOARD**

**"Glory to Soviet tank crews"**
Christie's suspension system became a key component of the Soviet Union's revolutionary T-34 tank.

Poland, who ordered a tank, but had their money returned when it wasn't delivered; the Soviet Union, who received two tanks and various plans that were delivered illegally as agricultural tractors; and Britain, who also bought a tank that was exported in pieces as an agricultural machine. These exported vehicles were influential in leading to the Russian BT series of fast tanks and the British A13 Cruiser tank.

Despite developing even more designs, Christie never found favor with the US military, and died a frustrated and bitter man.

**The flying tank**
Although the idea never took off, Christie designed the "flying tank"—a two-man vehicle with detachable wings that was intended to fly straight onto the battlefield.

**British tank factory**
Many of the tanks assembled at this British factory during World War II featured Christie's wheel and suspension design. These included the Covenanter, Crusader, Comet, Cromwell, and A13 Cruiser tanks.

# Vickers creates a global tank

The Vickers Mark E (or 6-Ton Tank) was designed as a private venture in the late 1920s by a team including designers John Valentine Carden and Vivian Loyd. It became a great export success. It was made in two key variants—the Type A, seen here, with two Vickers machine guns in separate turrets, and the Type B, which had a single turret with an innovative mounting housing a machine gun and a 3-pounder or 47 mm gun. It had riveted armor plates up to 1 in (25 mm) thick on the front, and its suspension consisted of two axles holding double trucks with leaf springs connecting the two sets; when one wheel set was raised, the springs pushed down on the second. An Armstrong Siddeley engine gave it a top speed of 22 mph (35 km/h) on the road.

Vickers exported over 150 Mark Es, and many more were built under licence, in some cases kick-starting the licencee nation's tank production. The Soviet Union bought 15 Type A vehicles and then built their own version, the T-26, in vast quantities, while many of the 17 countries that used the Mark E modified the design to fit their own requirements. The tank saw action worldwide: first in the Chaco War between Bolivia and Paraguay in 1933; in the Spanish Civil War; in the fighting between Finland and the Soviet Union; and in China, Poland, and Thailand.

**A Vickers Mark E tank** is displayed during trials in Warsaw, Poland in the 1930s, observed by a large crowd.

# Medium and Heavy Tanks

Slower and more powerful vehicles, the medium and heavy tanks were intended to take on enemy armor and fortifications, creating the breakthrough for faster vehicles to exploit. In general, armor protection and firepower were therefore emphasized over mobility. The Vickers Independent's multiple turrets influenced a number of these tanks, and Walter Christie's suspension system also began to find favor. Many nations purchased the Vickers Mark E, with some, like the Soviet Union, using it as a starting point to develop their own designs.

### ◁ Vickers Medium Mark II*

| | |
|---|---|
| **Date** 1926 | **Country** UK |
| **Weight** 15.1 tons (13.7 tonnes) | |
| **Engine** Armstrong-Siddeley V8 gasoline, 90 hp | |
| **Main armament** QF 3-pounder gun | |

The very similar Medium Mark Is and IIs served the Royal Tank Corps from 1923 to 1938. They were the first turreted tanks in British service, and although they saw no action, they had an enormous influence on the design work done between the wars. A total of 166 tanks were built.

### ▷ Vickers Mark E, 6 Ton

| | |
|---|---|
| **Date** 1928 | **Country** UK |
| **Weight** 8.3 tons (7.5 tonnes) | |
| **Engine** Armstrong-Siddeley 4-cylinder gasoline, 80 hp | |
| **Main armament** QF 3-pounder gun | |

A successful commercial design, Vickers sold this tank to 12 nations. It was not produced in large numbers, with only about 150 tanks built. The largest single order came from Poland for 38 tanks. However, its design was highly influential, and the 7TP (see pp.70–71) and T-26 were developed from it. The tank had two variants— Type A had two machine gun turrets, and Type B had a single turret, as shown here.

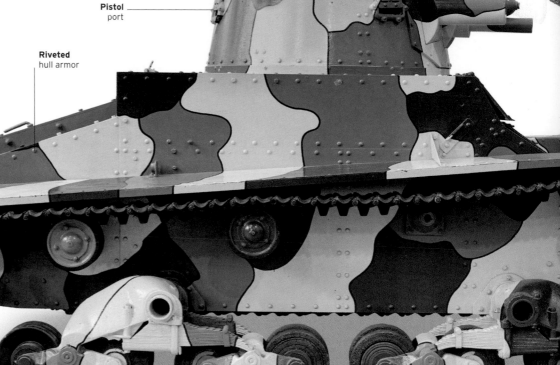

**Pistol** port

**Riveted** hull armor

**45 mm** main gun

### △ T-26

| | |
|---|---|
| **Date** 1931 | **Country** Soviet Union |
| **Weight** 10.4 tons (9.4 tonnes) | |
| **Engine** T-26 4-cylinder gasoline, 91 hp | |
| **Main armament** 45 mm 20K Model 1934 L/46 gun | |

The T-26 was by far the most widely produced tank of this period. A total of 12,000 tanks, including 2,000 twin-turreted vehicles and 1,700 variants, were built. It was used in the Spanish Civil War, but its weaknesses were soon exposed, and despite upgrades it was outclassed by 1939. In the Far East, some survived until 1945.

### ▽ T-28

| | |
|---|---|
| **Date** 1933 | **Country** Soviet Union |
| **Weight** 31.9 tons (29 tonnes) | |
| **Engine** Mikulin M17T gasoline, 500 hp | |
| **Main armament** 76.2 mm KT-28 L26 howitzer | |

A multiturreted design, the T 28 was intended for infantry support, so it was armed with a howitzer rather than an antitank gun. Around 500 were built. Experience in Poland and Finland led to extra armor being applied to some vehicles.

**Engine** exhaust

**Spare** road wheels on hull

**Smaller turrets** armed with machine guns

Driver's hatch

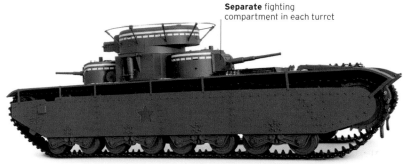

◁ **BT-7**

| | | | |
|---|---|---|---|
| **Date** | 1935 | **Country** | Soviet Union |

**Weight** 15.2 tons (13.8 tonnes)

**Engine** Mikulin M17T gasoline, 450 hp

**Main armament** 45 mm 20K Model 1934 L/46 gun

Based on Christie's M1931 (see pp.40–41), the BT-7 succeeded the BT-2 and BT-5. A total of 8,122 tanks of all three variants were built. They were fast and well armed but very lightly armored. They were used in Spain, the Far East, Poland, and Finland. Thereafter, thousands were lost in the German invasion of 1941, although like the T-26, some survived the war in the Far East.

**Separate** fighting compartment in each turret

Tracks could be removed for road driving

Camouflage paint

Drive sprocket

△ **T-35**

| | | | |
|---|---|---|---|
| **Date** | 1936 | **Country** | Soviet Union |

**Weight** 50.4 tons (45.7 tonnes)

**Engine** Mikulin M17T gasoline, 650 hp

**Main armament** 76.2 mm Model 1927/32 gun

A heavy tank, the T-35 shared many components with the T-28 in an effort to ease production, but ultimately just 61 were built. It had five turrets, one with the 76.2 mm gun, two with 45 mm 20K guns, and two with DT machine guns. Most were lost during the German invasion.

▷ **Medium Tank M2A1**

| | | | |
|---|---|---|---|
| **Date** | 1939 | **Country** | USA |

**Weight** 25.8 tons (23.4 tonnes)

**Engine** Wright Continental R-975 gasoline, 400 hp

**Main armament** 37 mm M3 L/56.6 gun

The M2 was the first US medium tank to enter production. Intended for infantry support, the tank was also armed with six .30 machine guns arranged to allow 360-degree fire. Although the M2 was clearly obsolete by 1940, its VVSS (see pp.46–47) and R-975 engine were not. Both were reused on the M3 and M4.

**Angled** turret armor

**Machine guns** cover 360 degrees

U.S.A. W-30444

**Spare road wheel** on turret

**Vertical volute** suspension

Headlamp

**Swedish** national symbol

◁ **Strv m/40L**

| | | | |
|---|---|---|---|
| **Date** | 1940 | **Country** | Sweden |

**Weight** 10.1 tons (9.1 tonnes)

**Engine** Scania-Vabis 1664 gasoline, 142 hp

**Main armament** 37 mm Bofors m/38 gun

Based on the Landsverk L-60, a total of 100 Strv m/40Ls were built. Interwar Swedish tanks were very capable, but as a neutral nation Sweden was left behind by rapid tank development during World War II. Twenty tanks were sold to the Dominican Republic in 1956. These were the only m/40Ls to see combat—against the US in 1965.

# Vickers Medium Mark II

Introduced in 1923, the Vickers Medium tank was the first British tank to see service equipped with a sprung suspension and a rotating turret. The design was so successful that the Medium was the main British tank from 1923 to 1935.

**DESIGNED TO FIGHT** on the move, the Medium's high speed of 30 mph (48 km/h) came from its air-cooled Armstrong Siddeley engine, which was mounted in the front of the tank. The tank itself had seven variants. The first, the Medium Mark I, had a 3-pounder gun in the turret, a Vickers machine gun in each side of the hull, and Hotchkiss light machine guns in the turret. This main gun was adequate against contemporary tanks, but it was useless against field fortifications and antitank guns, so a close support version of the tank was built. The Mark II dispensed with the Hotchkiss machine guns and had a coaxial Vickers machine gun instead. In addition to the gun tanks, command-post and bridge-laying versions were also produced.

Vickers Mediums formed the backbone of the British Army's Experimental Mechanised Force of 1928. This revolutionary combat formation performed maneuvers on Salisbury Plain that showed the potential of mechanized formations. For this reason, the mechanization of the British Army continued through the 1930s.

**REAR VIEW**

## SPECIFICATIONS

| Name | Tank, Medium, Mark II* |
| --- | --- |
| Date | 1923 |
| Origin | UK |
| Production | 100 |
| Engine | Armstrong Siddeley V8 gasoline, 90hp |
| Weight | 13 tons (11.75 tonnes) |
| Main armament | 3-pounder |
| Secondary armament | 3 x Vickers .303 machine guns |
| Crew | 5 |
| Armor thickness | 0.25-0.3 in (6.25-8 mm) |

Gunner
Gunner
Commander
Gunner
Driver

**3-pounder** main gun

**Metal track** with cast links

**Covered sprung** suspension

**THREE-QUARTER VIEW**

**Regimental HQ** tank tactical symbol

**Vickers .303** machine gun in ball mount

T199    ML8

T199    ML8642

**Mechanized cavalry**
This propaganda poster from 1940, featuring the Medium Mark II, illustrates the extent to which the British Army had changed since World War I. By 1941, all of its cavalry regiments had been mechanized.

**MIGHTIER YET !**

**Britain's Mechanised Army grows stronger every day**

E16

**Vehicle identification**
This particular Vickers Medium Mark II tank was used as a training vehicle, indicated by the insignia painted on its sides.

**Eminent export**
The Vickers Medium was influential not only because it proved the potential of armored formations, but also because it was widely exported. Fifteen tanks were sold to Russia, and the one sold to Japan led to the country's own Type 89 tank design.

## EXTERIOR

The Vickers Medium was constructed with riveted armor plate—0.25 in (6.25 mm) thick on the front, which was protection against bullets but little else. However, the Royal Tank Corps, formed in 1923, became highly skilled at firing the 3-pounder gun on the move, an achievement that enabled them to keep up their mobility and become a harder target for enemy gunners to hit.

1. HQ Command tank tactical sign   2. Light shroud
3. Headlight   4. Engine air intake   5. Driver's hatch
6. Coaxial Vickers machine gun mount   7. Hull wall ball-mount
Vickers machine gun   8. Main armament sight aperture
9. Turret vision port   10. "Mitre"-type commander's hatch
11. Track tensioner   12. Track return roller   13. Drive sprocket
14. Exhaust

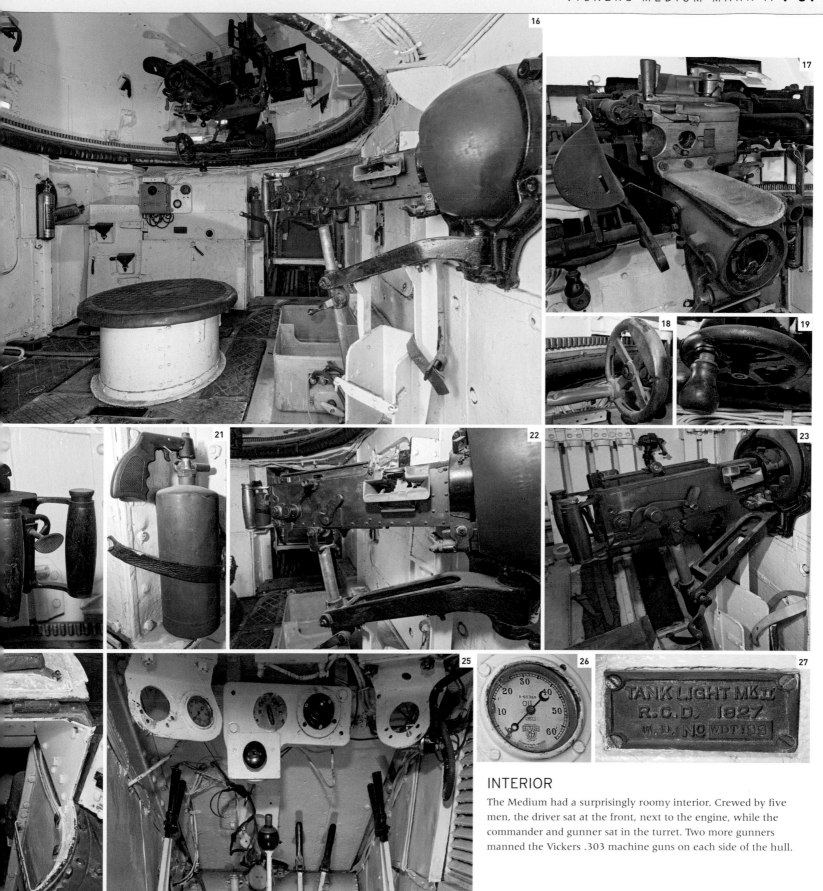

## INTERIOR

The Medium had a surprisingly roomy interior. Crewed by five men, the driver sat at the front, next to the engine, while the commander and gunner sat in the turret. Two more gunners manned the Vickers .303 machine guns on each side of the hull.

**15.** View through rear door **16.** Fighting compartment interior **17.** 3-pounder gun breach **18.** Gun elevation wheel **19.** Turret traverse wheel **20.** Coaxial Vickers machine gun **21.** Fire extinguisher **22.** Hull machine gun position **23.** Vickers .303 machine gun **24.** Driver's position from above **25.** Driver's controls **26.** Engine oil gauge **27.** Manufacturer's date plate

# 1939-1945
# WORLD WAR II

# WORLD WAR II

**The tank came of age** during World War II, seeing service all over the world in all climates and all terrains. The success of the German attacks of 1939–40 was largely due to the mobility of their Panzer forces. Although individually many of their tanks were outclassed by the latest Allied vehicles, the Germans concentrated their tank formations into larger units that were supported by artillery and airpower in a combination that overwhelmed their enemies. By contrast, French and British tanks were often spread too thinly across the front, and many were too lightly armed for antitank warfare.

In North Africa, the British enjoyed great success against the Italians, but once the German forces began to arrive, offensives and counteroffensives by both sides saw the front line move hundreds of miles in both directions. The Soviet Union had roughly 22,600 tanks when the Germans invaded. Many were outdated, and around 20,500 were lost in 1941 alone. The invasion forced the Soviets to move entire factories hundreds of miles to the east, where they began producing tanks and equipment on an unprecedented scale. In Europe, the Allied advances of 1944–45 were made possible by the mobility of their tank forces. Tanks also fought in Italy, where their mobility was tested by the terrain, and in the Far East, where older, lighter Allied tanks remained viable against Japanese forces.

The Allies built over 180,000 tanks during the war, and many remained in service around the world for decades, serving alongside newer vehicles whose designs incorporated the lessons learned during the conflict.

△ **German war poster**
A German Army recruitment poster enjoins the Dutch: "For your honour and conscience! Fight Bolshevism. The Waffen-SS is calling you!"

## Key events

▷ **September 1, 1939** German forces invade Poland. The Soviets invade on September 17, and Poland is defeated by October 6.

▷ **May 1940** The Battle of Arras. The experience of facing seemingly impenetrable British tanks spurs the development of the German Tiger.

▷ **April 1941** The Detroit Tank Arsenal delivers the first of 25,059 tanks to the US Army.

▷ **June 1941** Germany invades the Soviet Union. The next day, they encounter the T-34 for the first time.

▷ **November 1941** The first of over 12,000 British and American tanks supplied to the Soviet Union see action.

▷ **October 1942** The second Battle of El Alamein begins in Egypt. It marks the combat debut of the M4 Sherman.

▷ **July-August 1943** The Battle of Kursk is fought. The Soviets lose far more tanks than the Germans, but they gain the strategic initiative.

△ **Battle of Kursk**
Soviet infantry advance on a German position near Kursk in 1943. Their eventual victory was the beginning of the end of German ambitions in the east.

▷ **June 1944** On Saipan, the largest Japanese tank attack of the Pacific War is launched. Forty-four tanks take part, 12 survive.

▷ **April 1945** The invasion of Okinawa begins. Over 800 US tanks take part, reflecting how useful they have proven to be in the Pacific.

"**Nikolayev** and his loader Chernov **jumped** into the **burning machine**, **started** it, and sent it **right** into the **Tiger**. Both tanks **exploded** in the **collision**."
RUSSIAN MINISTRY OF DEFENSE ARCHIVE, ON THE BATTLE OF KURSK

◁ **A US War Production Board poster** reminds manufacturers of their priorities during the war.

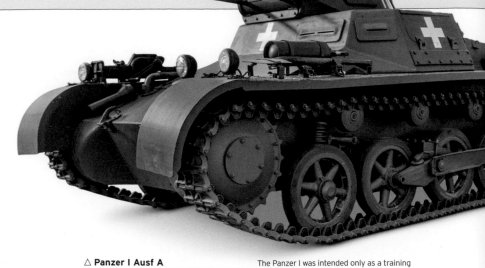

# German Tanks: 1939–40

Although the Treaty of Versailles in 1919 forbade Germany to own tanks, its army experimented with armored warfare in the Soviet Union during the 1920s. After Hitler came to power in 1933, Germany began openly building armored forces. The first tanks, Panzer I and II, were intended for training, but were used in the Spanish Civil War, which highlighted a number of weaknesses. Panzer IIIs and IVs incorporated these lessons, but they were scarce in 1939. The Panzer II remained the most common German tank throughout this period.

**Vision** ports

### △ Panzer I Ausf A

**Date** 1934 **Country** Germany

**Weight** 6 tons (5.5 tonnes)

**Engine** Krupp M305 gasoline, 57 hp

**Main armament** 2 x 7.92 mm MG13 machine guns

The Panzer I was intended only as a training vehicle. However, a shortage of other tanks meant the two-man Panzer I would ultimately see combat in Spain, Poland, France, Denmark, Norway, Russia, and North Africa. This Ausf A variant was underpowered and not really viable in combat; it proved invaluable for training, however.

### ◁ Panzer I Command Tank

**Date** 1935 **Country** Germany

**Weight** 6.6 tons (6 tonnes)

**Engine** Maybach NL38TR gasoline, 100 hp

**Main armament** 7.92 mm MG34 machine gun

The standard Panzer I only had space for a radio receiver, but unit commanders needed to transmit as well. This vehicle carried a transmitter and a third seat for the radio operator. It was used from 1935 until late 1942, when it was replaced by more advanced vehicles.

**2 cm** main gun

### ▷ Panzer II

**Date** 1937 **Country** Germany

**Weight** 10.6 tons (9.7 tonnes)

**Engine** Maybach HL62TR gasoline, 140 hp

**Main armament** 2 cm KwK 30 L/55 cannon

Although more heavily armed and armored than Panzer I, the Panzer II was also intended mainly for training. Due to a shortage of modern vehicles, it had to act as Germany's primary tank during 1939–40. Later, it proved effective as a light tank and for reconnaissance, serving until 1943.

**Drive sprocket** at front

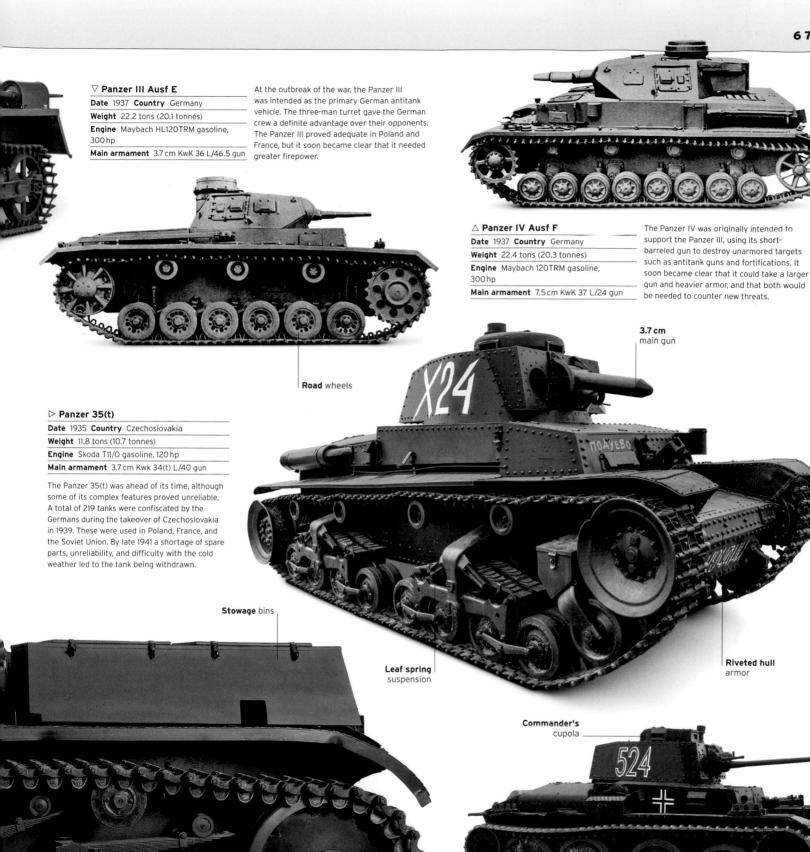

▽ **Panzer III Ausf E**

**Date** 1937 **Country** Germany

**Weight** 22.2 tons (20.1 tonnes)

**Engine** Maybach HL120TRM gasoline, 300 hp

**Main armament** 3.7 cm KwK 36 L/46.5 gun

At the outbreak of the war, the Panzer III was intended as the primary German antitank vehicle. The three-man turret gave the German crew a definite advantage over their opponents. The Panzer III proved adequate in Poland and France, but it soon became clear that it needed greater firepower.

△ **Panzer IV Ausf F**

**Date** 1937 **Country** Germany

**Weight** 22.4 tons (20.3 tonnes)

**Engine** Maybach 120TRM gasoline, 300 hp

**Main armament** 7.5 cm KwK 37 L/24 gun

The Panzer IV was originally intended to support the Panzer III, using its short-barreled gun to destroy unarmored targets such as antitank guns and fortifications. It soon became clear that it could take a larger gun and heavier armor, and that both would be needed to counter new threats.

**3.7 cm** main gun

▷ **Panzer 35(t)**

**Date** 1935 **Country** Czechoslovakia

**Weight** 11.8 tons (10.7 tonnes)

**Engine** Skoda T11/0 gasoline, 120 hp

**Main armament** 3.7 cm Kwk 34(t) L/40 gun

The Panzer 35(t) was ahead of its time, although some of its complex features proved unreliable. A total of 219 tanks were confiscated by the Germans during the takeover of Czechoslovakia in 1939. These were used in Poland, France, and the Soviet Union. By late 1941 a shortage of spare parts, unreliability, and difficulty with the cold weather led to the tank being withdrawn.

**Road** wheels

**Stowage** bins

**Leaf spring** suspension

**Riveted hull** armor

**Commander's** cupola

△ **Panzer 38(t) Ausf E**

**Date** 1938 **Country** Czechoslovakia

**Weight** 11 tons (10 tonnes)

**Engine** Praga EPA gasoline, 125 hp

**Main armament** 3.7 cm Kwk 38(t) L/47.8 gun

After annexing Czechoslovakia, Germany continued production of the Panzer 38(t), recognizing that it was more powerful and reliable than the Panzer I and II. Over 1,400 were built and used in France, Poland, and the Soviet Union until 1942. Its chassis was reused for a number of tank destroyers.

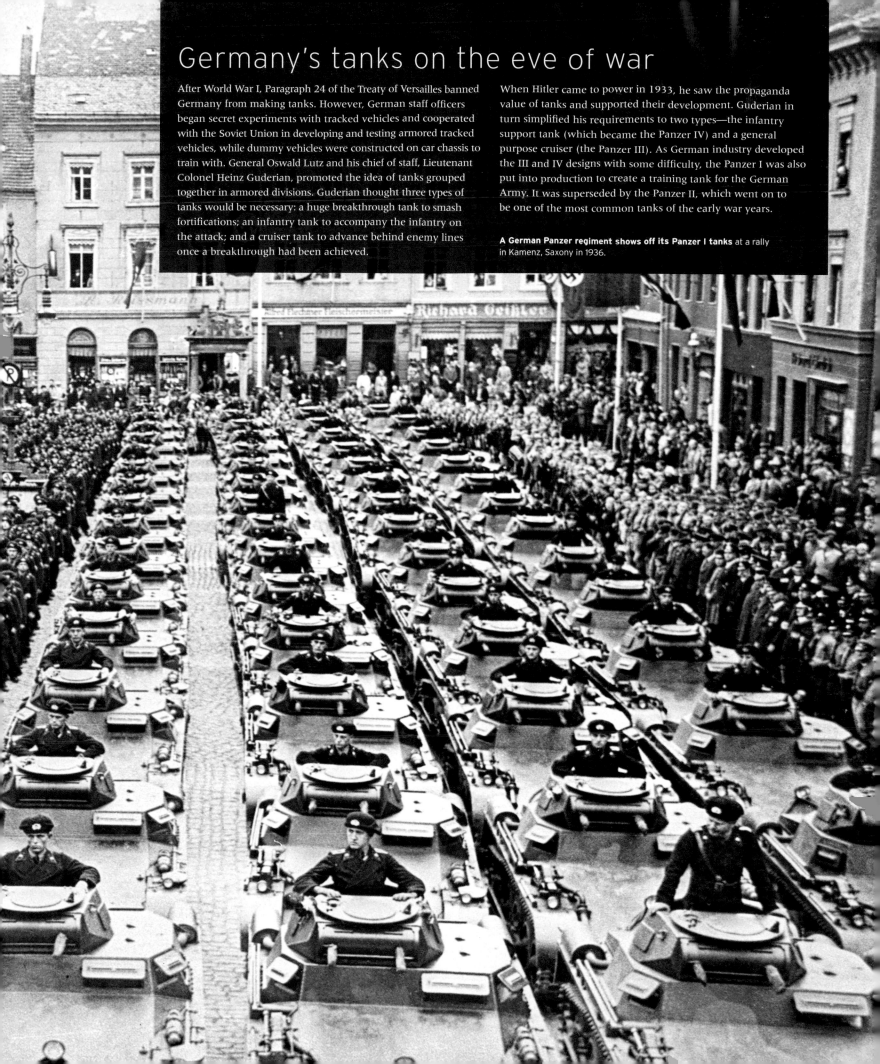

# Germany's tanks on the eve of war

After World War I, Paragraph 24 of the Treaty of Versailles banned Germany from making tanks. However, German staff officers began secret experiments with tracked vehicles and cooperated with the Soviet Union in developing and testing armored tracked vehicles, while dummy vehicles were constructed on car chassis to train with. General Oswald Lutz and his chief of staff, Lieutenant Colonel Heinz Guderian, promoted the idea of tanks grouped together in armored divisions. Guderian thought three types of tanks would be necessary: a huge breakthrough tank to smash fortifications; an infantry tank to accompany the infantry on the attack; and a cruiser tank to advance behind enemy lines once a breakthrough had been achieved.

When Hitler came to power in 1933, he saw the propaganda value of tanks and supported their development. Guderian in turn simplified his requirements to two types—the infantry support tank (which became the Panzer IV) and a general purpose cruiser (the Panzer III). As German industry developed the III and IV designs with some difficulty, the Panzer I was also put into production to create a training tank for the German Army. It was superseded by the Panzer II, which went on to be one of the most common tanks of the early war years.

**A German Panzer regiment shows off its Panzer I tanks** at a rally in Kamenz, Saxony in 1936.

# Allied Tanks: 1939-40

After the German invasion of Poland on September 1, 1939, the Polish forces fought bravely, but were overwhelmed by the Germans and their Soviet allies. In May 1940, the French and British forces, facing the German invasion of Western Europe, had more tanks than their opponents, and many were superior on paper. However, they were spread thinly rather than concentrated into large units, and the shock of the German invasion, combined with poor tactics, had a strong psychological impact on Allied commanders. As a result, most of the Allied tanks that fought in 1940 were captured or abandoned.

**Sharply angled** hull

### △ 7TP

| | |
|---|---|
| **Date** 1937 | **Country** Poland |

**Weight** 10.5 tons (9.6 tonnes)

**Engine** Saurer VLDBb diesel, 110 hp

**Main armament** 37 mm Bofors wz.37 L/45 gun

The 7TP was a Polish development of the Vickers Mark E. A small number of 7TPs had twin machine gun turrets, but most of the approximately 150 tanks built had a single turret armed with a 37 mm gun. The 7TPs were superior to most German tanks in 1939, but they were too few to affect the outcome of the invasion of Poland.

**Rounded** hull areas deflect projectiles

**Armor** covers road wheels

### △ SOMUA S35

| | |
|---|---|
| **Date** 1935 | **Country** France |

**Weight** 21.5 tons (19.5 tonnes)

**Engine** Somua V-8 gasoline, 190 hp

**Main armament** 47 mm SA 35 gun

The S35 was made of cast steel, which provided much better armor protection than riveted panels. It had a crew of three, but only a one-man turret, so the commander had to load, aim, and fire the gun, as well as command the tank.

**Hexagonal** one-man turret

**Vision** port

### △ Char léger Modéle 1935 R

| | |
|---|---|
| **Date** 1935 | **Country** France |

**Weight** 12.1 tons (11 tonnes)

**Engine** Renault V-4 gasoline, 85 hp

**Main armament** 37 mm Puteaux SA 18 L/21 gun

Commonly known as the Renault R35, this was a light, two-man infantry tank. It had thick armor and a gun that was intended to destroy fortifications and eliminate infantry rather than knock out tanks. It was designed to operate alongside infantry, so its top speed was only 12½mph (20 km/h).

**Engine** exhaust pipe

### ▷ Char B1 bis

| | |
|---|---|
| **Date** 1936 | **Country** France |

**Weight** 34.7 tons (31.5 tonnes)

**Engine** Renault V12 gasoline, 307 hp

**Main armament** 1 x 75mm ABS 1929 SA 35 L/17.1 howitzer, 1 x 47 mm SA 35 gun

The most powerful French tank in 1940, the B1 bis was armed with a 75mm infantry support gun in the hull and a 47mm antitank gun in the usual one-man turret. It was very heavily armored, but suffered from slow speed and limited range. This was a result of being in development since the 1920s; by the time it was ready, it had already been overtaken by other models.

**Welded** armor

### △ Char léger Modéle 1936 FCM

**Date** 1936 **Country** France

**Weight** 13.7 tons (12.4 tonnes)

**Engine** Berliet 4-cylinder diesel, 91 hp

**Main armament** 37 mm Puteaux SA 18 L/21 gun

This two-man infantry tank, commonly known as the FCM 36, was one of the first tanks to use welded armor, which gave it excellent protection. However, its SA 18 gun was inadequate against enemy armor, making the FCM less useful against the German Panzer forces. Only 100 were produced.

**T7230**

### △ A9 Cruiser

**Date** 1937 **Country** UK

**Weight** 13.4 tons (12.2 tonnes)

**Engine** AEC Type 179 gasoline, 150 hp

**Main armament** QF 2-pounder gun

The A9 was the first cruiser tank, a British concept intended for independent operations rather than infantry support. It was therefore fast, but lightly armored. The A9 had capable suspension and probably the most powerful antitank gun in the world at the time—the 2-pounder.

**Cast** turret

### △ Char léger Modèle 1939 H

**Date** 1935 **Country** France

**Weight** 13.2 tons (12 tonnes)

**Engine** Hotchkiss 6-cylinder gasoline, 120 hp

**Main armament** 37 mm Puteaux SA 38 L/33 gun

The H39 was an upgraded version of the H35, a two-man light tank. Intended to operate with the infantry, the H35 was rejected because of its poor cross-country performance and was passed to the cavalry. The H39 solved this problem and improved the tank's firepower. Around 1,200 tanks of both versions were built in total. After the fall of France in 1940, several hundred of these were used by the Germans.

**Front-mounted** drive sprocket

**Camouflage** designed by Major Denys Pavitt

**Allied** insignia

**One-man** turret

**47 mm** antitank gun

**Metal** tracks

**T10245**

### △ Infantry Tank Mark IIA A12

**Date** 1939 **Country** UK

**Weight** 29.7 tons (26.9 tonnes)

**Engine** 2 x AEC 6-cylinder diesel, 95 hp each

**Main armament** QF 2-pounder gun

Commonly known as Matilda II, this infantry tank was a far more capable vehicle than its predecessor. It had even heavier armor and a 2-pounder gun. In late 1940 and early 1941, this "Queen of the Desert" dominated the battlefields of North Africa. Although outclassed by later German tanks, it fought on in Australian hands against the Japanese. It was the only British tank to serve throughout World War II.

### ▽ A13 Cruiser Mark III

**Date** 1939 **Country** UK

**Weight** 15.9 tons (14.4 tonnes)

**Engine** Nuffield Liberty V12 gasoline, 240 hp

**Main armament** QF 2-pounder gun

The Mark III A13 was the first British tank to use Christie suspension (see pp.52–53). This and the Mark III's powerful engine gave it greater mobility, but its armor was only 0.55 in (14 mm) at its thickest. The Mark III—and the better-armored but otherwise identical Mark IV—served in France in 1940 and the Western Desert in 1941.

**Crew kit** on turret

**AGILITY**

**T 9143**

# Axis Tanks: 1941–45

The North African Campaign, which began in 1940, was followed in 1941 by the German invasion of the Soviet Union and the Japanese attack on Pearl Harbor. As fighting intensified, tank technology evolved—so much so that by the end of the war tanks had the kind of firepower, protection, and reliability that were undreamed-of in 1939. However, technology wasn't everything. The Germans built ever more formidable vehicles, but these were plagued by mechanical failure and inexperienced crews. Tanks produced by Italy and Japan (the other Axis powers), being less advanced, were increasingly outclassed against the Allied armies.

**Commander's** cupola

**Riveted** hull

### △ Type 95 Ha-Go

**Date** 1936  **Country**  Japan

**Weight**  8.3 tons (7.5 tonnes)

**Engine**  Mitsubishi 6-cylinder diesel, 110 hp

**Main armament**  37 mm Type 98 gun

The Type 95 was popular with its crews and remained in front-line Japanese service throughout World War II. It was successful against the Chinese in the late 1930s, and in the early Japanese victories in 1942, but as Allied tanks began to enter combat it was soon outmatched. Its engine was powerful for its size, and its light weight made it useful on difficult terrain.

**37 mm** main gun

**Stowage** container

**Bell crank** suspension

### ◁ Type 97 Chi-Ha

**Date** 1937  **Country**  Japan

**Weight**  16.8 tons (15.2 tonnes)

**Engine**  Mitsubishi Type 97 diesel, 170 hp

**Main armament**  47 mm Type 1 gun

The Type 97 medium tank had a similar design to the Ha-Go, and featured a 57 mm gun optimized for infantry support. However, shortcomings in its firepower were exposed in the Battle of Khalkin Gol in 1939. The Japanese responded with the improved Shinhoto Chi-Ha, which had a 47 mm antitank gun.

**7.92 mm** MG 34 machine gun

### ▷ Panzer IV Ausf H

**Date** 1937  **Country**  Germany

**Weight**  28 tons (25.4 tonnes)

**Engine**  Maybach 120TRM petrol, 300 hp

**Main armament**  7.5 cm KwK 40 L/48 gun

First produced in 1937, the Panzer IV was upgraded in 1942. The addition of the long 7.5 cm gun promoted it from its original role as a support tank to that of the German Army's primary antitank vehicle. Its armor protection was also improved, including large add-on skirts and turret armor. Roughly 8,500 were built, making it the most commonly used German tank of World War II.

**Rubber-rimmed** road wheels

### △ Panzer III Ausf L

**Date** 1937  **Country**  Germany

**Weight**  25.4 tons (23.1 tonnes)

**Engine**  Maybach HL120TRM gasoline, 300 hp

**Main armament**  5 cm Kwk 39 L/60 gun

The Panzer III's armor and gun were both upgraded after combat experience in France. This version, the Ausf L, had 50 mm armor and a 5 cm gun. It fought in the Soviet Union and North Africa, but was replaced by the Panzer IV from 1942. The final Panzer III variant mounted the same 7.5 cm howitzer as the first Panzer IVs.

**Leaf-spring** suspension

**Breda 38** machine guns

### ▷ M14/41

**Date** 1940  **Country**  Italy

**Weight**  16 tons (14.5 tonnes)

**Engine**  SPA 15T M41 diesel, 145 hp

**Main armament**  47 mm M35 L/32 gun

Italy learned lessons from sending tanks into the Spanish Civil War. New vehicles were designed, as a result of that experience, and first saw service in North Africa in 1940. The M14/41 was an upgraded version of the M13/40 that was optimized for desert conditions. It was well armed, but its armor was no match for the Allies' 2-pounder gun.

**Large** drive sprocket

◁ **Tiger**

**Date** 1942 **Country** Germany

**Weight** 63.8 tons (57.9 tonnes)

**Engine** Maybach HL210P45 gasoline, 650 hp (see p.75)

**Main armament** 8.8 cm KwK 36 L/56 gun

The Tiger was the product of Germany's experience of fighting in France in 1940. Heavily armored and armed with the powerful 8.8 cm gun, it proved a formidable opponent for Allied tank crews. However, the Tiger was not only expensive; its mechanical complexity also made it prone to technical problems. Only 1,347 were built.

**Interleaved**
road wheels

**7.5 cm** main gun

**Spare track links**
on hull

◁ **Panther**

**Date** 1943 **Country** Germany

**Weight** 51 tons (46.2 tonnes)

**Engine** Maybach HL230P30 gasoline, 700 hp

**Main armament** 7.5 cm KwK 42 L/70 gun

Designed in response to the Soviet T-34, the Panther was more heavily armored and boasted far greater firepower. First used at Kursk in July 1943, it was fast and maneuverable, with strong frontal armor, and a very accurate and powerful gun. However, like the Tiger, it was often unreliable; engine fires were common.

**Commander's**
cupola

**7.92 mm** MG 34
machine gun

**Glacis**
plate armour

**Armor** sloped
variably between
25 and 50 degrees

▷ **Tiger II (King Tiger)**

**Date** 1944 **Country** Germany

**Weight** 76.2 tons (69.1 tonnes)

**Engine** Maybach HL230P30 gasoline, 700 hp

**Main armament** 8.8 cm KwK 43 L/71

The Tiger II was perhaps the most formidable tank of World War II. Its frontal armor could withstand all Allied anti-tank weapons, and its 8.8 cm gun was a threat even at long range. Its engine was unreliable, however, and only 489 were built—too few to influence the outcome of the war.

# Tiger I

Of all the tanks of World War II, none has inspired such a fearsome reputation as the Tiger. With its 88 mm gun, thick frontal armor, wide tracks, and sheer size, it was a devastating weapon that struck terror into Allied forces on the battlefield. However, it was dogged by technical difficulties that compromised its tactical effectiveness.

HITLER ORDERED the production of a heavy tank in May 1941, after the failure of German weaponry to penetrate the armor of the Matilda 2 and Char B. The Tiger's boxy shape and layout were similar to earlier German tanks, but on a huge scale—over twice the weight of the Panzer IV. The heavy tank was a stable platform for the accurate 88 mm KwK 36 gun, for which it carried 92 rounds. Its engine was upgraded from 650 hp to 700 hp during production: even so, the engine and transmission struggled to cope with the vehicle's weight, which grew from a planned 55 tons (50 tonnes) to 63.8 tons (57.9 tonnes).

**REAR VIEW**

The Tiger was rushed into service and suffered numerous growing pains. It was mainly used defensively, rather than to punch through enemy lines as intended: the cost of production, and a shortage of skilled crews, meant that it failed to have the desired impact on the battlefield. However, it had a huge psychological effect on the enemy, and remains the most mythologized tank of the war.

| SPECIFICATIONS | |
|---|---|
| Name | PzKpfw VI Tiger Ausf E |
| Date | 1942 |
| Origin | Germany |
| Production | 1,347 |
| Engine | Maybach HL210P45 V-12 gasoline, 650 hp |
| Weight | 63.8 tons (57.9 tonnes) |
| Main armament | 8.8 cm KwK 36 |
| Secondary armament | 7.92 mm MG34 |
| Crew | 5 |
| Armor thickness | Max 4.72 in (120 mm) |

Radio operator
Loader
Commander
Driver
Gunner

**Muzzle** brake expels propellent gases to stabilize the main gun

**Ball mount** offers both protection and range of fire

**Spare track** links can also act as extra armor

**THREE-QUARTER VIEW**

**Interleaved** road wheels help to distribute weight

**Propaganda machine**
The Tiger was heavily used for German propaganda during the war. Here the *Berliner Illustrierte Zeitung*, a popular wartime illustrated magazine, features the tank on its cover.

**Tactical number**
The number "131" indicates that this tank belonged to the 1st Company, 3rd Platoon of its tank regiment, and that it was the 1st tank of its platoon.

**One of a kind**
This tank, Tiger 131, was captured in Tunisia in April 1943. As the first complete Tiger captured, it was taken to Britain for extensive analysis. An early example, it had the original HL210P45 engine rather than the more common HL230P30 700 hp. The tank has been restored to running order.

## EXTERIOR

To spread out the large weight of the tank, the road wheels are positioned in an interleaved system, copied from earlier German half-track designs. Sixteen torsion bars provide suspension—eight arms on each side, each arm holding three wheels, which meant that to replace just one of the inner wheels, nine had to be removed. The size of the tank led to innovations such as removing outer road wheels and installing thinner transportation tracks for train travel. This tank, Tiger 131, still shows exterior battle damage from the day of its capture.

**1.** National recognition symbol  **2.** Driver's vision port  **3.** Turret lifting lug  **4.** Radio operator's machine gun  **5.** Smoke grenade dischargers  **6.** Drive sprocket and interleaved road wheels  **7.** Commander's hatch  **8.** Turret pistol port  **9.** Towing cables and wire cutters on hull  **10.** Fiefel air filter tubes  **11.** Track toolbox

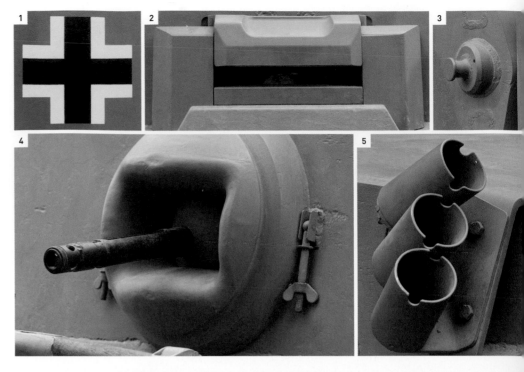

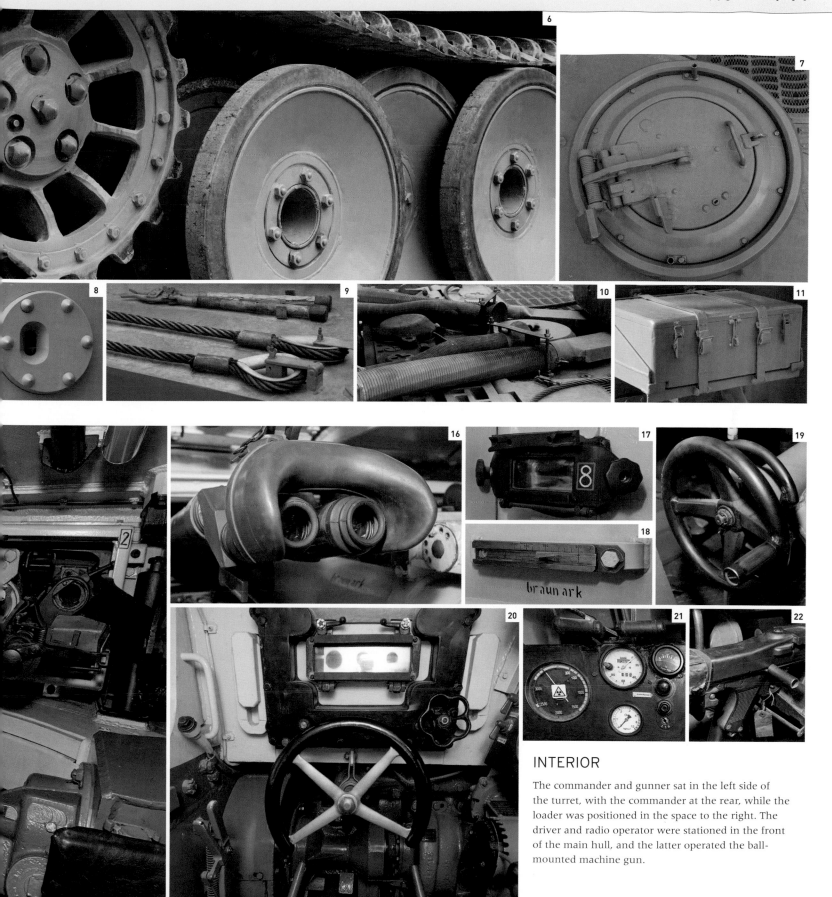

## INTERIOR

The commander and gunner sat in the left side of the turret, with the commander at the rear, while the loader was positioned in the space to the right. The driver and radio operator were stationed in the front of the main hull, and the latter operated the ball-mounted machine gun.

**12.** Commander's hatch (open)   **13.** Commander's periscope
**14.** Turret traverse wheel   **15.** Loader's position and main gun breech   **16.** Binocular gun sight   **17.** Turret side vision port
**18.** Gun recoil return gauge   **19.** Barrel elevation wheel
**20.** Driver's controls and vision port   **21.** Driver's instrument panel   **22.** Co-driver's machine gun

# The flying tanks of D-Day

The idea of carrying tanks by air dates back to the early 1930s, but it was not achieved until 1944—D-Day. On the morning of June 6, a few tanks were flown from an airfield in southern England and landed on the French coast near the mouth of the Orne river. The tanks were Tetrarch Light Tanks (see p.92) and the aircraft were Hamilcar Gliders.

The Hamilcar was a large aircraft for its time, with a wingspan of 110 ft (34 m) and a weight of around 7 tons (6.3 tonnes). Built almost entirely of wood, it required a crew of two. It dropped its undercarriage on takeoff and landed on skids—as soon as the glider stopped, the tank started up and, as it moved forward, it activated a rope that opened the nose door.

On D-Day, each Hamilcar carried either a pair of Universal Carriers (see p.122) or one Tetrarch. Hamilcars were used again on the Rhine Crossing in March 1945, in this case carrying US Locust light tanks. Built in the US to replace the Tetrarch, the Locust had many growing pains, and by the time it reached Europe it was too weak to be of much use. Of the eight tanks used in the Rhine crossing, one was lost as a glider broke up in flight, three were damaged on landing, and another was rapidly knocked out by a German assault gun.

**A Locust light tank** disembarks from the folding nose of a Hamilcar glider in 1944.

# M3 Stuart

As World War II drew near, the US military set about replacing its outdated M2 light tank with a newer, better-armored version. The M3 was armed with a 37 mm M6 main gun supported by five machine guns, later reduced to two; its armor and weapons were no match for most tanks, but it was well-liked for its speed and mechanical performance.

**USED BY BOTH BRITISH** and US armed forces, the M3 was christened "Stuart" after the Confederate General J. E. B. Stuart, in keeping with the British military tradition that named US-made tanks after US generals. Later, British troops gave it the affectionate nickname "honey" in honor of its reliablity.

The M3 had a Continental air-cooled radial engine with a heavy fuel consumption. This affected its operational range, which could be as low as 75 miles (120 km) before refueling was necessary. However, British troops liked the reliability of the tank, and even though many Stuarts were knocked out in early encounters in the North African desert, this was mainly due to poor tactical use, not through any particular fault of the vehicles themselves.

An improved model of the tank—the M5, with a redesigned hull and Cadillac V-8 engine—began replacing earlier models of the M3 from 1943 (see p.84). However, by this time it was clear that the 37 mm gun was inadequate as an antitank gun against the heavier vehicles in use in Europe. The M3 and M5 were still used for reconnaissance in British service, sometimes with turrets removed for speed, and the tank was still a match for the less well-protected Japanese armored vehicles in the Pacific theater of war.

**REAR VIEW**

## SPECIFICATIONS

| Name | M3A1 Stuart |
| --- | --- |
| Date | 1941 |
| Origin | USA |
| Production | 22,700 |
| Engine | Continental R-670 7-cylinder gasoline, 250 hp |
| Weight | 14.2 tons (12.9 tonnes) |
| Main armament | 37 mm M6 |
| Secondary armament | .30 Browning M1919 |
| Crew | 4 |
| Armor thickness | 2 in (51mm) max |

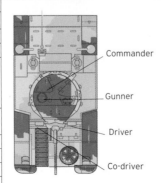

Commander

Gunner

Driver

Co-driver

**Two-man** turret holds commander and gunner

**37 mm** main gun with up to 174 rounds

**Co-driver's** machine gun

**Serial** number

**Vehicle** name

**Towing cable** for quick battlefield recovery

**THREE-QUARTER VIEW**

**Vertical** volute suspension system

## CLEMENTINE

**Vehicle name "Clementine"**
Some units allowed the naming of tanks after troops' sweethearts, while others used place names or the initial letter of the unit.

## T37765

**Serial number**
The unique serial number issued to each tank remained with the vehicle, even if it was allocated to a new unit.

**Reconnaissance tank**
This tank, called Clementine (see above), saw action with A Squadron, 3rd Royal Tank Regiment, part of the 4th Armoured Brigade, in November 1942 at the beginning of the Tunisian campaign. By this stage of the war, the Stuart was being used as a reconnaissance vehicle, since German tanks and antitank guns could easily pierce its 1.49 in (38 mm) frontal armor.

## EXTERIOR

The M3's compact two-man turret gave it a slim profile, but offered very little space for the commander and gunner. The lack of a loader put additional pressure on the commander to load the main gun, as well as constantly focusing on the enemy's position and the best direction of attack. Later models were equipped with a commander's cupola to improve visibility; this version relied on periscopes and pistol ports around the turret. The driver's vision, meanwhile, was limited to a single armored port at the front of the vehicle.

**1.** Insignia  **2.** Co-driver's machine gun  **3.** Driver's hatch (open)  **4.** Driver's vision port  **5.** Commander's periscope  **6.** Turret pistol port  **7.** Drive sprocket **8.** Track tensioner  **9.** Suspension and road wheels **10.** Engine  **11.** Fire-extinguisher release  **12.** Rear light **13.** Toolbox

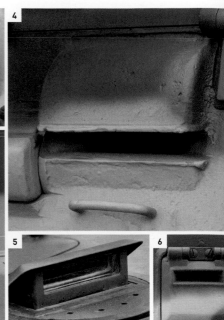

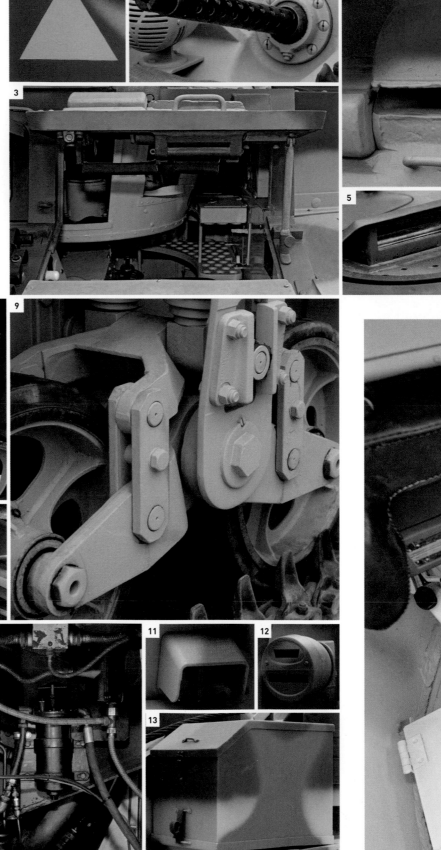

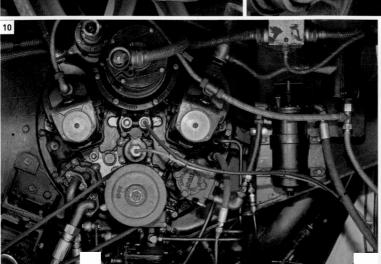

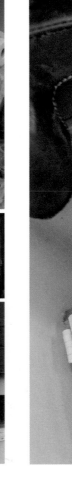

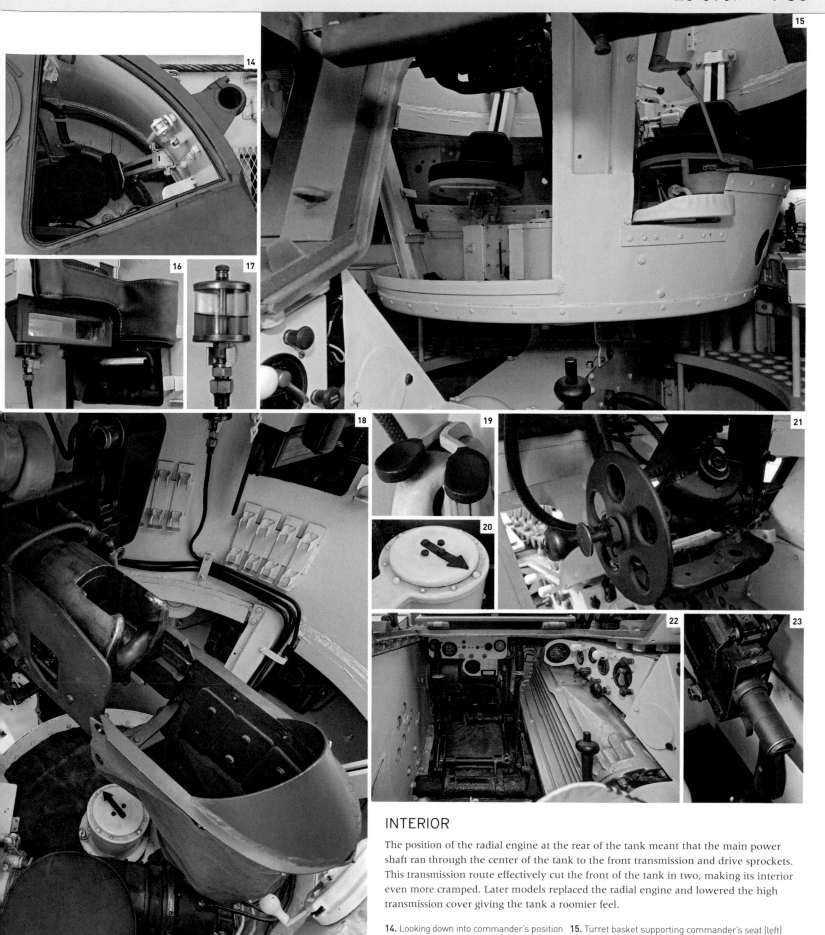

## INTERIOR

The position of the radial engine at the rear of the tank meant that the main power shaft ran through the center of the tank to the front transmission and drive sprockets. This transmission route effectively cut the front of the tank in two, making its interior even more cramped. Later models replaced the radial engine and lowered the high transmission cover giving the tank a roomier feel.

**14.** Looking down into commander's position  **15.** Turret basket supporting commander's seat (left) and gunner's seat (right)  **16.** Commander's periscope  **17.** Hydraulic fluid  **18.** Gunner's position
**19.** Automatic turret traverse controls  **20.** Direction of travel indicator  **21.** Manual barrel elevation wheel  **22.** Driver's position  **23.** Co-driver's machine gun

# US Tanks: 1941-45

In 1940, the US had around 350 modern tanks in service. The well-developed American automotive industry turned its hand to tank manufacturing, and expanded massively. By 1945 it had built over 60,000 vehicles and supplied them to every Allied power. Successful design components were kept from model to model to ease production. The M4 Sherman in particular proved capable of being upgraded extensively. American tanks were robust, well built, and powerful: while German designs were sometimes more powerful on paper, US crews' good tactics, logistics, and training were often enough to prevail.

**Air** filter

△ **M3A1 (Stuart)**

**Date** 1940 **Country** USA

**Weight** 14.2 tons (12.9 tonnes)

**Engine** Continental R-670-9A gasoline, 250 hp

**Main armament** 37 mm M6 L/56.6 gun

The Stuart was an improved version of the 37 mm-armed M2A4. It benefited from mass production techniques that made it reliable and easy to repair. It was used by all the Allied powers in every theater of war. By 1944 it was obsolete as a tank, but remained in service for reconnaissance.

**Riveted** armor

**37 mm** gun

**75 mm** main gun

△ **M3 (Grant)**

**Date** 1941 **Country** USA

**Weight** 30 tons (27.2 tonnes)

**Engine** Wright Continental R-975 gasoline, 340 hp

**Main armament** 1 x 75 mm M2 L/31 gun, 1 x 37 mm M5 L/56.5 gun

The M3 stemmed from an urgent need to field a 75 mm gun before a suitable turret was ready. The gun was mounted in a sponson on the hull, which limited its field of fire. The M3 kept the successful engine and Vertical Volute Suspension System (VVSS) from the M2 medium. British M3s used a modified turret and named it the Grant. The original version was named the Lee.

▷ **M4A1 (Sherman)**

**Date** 1942 **Country** USA

**Weight** 33.3 tons (30.2 tonnes)

**Engine** Wright-Continental R-975 gasoline, 400 hp

**Main armament** 75 mm M3 L/40 gun

The Sherman used the M3 chassis, combined with a turret for the 75 mm gun. There were five main variants of the Sherman, the primary difference being the engine used. The M4A1 had a cast rather than welded hull. Almost 50,000 were built; this tank was the second ever produced and is the oldest survivor.

**Headlight** cage

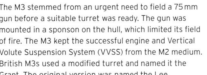

**Aerial** mount

△ **M5A1 (Stuart)**

**Date** 1942 **Country** USA

**Weight** 16.9 tons (15.3 tonnes)

**Engine** 2 x Cadillac Series 42 gasoline, 148 hp each

**Main armament** 37 mm M6 L/56.6 gun

The M5 was developed from the M3 to free up R-670 engines for aircraft. The hull was also redesigned to improve protection. The new engine arrangement allowed more space inside for the crew and made the tank quieter. Unlike the M3, the M5 was not used by the Soviet Union, but both were used for the same roles in British and American service.

▷ **M4A3E8 (76) (Sherman)**

**Date** 1944 **Country** USA
**Weight** 35.6 tons (32.3 tonnes)
**Engine** Ford GAA V8 gasoline, 500 hp
**Main armament** 76 mm M1A2 L/52 gun

A late model of M4A3, this "Easy 8" Sherman was armed with the more powerful 76 mm gun in the new T23 turret. The frontal armor was sloped at 47 degrees, giving improved protection. The new Horizontal Volute Suspension System (HVSS) and wider tracks improved the tank's mobility. This example appeared in the 2014 movie *Fury*.

Upgraded 76 mm gun

Horizontal Volute Suspension System

Gunsight aperture

◁ **M24 (Chaffee)**

**Date** 1944 **Country** USA
**Weight** 20.2 tons (18.3 tonnes)
**Engine** 2 x Cadillac Type 44T24 gasoline, 110 hp each
**Main armament** 75 mm M6 L/39 gun

The M24 was designed to have superior mobility and firepower compared to the Stuart. However, due to delays in production, it did not fully replace the Stuart before the end of the war. It was the first US tank to use torsion bars instead of the Vertical Volute Suspension System.

Muzzle brake

Air vent

Idler wheel

Pistol port

△ **M26 (Pershing)**

**Date** 1945 **Country** USA
**Weight** 45.9 tons (41.7 tonnes)
**Engine** Ford GAF V8 gasoline, 500 hp
**Main armament** 90 mm M3 L/53

After a prolonged development process, production of the M26 was further delayed, and only 20 reached Europe to see combat. The powerful 90 mm gun was capable against the Panther and the Tiger. Like the Chaffee, it had torsion bar suspension. As it used the same engine as the M4A3, but was heavier, it proved underpowered.

MICHAEL

T 74195

Track links

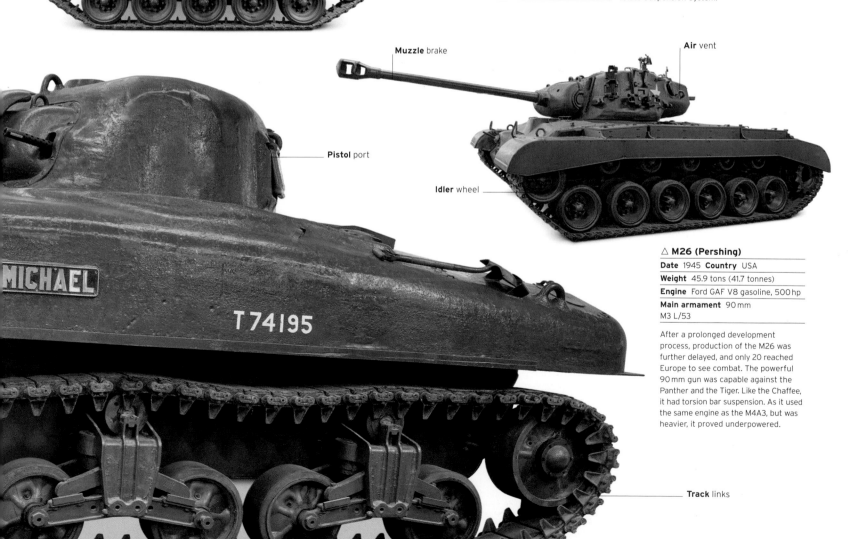

# M4 Sherman

Like the T-34 and Tiger, the Sherman's story is often clouded by myths and misinformation. The US had made just 365 modern tanks by the end of 1940, but had made 49,234 Shermans alone by the war's end—an amazing achievement, and one that should not be overlooked when comparing the Sherman with late-war German tanks on a one to one basis.

**IN 1940, THE US DOCTRINE** for the use of tanks centered around their role as weapons of exploitation—armored cavalry that could dash forward after a breakthrough and cause mayhem behind enemy lines. Designed in 1940 as the successor to the interim model M3 Lee medium tank, the Sherman met this criteria perfectly: it was speedy, and was armed with a good dual-purpose gun. It was also simple to maintain, reliable, and rugged. It was built in 11 different plants across the US, most of which had had no prior experience in tank manufacturing.

The Sherman soon proved itself well suited to the needs of World War II, and was made in a number of subvariants, adapted for many roles, and produced in such numbers (63,181, including derivatives) that it could arm the US, British and Commonwealth, Russian, and other Allied armies. The Sherman saw service in many nations' armies after World War II, and was still in service in Paraguay in 2016.

REAR VIEW

| SPECIFICATIONS | |
| --- | --- |
| Name | M4A1 Sherman |
| Date | 1940 |
| Origin | US |
| Production | 49,234 |
| Engine | Wright-Continental R-975 radial gasoline, 400 hp |
| Weight | 33.3 tons (30.2 tonnes) |
| Main armament | 75 mm M3 |
| Secondary armament | .30 Browning M1919 machine guns |
| Crew | 5 |
| Armor thickness | 4.6 in (118 mm) |

Loader
Commander
Gunner
Driver
Co-driver

75 mm medium velocity gun

Gun mantlet

Barrel clamp

Extra stowage along the front glacis

**THREE-QUARTER VIEW**

Rubber-blocked track

Additional armor

### Uparmored model
This Sherman M4A1 has a cast hull and additional armor welded over the hull sides to protect the ammunition stowage. In spite of crew stories, reports showed ammunition caused more "brew-ups" (fires) in Sherman tanks than the engine did, so protecting ammunition with extra armor and later "wet" ammunition stowage was vital.

### "Havoc"
The tank has the markings of a vehicle from H Company, 66 Armoured Regiment of the 2nd US Armored Division. Tank names in H company began, understandably, with the letter H.

### Tank serial number
While tanks could change units, be rebuilt, and reassigned, meaning a change in markings, the unique serial number remained with the vehicle as a permanent reference.

## EXTERIOR

As the war progressed, the design of the Sherman was modified with thicker armor, wider tracks, and a new, upgraded 76 mm gun. With 11 different factories building the tank around four main engine types, the variations between the models can be considerable. This tank, produced by the Lima tank works in Ohio, US in 1943, has upgraded armor and went on to see service as a training vehicle in the French army after World War II.

1. Allied Forces recognition symbol  2. Tow hook
3. Headlight  4. Front drive sprocket  5. Co-driver's machine gun  6. Armored roof fan cover  7. Driver's periscope  8. Driver's hatch (closed)  9. Paired road wheels  10. Air filter  11. Spotlight  12. Turret hatch and commander's cupola  13. Engine bay

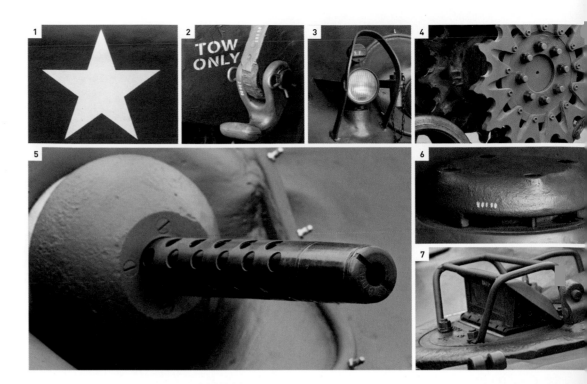

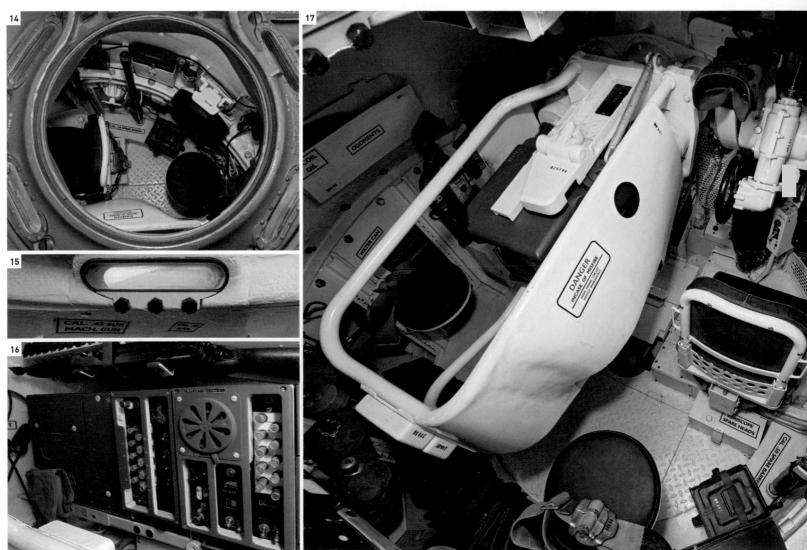

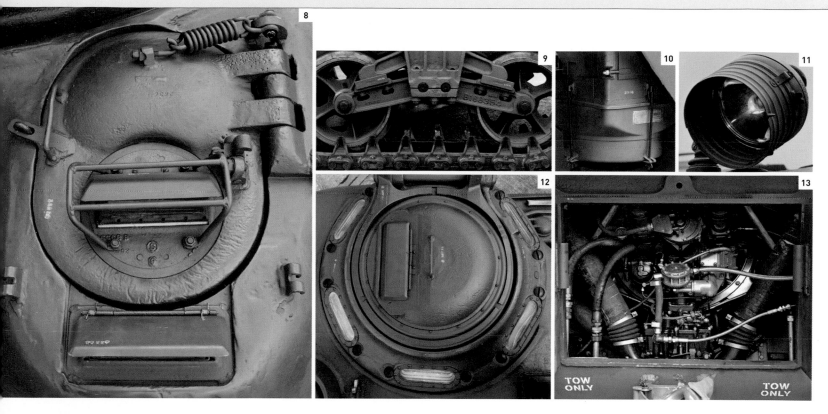

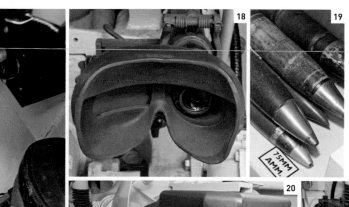

## INTERIOR

This version features the early turret design, with only one turret hatch shared by the fighting crew of commander, gunner, and loader; later models had a second hatch. The commander's cupola offered a wide range of view, with vision ports all the way around.

**14.** Looking down into the commander's position **15.** Commander's vision cupola block **16.** SCR 508 radio set **17.** Turret interior showing commander's and gunner's position **18.** 75 mm gunsight **19.** 75 mm ammunition **20.** Main gun breech **21.** Coaxial machine gun **22.** Azimuth indicator **23.** Main gun elevation wheel **24.** Driver's hatch **25.** Driver's position **26.** Driver's instrument panel

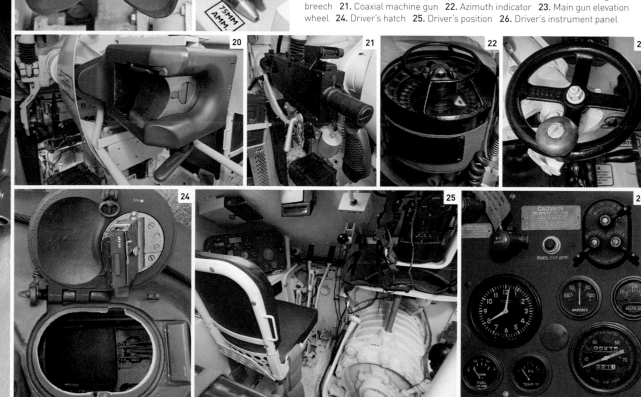

# Engine change behind enemy lines

"Hurricane," a Sherman serving with Company H, 66th Armored Regiment of the 2nd Armored Division, came ashore at Utah Beach on June 9, 1944. By August 16, it was in need of a new engine and here, behind the lines at Teilleul in Normandy, France, a new Continental R-975-C4 engine was readied to be dropped into the hull by a wrecker.

Tanks—because of the stresses and strains they undergo— wear out components quickly. Climate and terrain have an obvious effect: dust in hot climates can enter the engine and act as a grinding paste along with sand and gravel, while in cold climates metal can become brittle, and fluids within the tank can freeze, causing damage. Inexperienced or undertrained

crews could also damage vehicles, and the nature of battle meant that maintenance could not always be properly carried out, leading to breakdowns and component failures.

When the British Army first received US tanks in 1941, there was general agreement that maintenance of US vehicles was much easier than contemporary British designs. For a tank crew in the field, easier maintenance meant less time spent carrying it out, and that meant the greater possibility of a good night's sleep.

**M4 Sherman "Hurricane"** has its engine changed in Normandy, France, in 1944. The Sherman's manual dedicated 16 pages to engine changes.

# UK and Commonwealth Tanks

After evacuating from France, Britain had very few tanks available, and a German invasion was believed to be imminent. Due to this danger, it was decided to continue building older, less capable vehicles rather than accept the delays in production that would result from designing new vehicles and modifying factories to build them. This, combined with a restriction on size and weight, brought about by the need to fit tanks on railroad cars, meant that throughout the war British tanks were almost always less well-armored than their opponents.

△ **Covenanter**

**Date** 1940 **Country** UK

**Weight** 20.2 tons (18.3 tonnes)

**Engine** Meadows Flat 12 gasoline, 300 hp

**Main armament** QF 2-pounder gun

The A13 Covenanter shared only the Christie suspension with earlier A13s. It had several faults. The engine radiators were attached to the hull front, leading to cooling problems. The tank used steel wheels instead of aluminum, which increased weight and stressed the suspension. It was mostly used for training.

▷ **Valentine Mark II**

**Date** 1940 **Country** UK

**Weight** 17.9 tons (16.3 tonnes)

**Engine** AEC Type 190 diesel, 131 hp

**Main armament** QF 2-pounder gun

The Valentine used parts from the A10 Cruiser, making it cheaper than the Matilda (see p.71). It also carried less armor but was easier to make. Early variants, such as this, mounted the 2-pounder gun in a two-man turret. A three-man turret was later developed, as was a two-man turret with a larger 6-pounder gun.

**Coaxial** machine gun

**Driver's** vision port

**Three-wheel** bogies

**Idler** wheel

**Anti-infantry** machine-gun

**Fuel container** on hull

**Driver's** vision port

◁ **Tetrarch (Close Support)**

**Date** 1940 **Country** UK

**Weight** 8.4 tons (7.6 tonnes)

**Engine** Meadows 12-cylinder gasoline, 165 hp

**Main armament** 3 in howitzer

A prewar design with a 2-pounder gun, the Tetrarch was intended to improve the firepower of British light tanks. However, the Battle of France proved their vulnerability. The few Tetrarchs produced were allocated to airborne forces, with some used during D-Day landings in June 1944. These were withdrawn by August.

◁ **Crusader III**

**Date** 1941 **Country** UK

**Weight** 22.1 tons (20.1 tonnes)

**Engine** Nuffield Liberty Mark III V12 gasoline, 340 hp

**Main armament** QF 6-pounder gun

Around 5,300 Crusaders were built, and they played a major role in North Africa. The Mark I and II were lightly armored and equipped with the aging 2-pounder gun. This version, the Crusader III, had better protection and used the 6-pounder. The engine and Christie suspension made it very fast, but it proved to be unreliable in the desert.

**Drive** sprocket

**2-pounder** main gun

▷ **Churchill Mark I**

**Date** 1941 **Country** UK

**Weight** 43.1 tons (39.1 tonnes)

**Engine** Bedford 12-cylinder gasoline, 350 hp

**Main armament** 1 x QF 2-pounder gun, 1 x 3 in howitzer

The Mark I was armed with a 2-pounder gun for antitank operations and a 3 in howitzer for supporting infantry with high explosive rounds. The howitzer was removed from later versions. Due to rushed production, early Churchills had many flaws, and the Mark I was only used in action at Dieppe in August 1942.

**Coiled spring** suspension

**Thin metal armor** covers idler wheel

**Armored** machine gun

◁ **Sentinel**

**Date** 1942 **Country** Australia

**Weight** 31.4 tons (28.4 tonnes)

**Engine** 3 x Cadillac V8 41-75 gasoline, 117 hp

**Main armament** QF 2-pounder gun

In 1940, Britain could not spare any tanks for its allies, which led the Australians to design and build the Sentinel. Its turret and hull were large, complicated castings. More tanks became available after the US entered the war, and the 65 Sentinels produced were used only for training.

**Horizontal** volute spring suspension

**Tracks**

▷ **Cavalier**

**Date** 1940 **Country** UK

**Weight** 29.7 tons (26.9 tonnes)

**Engine** Nuffield Liberty gasoline, 410 hp

**Main armament** QF 6-pounder gun

The first of three very similar Cruiser tanks designed to replace the Crusader, the Cavalier was an interim model that used the Crusader's Liberty engine, as the Meteor engine that had been intended for these vehicles was not yet available. It was never used in battle.

**Rear** drive sprocket

**95 mm howitzer** main gun

**Turret** powered by hydraulics

◁ **Centaur IV (Close Support)**

**Date** 1942 **Country** UK

**Weight** 30.8 tons (27.9 tonnes)

**Engine** Nuffield Liberty gasoline, 395 hp

**Main armament** 95 mm howitzer

The second Crusader replacement, the Centaur, used the Liberty engine, but was modified so the Meteor would also fit with minimal changes. Most versions carried 6-pounder or 75 mm guns, but the only ones to see action were Close Support variants with a 95 mm howitzer, used on D-Day.

# UK and Commonwealth Tanks (cont.)

British tank doctrine, dating back to the mid-1930s, required two types of tank. Cruisers such as the Cromwell were intended for independent action and needed to be fast—however, this limited the amount of armor they could carry. Infantry tanks such as the Valentine, on the other hand, operated alongside footsoldiers: they could be slower, but needed thick armor. Britain also used US tanks, some of which were modified.

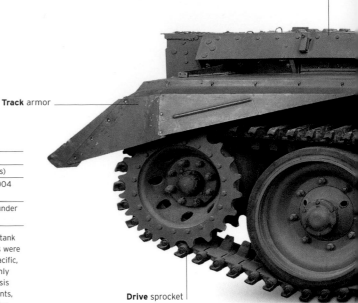

**Meteor** engine

**Track** armor

**Drive** sprocket

**Stowage** bin

**Coil-sprung** suspension

◁ **Valentine Mark IX**

**Date** 1942 **Country** UK

**Weight** 19 tons (17.3 tonnes)

**Engine** General Motors 6004 diesel, 138 hp

**Main armament** QF 6-pounder gun

The most-produced British tank of World War II, Valentines were used in North Africa, the Pacific, and in Eastern Europe. Highly versatile, it formed the basis for many specialized variants, such as a bridge layer, Duplex Drive amphibious tank, and flamethrower.

**Cast** hull

**6-pounder** main gun

◁ **Ram**

**Date** 1943 **Country** Canada

**Weight** 32.5 tons (29.5 tonnes)

**Engine** Wright Continental R975-C4 gasoline, 400 hp

**Main armament** QF 6-pounder gun

Canada started producing tanks in 1940, and after building 1,400 Valentines it began work on the Ram. The Ram used many features of the M3 medium tank, along with a Canadian-designed hull and turret. Nearly 2,000 were built and most were used to train tank crews.

▽ **Churchill Mark VI**

**Date** 1943 **Country** UK

**Weight** 44.8 tons (40.6 tonnes)

**Engine** Bedford 12-cylinder gasoline, 350 hp

**Main armament** QF 75 mm gun

After extensive upgrades and improvements for better reliability, the Churchill Mark VI was very different from the Mark I (see pp.92–93). It was now armed with a 6-pounder or 75 mm gun, and its armor protection was greatly improved. It was renowned for being able to climb seemingly impossible hills, and for shrugging off antitank fire.

**75 mm** main gun

**Angled** turret armor

△ **Harry Hopkins**

**Date** 1943 **Country** UK

**Weight** 9.5 tons (8.6 tonnes)

**Engine** Meadows gasoline, 148 hp

**Main armament** QF 2-pounder gun

The Harry Hopkins, as it was known, was a larger and better armored variant of the Tetrarch (see pp.78–79). It used the same unusual steering technique, where the road wheels moved sideways and twisted the tracks. Unlike the Tetrarch, it was too heavy to be airlifted and saw no service.

**Engine** vent

**Muzzle** brake

△ **Cromwell IV**

**Date** 1944 **Country** UK

**Weight** 30.8 tons (27.9 tonnes)

**Engine** Rolls-Royce Meteor Mark IB gasoline, 600 hp

**Main armament** QF 75 mm gun

A version of the Merlin aircraft power plant, the Cromwell's Meteor engine made it one of the fastest tanks of the war. This, and the tank's low height, made it popular with the Armored Reconnaissance Regiments in northwest Europe. However, it was outclassed by heavier German tanks. The Cromwell IV, shown here, was the most common variant produced.

**Stowage** bin

△ **Comet**

**Date** 1944 **Country** UK

**Weight** 36.4 tons (33 tonnes)

**Engine** Rolls-Royce Meteor Mark III gasoline, 600 hp

**Main armament** QF 77 mm HV gun

Arguably the best British tank of the war, the Comet only reached the front lines in limited numbers in early 1945. It was more heavily armored but its stronger suspension gave it similar mobility to the lighter Cromwell. The 77 mm gun, which could fit in its smaller turret, was slightly less powerful than the 17-pounder.

**Camouflage** netting

△ **Challenger A30**

**Date** 1944 **Country** UK

**Weight** 35.3 tons (32 tonnes)

**Engine** Rolls-Royce Meteor gasoline, 600 hp

**Main armament** QF 17-pounder gun

The Challenger's 17-pounder gun was much more capable than previous British weapons, but also much larger. The tank's hull was based on the Cromwell, but lengthened to support the wider and taller turret. Just 200 Challengers were built, and they were used to provide long-range antitank support to units using Cromwells.

**Engine** exhaust

▷ **Sherman Firefly**

**Date** 1944 **Country** UK

**Weight** 38.4 tons (34.9 tonnes)

**Engine** Chrysler A57 Multibank gasoline, 400 hp

**Main armament** QF 17-pounder gun

The British upgraded the Sherman with the 17-pounder gun. Fireflys never fully replaced 75 mm-armed Shermans, as the 17-pounder was less effective against non-armoured targets. It was a target for the Germans, so many crews camouflaged the long barrel. This is an M4A4 variant, with a longer hull due to its engine size.

**QF 17-pounder** main gun

# Soviet Tanks: 1941–45

A huge number of Soviet soldiers and tanks were lost in the first few months of the German invasion of the Soviet Union. Soviet tank factories were relocated east, beyond the Ural Mountains; until they were able to resume full operations, British and American tanks were also used. As the war progressed, production was standardized as much as possible in order to increase output. The tanks were accordingly simple, reflecting the limited skills of their crews, who were very often inexperienced or poorly trained.

**Armor** impervious to antitank guns

**Tall**, heavy turret

**152 mm** howitzer

**Torsion bar** suspension

### △ Kliment Voroshilov-1 (KV-1)

| | |
|---|---|
| **Date** 1939 | **Country** Soviet Union |
| **Weight** 53.2 tons (48.3 tonnes) | |
| **Engine** Kharkiv Model V-2K diesel, 500 hp | |
| **Main armament** 76.2 mm ZiS-5 L/41.5 gun | |

A heavy tank, the KV-1 was virtually immune to the German antitank weapons of 1941. It was one of the few tanks to continue in production after the Soviet factories were relocated. It used the same engine and gun as the T-34, but, being heavier, had poorer mobility. Around 4,700 KV-1s were built before production halted in April 1943.

### ◁ Kliment Voroshilov-2 (KV-2)

| | |
|---|---|
| **Date** 1939 | **Country** Soviet Union |
| **Weight** 59.4 tons (53.9 tonnes) | |
| **Engine** Kharkiv Model V-2K diesel, 550 hp | |
| **Main armament** 152 mm M-10T L/20 howitzer | |

After facing well fortified Finnish bunkers during 1939–40, the Soviets were convinced that a tank armed with an artillery piece was vital—and the KV-2 was their initial response. It was a good concept, but it failed to work in practice: the KV-2's tall turret made the tank heavier, slower, and easier to target. Just 334 were built, production ending when the Germans invaded Russia in 1941.

### ▷ T-34

| | |
|---|---|
| **Date** 1941 | **Country** Soviet Union |
| **Weight** 34.6 tons (31.4 tonnes) | |
| **Engine** Kharkiv Model V-2-34 diesel, 500 hp | |
| **Main armament** 76.2 mm F-34 L/41 gun | |

One of the most important tanks in history, the T-34 began development as early as 1938. Wartime pressures precluded cosmetic considerations, the focus being more on reducing cost and accelerating production.

**45 mm** rear hull armor

## ▽ T-60

**Date** 1941 **Country** Soviet Union

**Weight** 6.4 tons (5.8 tonnes)

**Engine** GAZ-202 6-cylinder diesel, 70 hp

**Main armament** 20 mm TNSh cannon

Intended to replace the prewar light tanks, the two-man T-60 was used as a reconnaissance vehicle. Early encounters with the Germans showed that it was under-gunned and too lightly armored. Adding thicker armor reduced its mobility, and the turret was too small to take a larger gun. It was unpopular, and gave way to the T-70.

**Engine** exhaust

**20 mm** TNSh cannon

**Rubber-clad** road wheels

## △ T-70

**Date** 1942 **Country** Soviet Union

**Weight** 10.1 tons (9.2 tonnes)

**Engine** 2 x GAZ-202 6-cylinder diesel, 70 hp each

**Main armament** 45 mm ZiS-19BM gun

Although more heavily armed and armored than its predecessor (the T-60) the T-70 was still outclassed by the advanced German tanks. By 1943, the Soviets had realized that light tanks had no place on the battlefield, and relegated them to secondary roles. The SU-76 assault gun (see pp.110–11) was developed from the T-70 chassis.

**85 mm** ZiS S-53 gun

**External** diesel fuel tanks

## ▷ T-34/85

**Date** 1944 **Country** Soviet Union

**Weight** 35.3 tons (32 tonnes)

**Engine** Kharkiv Model V-2-34 diesel, 500 hp

**Main armament** 85 mm ZiS S-53 L/55 gun

Despite its initial success, the T-34's shortcomings were clear by late 1943. Its two-man turret was too cramped for the crew to work effectively, and the gun was no longer sufficiently powerful. The T-34/85 resolved both of these issues. It went on to have a long postwar career with the Soviets and their client states, with one used in Yemen as late as 2015.

**76.2 mm** main gun

**74 mm** frontal hull armor

**122 mm** main gun

**Turret** welded for greater protection

## ◁ Iosif Stalin-2 (IS-2)

**Date** 1944 **Country** Soviet Union

**Weight** 49.3 tons (44.7 tonnes)

**Engine** Kharkiv Model V-2IS diesel, 520 hp

**Main armament** 122 mm D-25T L/45 gun

The need to face the threat of German Panthers and Tigers revitalized Soviet heavy tank production. The IS series was a development of the KV-1, with a new hull and transmission. On entering service, the IS-2 replaced both the IS-1 and the 85 mm-armed KV-85, and became organized into separate Heavy Tank Regiments. These were used to spearhead attacks on German positions.

**Wide** tracks

## ▷ Iosif Stalin-3M (IS-3M)

**Date** 1945 **Country** Soviet Union

**Weight** 51.3 tons (46.5 tonnes)

**Engine** Kharkiv Model V-2IS diesel, 600 hp

**Main armament** 122 mm D-25T L/45 gun

Limitations in the speed and armor of the IS-2 led to the development of the IS-3, which, although rushed into service, arrived too late for World War II. Initially it developed multiple mechanical problems, but these were resolved in the improved IS-3M model. The IS-3's sloped sides gave better armor protection, and became a feature of postwar Soviet tank designs.

**Rounded** "upturned soup-bowl" turret

**Diesel** tanks

**Christie** suspension system

# T-34/85

The T-34 was described as the "best tank in the world" by the German General Paul Ludwig Ewald von Kleist when his forces first encountered it in the summer of 1941. Its success was based partly on its design, and partly on its use in huge numbers, and it was able to defeat more technically advanced opposition vehicles.

**THE T-34 WAS** a powerfully armed and well-protected medium tank designed by Mikhail Koshkin at the end of the 1930s (see pp.102–103) to replace the earlier BT series of fast tanks. Its groundbreaking design was influenced by lessons learned fighting the Japanese at Khalkhin Gol in 1939. It had thicker armor and a larger gun than its predecessors, and a diesel engine that was considered less of a fire risk than earlier gasoline engines, which had been vulnerable to incendiary devices.

During trials of the new tank in the spring of 1940, Koshkin caught pneumonia, of which he was to die in September—the same month that the first production tanks rolled out of the factory. Improvements to the design continued throughout the war, many of which intended to reduce production costs and times: the cost of a T-34 dropped from 269,500 to 135,000 rubles. This need for simplicity was partly driven by production facilities moving to new sites behind the Ural Mountains due to the advancing German armies. The T-34 went on to be made in Poland and Czechoslovakia, and tens of thousands of them saw service in armies worldwide. This version, the T-34/85, has an enlarged turret to house the commander, gunner, and loader, and is named after its upgraded 85 mm gun.

**REAR VIEW**

| SPECIFICATIONS | |
| --- | --- |
| Name | T-34/85 |
| Date | 1940 |
| Origin | Soviet Union |
| Production | 84,700 |
| Engine | Model V-2-34 V12 diesel, 500 hp |
| Weight | 35.3 tons (32 tonnes) |
| Main armament | 85 mm ZiS S-53 |
| Secondary armament | 2 x 7.62 mm DT machine guns |
| Crew | 5 |
| Armor thickness | Max 2.4 in (60 mm) |

Gunner

Loader

Engine

Commander

Driver

**Commander's cupola**, added to later models

**More powerful 85 mm** main gun

**Coaxial machine gun** operated by the co-driver

**THREE-QUARTER VIEW**

**Idler wheel** set at the front

**Road wheels** rimmed with rubber

**Battalion insignia**
This particular tank was deployed in the second company (2) of the first battalion, and was the command tank (number 11) of the first platoon. The small Russian letter on the right ("I" in English) is the initial of the first battalion's commander, Ivanov.

**Influential design**
When the T-34 first entered service in World War II, its armor and firepower were groundbreaking. However, its crews were not always sufficiently trained to operate it effectively.

## EXTERIOR

The finish on early T-34 models was good,
but standards dropped as production moved
to improvised factories farther east in Russia
following the German invasion. The Red Army
realized the crude cast marks on the turret made
no difference to the tank's fighting ability, so
time was not wasted on removing them. The
T-34's armor consisted of homogenous rolled
and welded nickel steel.

1. Regimental insignia of 4th Guards Tank Corps
2. Driver's hatch (closed)  3. Co-driver's machine gun
4. Road wheels  5. Spare track links  6. Axle joint
7. Fuel cap  8. Commander's (right) and gunner's (left)
hatches  9. Commander's periscope  10. Fuel drum
11. Exhaust  12. Engine bay

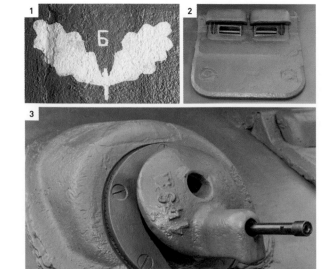

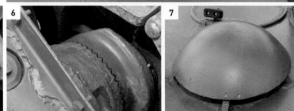

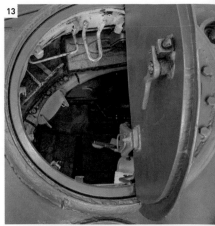

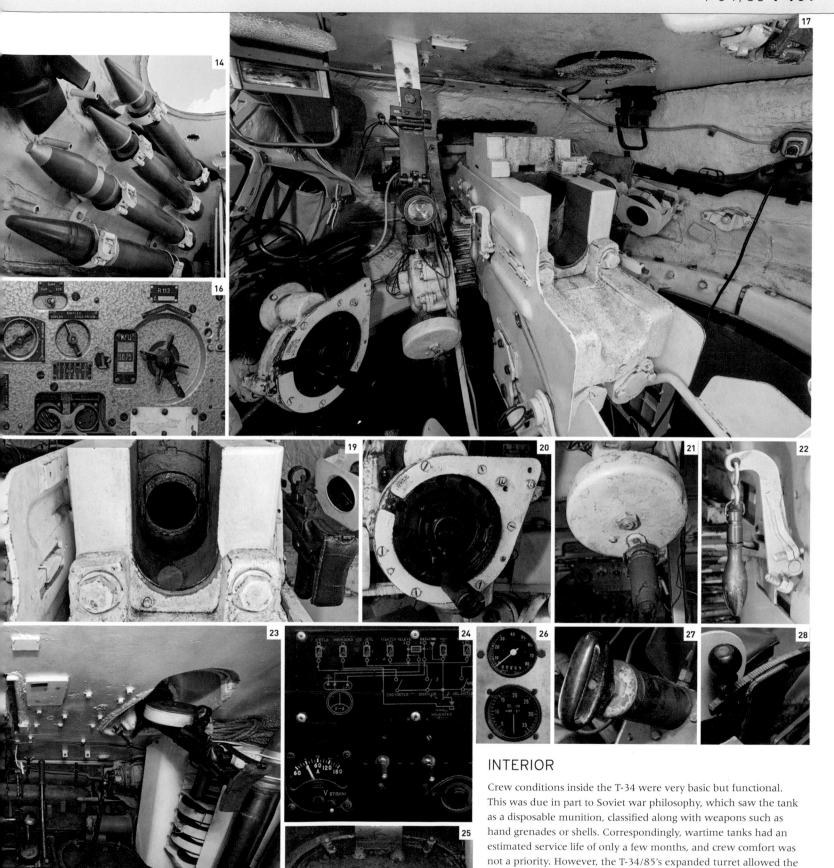

## INTERIOR

Crew conditions inside the T-34 were very basic but functional. This was due in part to Soviet war philosophy, which saw the tank as a disposable munition, classified along with weapons such as hand grenades or shells. Correspondingly, wartime tanks had an estimated service life of only a few months, and crew comfort was not a priority. However, the T-34/85's expanded turret allowed the crew slightly more room than earlier variants.

**13.** Looking down into commander's position **14.** Spare shells **15.** Gunner's periscope **16.** Radio **17.** Commander's position showing main gun breech **18.** Coaxial machine gun **19.** Main gun breech (open) **20.** Barrel elevation handle **21.** Turret traverse handle **22.** Fire extinguisher release **23.** Driver's position **24.** Instrument panel **25.** Escape hatch **26.** Instrument dials **27.** Pressure pump **28.** Gearshift

T-34 tanks under construction in a Soviet factory

# Great designers
# Mikhail Koshkin

As the head of the design team at the Kharkov tank factory in the Ukraine, Mikhail Koshkin's main legacy was the T-34, the medium tank that changed the course of World War II (see pp.98-101). Its background is rooted in the history of Soviet tank design.

**UNDER JOSEPH STALIN'S** leadership, the officials of the Soviet Union saw the tank as not only an important military asset, but also a vital symbol of power—and just like Adolf Hitler, the other major European dictator, Stalin took personal interest in the matter, influencing tank design and production in his country.

Russia, and later the Soviet Union, had a comparatively slow start in tank manufacturing. During World War I, no Russian tank designs saw production, but in the postwar period, captured vehicles such as the French Renault FT-17 were copied in Russian factories. As in other European countries, the 1920s and '30s was a period of experimentation in armored vehicle design, but Soviet industrial experience with heavy vehicles was scarce. Since it was a Communist power, the Soviet Union's only option

**Mikhail Koshkin**
(1898-1940)

for international industrial cooperation was with the other European pariah, Germany, which led to secret trials of German armored vehicles at a Soviet testing center at Kazan. As industrial experience and capacity grew with the Soviet Five Year Plans, new tanks were imported to copy and build under licence. These included the Vickers Mark E and Carden-Loyd tankettes from Britain, and an example of J. Walter Christie's M1931 wheel-cum-track vehicle from the US. The latter was designed so that its tracks could be removed and it could run at speed on its wheels on roads. These tanks became the basis of major tank production in the Soviet Union, leading to the design of the T-26, BT-2, and T-27 vehicles.

Meanwhile, Mikhail Koshkin, who was born of humble stock, had been drafted into the army in 1917 and sent to various fronts. He later studied at a university and enrolled in technical college, ending up working in the Kirov factory in Leningrad on the T-29 and T-111 prototypes. By the time the Soviet military called for the development of a new replacement tank for the light BT series in 1937, Koshkin had risen to be the head of the design team at the Kharkov tank factory. He argued for abandoning wheel-cum-track vehicles, thickening vehicles' armor protection, and increasing the firepower of the proposed new models.

Despite internal arguments from rival factory teams and a lack of Red Army support, Koshkin presented his design directly to Stalin, who approved it. The vehicle became the famous T-34, a tank that began its service life with many mechanical and design issues—but successfully combined mobility, armor protection, and firepower. It was comparatively simple to manufacture and was produced in huge numbers, proving a fearsome surprise for the invading German Wermacht in 1941.

**KV-1 being assembled in Leningrad**
The rival to Koshkin's T-34 design, the KV-1's heavy armor made it a formidable weapon. However, its high cost of manufacture led to production being discontinued.

However, the T-34 was not the only Soviet tank in development at the time. A rival design team led by S. J. Kotin designed a new heavy tank—the KV (named after Kliment Voroshilov, the People's Commissar of Defense), which had heavy armor and the same 76 mm gun as the T-34. Like Koshkin, Kotin and his team argued that the earlier fashion for multiple turreted tanks had to be abandoned, and the KV had same diesel engine as proposed for the T-34 tank, lessening fire risks. Although the KV's variants were produced in much smaller numbers than the T-34, they subsequently formed the basis of other tanks including the heavy IS (Josef Stalin) series.

Perhaps the greatest achievement of Soviet tank manufacturing was the production of so many vehicles under such hardships. The German invasion not only led to the loss of huge numbers

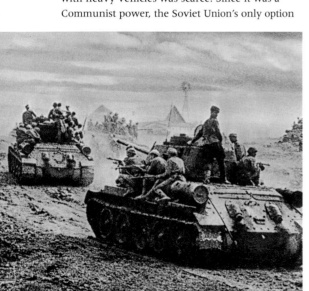

**Soviet T-34s on the move**
The T-34's wide tracks and effective suspension gave it the ability to travel over muddy or snowy conditions.

# "Quantity has a quality all of its own."

**ATTRIBUTED TO JOSEPH STALIN**

**Soviet war bond and stamp featuring the T-34**
Koshkin's design became an icon of Soviet military supremacy. Koshkin himself received various state honors posthumously, the last of them in 1990.

of tanks in battle, but also the need to move factories to relative safety behind the Ural Mountains. New and simplified production methods became a necessity— workers produced tanks for the front line using the most basic of factory facilities. Production costs went down, speed of manufacture increased, and a staggering 112,000 tanks of different types were made between 1940 and 1945.

Koshkin himself died after contracting pneumonia while on a lengthy cross-country test-drive of the T-34 prototypes, and although his contributions were only formally acknowledged years after his death, his T-34 was vital in the eventual defeat of Germany.

**Soviet tank factory**
Workers assemble an IS-2 heavy tank in 1943. The IS-2's design was a deliberate move to a heavier gun than Koshkin's T-34, whose effectiveness had spurred the arms race in tank design between Germany and the Soviet Union.

# Preparing for battle

Whatever their specifications and qualities, tanks are only as effective as the crews inside them. The work of the best engineers and designers, and the huge costs involved in manufacturing such complex machines, plus the testing and issuing of the equipment, is all wasted if the crew is unable to work the tank effectively. History has shown that experienced, motivated, and well-trained crews working technically inferior tanks have beaten superior vehicles crewed by less experienced or less motivated men. As in many other areas of warfare, the effect of motivation, morale, belief, and leadership, however hard to quantify, is of huge importance to a tank crew, and can have an enormous effect on their performance in battle.

American crewmen, for instance, in late 1944 or early 1945, could find themselves fighting against far superior German tanks—and winning. Later analysis revealed that at this stage of the war German tank crews were indeed insufficiently trained, and so suffered in spite of their own technical superiority. Studies also show that the stress of combat often led men to seek help, guidance, and comfort in religion. Statistics reveal that soldiers' reliance on prayer rose from 32 percent to 74 percent as the battle intensified.

**US chaplain Major George F. Daum** leads Sherman tank crews in prayer before their advance into Germany in 1945.

# German Tank Destroyers

The earliest German tank destroyers used captured or obsolete light-tank hulls, with antitank guns affixed on top. Usually open-topped, they were issued to the Panzerjäger, or antitank artillery soldiers, to replace towed guns, thus improving their mobility. By contrast, Germany's Sturmgeschütz ("assault gun") vehicles were not originally optimized for destroying tanks. Rather, they were infantry support vehicles operated by the artillery and armed with low-velocity guns. Combat experience forced them to adapt, and they were soon upgraded with antitank guns.

**Panzer I** hull

**4.7 cm** PaK(t) gun

**Leaf spring** suspension

### ▷ StuG III

**Date** 1940 **Country** Germany

**Weight** 26.8 tons (24.3 tonnes)

**Engine** Maybach HL120TRM gasoline, 300 hp

**Main armament** 7.5 cm StuK 40 L/48 gun

The first StuGs were armed with the same short-barreled 7.5 cm L/24 gun as early Panzer IVs. The StuG's low height and armor made it an ideal tank destroyer, and in 1942 the longer-barreled L/48 gun was attached to optimize it for that role. With over 11,000 built, it was Germany's most-produced armored vehicle.

### ◁ Panzerjäger I

**Date** 1940 **Country** Germany

**Weight** 7.2 tons (6.5 tonnes)

**Engine** Maybach NL38TR gasoline, 100 hp

**Main armament** 4.7 cm PaK(t) L/43.4 gun

The first German attempt to provide their forces with mobile antitank firepower, the Panzerjäger I matched captured Czech guns with Panzer I hulls. This was obsolete as a tank, but had much greater mobility than a towed gun. A total of 202 vehicles were built and used in France and North Africa.

### ▷ Marder I

**Date** 1942 **Country** Germany

**Weight** 9.3 tons (8.4 tonnes)

**Engine** DelaHaye 103TT gasoline, 70 hp

**Main armament** 7.5 cm PaK 40 L/46 gun

In 1941 German antitank guns proved to be ineffective against heavily armored Soviet tanks. The Marder vehicles were an urgent response to the German requirement to give greater mobility to their new PaK 40 towed gun by attaching it to tracked vehicles. Marder I used the chassis of the French Lorraine 37L supply tractor.

**Lorraine** tractor chassis

**7.62cm** PaK 36(r) gun

**7.5 cm** PaK 40/2 gun

**Panzer II** chassis

### △ Marder II

**Date** 1942 **Country** Germany

**Weight** 12.1 tons (11 tonnes)

**Engine** Maybach HL62TRM gasoline, 140 hp

**Main armament** 7.5 cm PaK 40/2 L/48 gun

The Marder II used the chassis of the Panzer II, which was obsolete as a tank. A total of 650 vehicles were built and armed with the PaK 40 gun. Another 200, called the Sd Kfz 132, were armed with captured Soviet 76.2 mm F-22 field guns that had been converted to antitank guns by the Germans.

### ▷ Marder III

**Date** 1942 **Country** Germany

**Weight** 12 tons (10.9 tonnes)

**Engine** Praga EPA/2 gasoline, 140 hp

**Main armament** 7.62 cm PaK 36(r) L/51.5 gun

The Marder III series was based on the Czech Panzer 38(t) (see pp.66-67). This version used the converted Russian F-22 gun, like the Sd Kfz 132 Marder II. A total of 344 examples of this variant were built. Although they were mainly used in the Soviet Union, 66 were also sent to North Africa.

**Torsion bar** suspension

**Idler** at rear

▷ **Marder III Ausf H**

**Date** 1942 **Country** Germany

**Weight** 12.1 tons (11 tonnes)

**Engine** Praga EPA/2 diesel, 140 hp

**Main armament** 7.5 cm PaK 40/3 L/46 gun

This variant of the Marder III had an improved superstructure that was lighter and provided better protection for the crew. Around 410 were built or converted from the standard tank. The Marder III was mainly used in the Soviet Union, where it performed best in defensive roles or as long-range fire support.

**Modified** Panzer 38(t) chassis

**Fighting compartment** at rear

**Steeply sloped** frontal armor

**Modified** Panzer 38(t) chassis

◁ **Marder III Ausf M**

**Date** 1943 **Country** Germany

**Weight** 11.8 tons (10.7 tonnes)

**Engine** Praha AC gasoline, 140 hp

**Main armament** 7.5 cm PaK 40/3 L/46 gun

The Ausf M used a modified Panzer 38(t) chassis that was designed to be used with self-propelled guns. The engine was moved to the center, allowing the gun to be mounted at the rear. Like all the Marder vehicles, it was open-topped. A total of 975 were built.

**15 cm** StuH 43 howitzer

▷ **Brummbar**

**Date** 1943 **Country** Germany

**Weight** 31.6 tons (28.7 tonnes)

**Engine** Maybach HL120TRM gasoline, 300 hp

**Main armament** 15 cm StuH 43 L/12 howitzer

As StuGs were increasingly used as tank destroyers, there was still a need for an armored infantry support vehicle that could fire high-explosive shells, especially to deal with solidly built city buildings. This role was met by the Stug III-derived StuH 42, and by the Brummbar, based on the Panzer IV.

# German Tank Destroyers (cont.)

Lacking complicated and expensive turrets, tank destroyers were quicker and cheaper to manufacture than conventional tanks. They could usually mount a more powerful gun on the same hull, and as the Germans retreated in the face of overwhelming Allied numbers and firepower, this became a distinct advantage. Later Jagdpanzers were fully armored and generally based on heavy tank hulls. In the last months of the war, tank destroyers increasingly began to take the place of actual tanks.

**▷ Nashorn (Hornisse)**

**Date** 1943 **Country** Germany

**Weight** 26.9 tons (24.4 tonnes)

**Engine** Maybach HL120TRM gasoline, 300 hp

**Main armament** 8.8 cm PaK 43/1 L/71 gun

The Nashorn was an interim design that used a chassis developed from the Panzer IV. It was later renamed Hornisse, and was the first German tank destroyer to mount the highly effective PaK 43 gun. The gun's very long range allowed the vehicle to stand off from the enemy.

**Augmented**
Panzer IV chassis

**7.5 cm** StuK
40 gun

**Modified**
PaK 43 gun

**△ Ferdinand**

**Date** 1943 **Country** Germany

**Weight** 72.8 tons (66 tonnes)

**Engine** 2 x Maybach HL 120TRM petrol, 300 hp each

**Main armament** 8.8 cm PaK 43/2 L/71 gun

The Ferdinand hull was an unsuccessful design for the Tiger tank. A total of 90 tanks were built, and they were equipped with the PaK 43 in a fully enclosed and very heavily armored superstructure. The firepower and armor served them well as antitank platforms, but their huge size and weight restricted their mobility.

**△ StuG IV**

**Date** 1944 **Country** Germany

**Weight** 25.8 tons (23.4 tonnes)

**Engine** Maybach HL120TRM gasoline, 300 hp

**Main armament** 7.5 cm StuK 40 L/48

High demand for the StuG III meant that after a bombing raid on the factory, the Germans adapted the design for the Panzer IV chassis in order to maintain production. Around 1,140 Stug IVs were built. Both variants proved highly effective as defensive antitank vehicles.

**△ Jagdpanzer IV/70**

**Date** 1944 **Country** Germany

**Weight** 26.9 tons (24.4 tonnes)

**Engine** Maybach HL120TRM gasoline, 300 hp

**Main armament** 7.5cm PaK 42 L/70 gun

Like the StuG IV, the Jagdpanzer IV was also based on the Panzer IV chassis. A total of 769 of the original vehicle were built. A dedicated tank hunter, it was armed with a PaK 39 L/48 gun. This version was equipped with the longer and more powerful PaK 42 L/70, and replaced the earlier vehicle from 1944. Around 1,200 of these tanks were built.

**7.5 cm**
PaK 42 gun

**Hull** based on
Panzer 38(t)

**Idler** at rear

8.8 cm PaK 43/3 gun

◁ **Jagdpanther**

**Date** 1944 **Country** Germany

**Weight** 51.5 tons (46.7 tonnes)

**Engine** Maybach HL230P30 gasoline, 700 hp

**Main armament** 8.8 cm PaK 43/3 L/71 gun

The Jagdpanther was based on the Panther (see pp.72–73) chassis, and was well armored, mobile, and possessed heavy firepower. It was a capable weapon, especially when used in ambush or defensive positions. However, only 392 were built and they were plagued by poor maintenance and crew training. The Jagdpanther was thus too scarce to affect the course of the war.

**Interleaved** road wheels

12.8 cm PaK 44 gun

34 ft 11 in (10.65 m) long, including gun

▽ **Jagdpanzer 38(t) Hetzer**

**Date** 1944 **Country** Germany

**Weight** 17.6 tons (16 tonnes)

**Engine** Praga AC/2 gasoline, 150 hp

**Main armament** 7.5 cm PaK 39 L/48 gun

Using a hull based on the Panzer 38(t) (see pp.66–67), the Hetzer was smaller, lighter, and cheaper than other late-war Jagdpanzers. Due to its small size, it could easily hide and ambush enemy forces on the battlefield. However, the Hetzer was not popular with its crews, who found it extremely cramped, with a poorly laid-out interior. Around 2,584 were built.

△ **Jagdtiger**

**Date** 1944 **Country** Germany

**Weight** 78.4 tons (71.1 tonnes)

**Engine** Maybach HL230P30 gasoline, 700 hp

**Main armament** 12.8 cm PaK 44 L/55 gun

The Jagdtiger was the heaviest armored vehicle of World War II. It used the same suspension as the Tiger II (see pp.72–73), but had a longer hull. Its gun could defeat any Allied tank at long range. Many Jagdtigers were lost due to breakdowns, some being destroyed by their crews.

**Torsion bar** suspension

7.5 cm PaK 39 gun

*max*

38 cm mortar

**Sprocket wheel** at front

△ **Sturmtiger**

**Date** 1944 **Country** Germany

**Weight** 72.8 tons (66 tonnes)

**Engine** Maybach HL230P45 gasoline, 700 hp

**Main armament** 38 cm Stu M RW61 L/5.4 mortar

An assault gun based on the Tiger chassis, the Sturmtiger was heavily armored in order to survive close-range street fighting. Its powerful rocket-assisted mortar gave it devastating firepower, but the round's huge size meant that only 14 could be carried. Only 18 Sturmtigers were ever built.

# Allied Tank Destroyers

There was a clear difference in design between Soviet and US tank destroyers and assault guns. The Soviets favored turretless vehicles for the same reasons as the Germans: they were quicker and cheaper to build, and could mount a larger gun and heavier armor than the tank they were based on. American tank destroyers, meanwhile, were intended to be used in counterattacks, outmaneuvering enemy tanks; they emphasized mobility over protection, and kept the more versatile turret. In reality, both countries used them as artillery pieces and to support infantry.

## ▷ M10

**Date** 1942 **Country** USA

**Weight** 32.5 tons (29.5 tonnes)

**Engine** General Motors 6046 diesel, 375 hp

**Main armament** 3 in M7 L/40 gun

The M10 was based on the M4A2 Sherman chassis, and the M10A1 used the gasoline-engined M4A3, easing logistics. Both were lightly armored with an open-topped turret to enhance mobility and situational awareness. Around 6,500 were built. Many vehicles supplied to the UK were later upgunned with the 17-pounder, renamed the Achilles.

**Main gun** muzzle brake

**Rubber-rimmed** road wheels

**122 mm** howitzer

## △ SU-76M

**Date** 1943 **Country** Soviet Union

**Weight** 11.4 tons (10.4 tonnes)

**Engine** 2 x GAZ-203 6 cylinder diesel, 85 hp each

**Main armament** 76.2 mm ZiS-3Sh L/42.6 gun

With over 12,600 built, the SU-76M was the second most-produced Soviet armored vehicle of the war. Based on a stretched T-70 light tank chassis, it was used as a light assault gun and mobile artillery piece, and had the capability to destroy lighter German tanks. Although reliable and popular with the infantry, due to its light armor and open top its crew did not always feel the same.

## ◁ SU-122

**Date** 1943 **Country** Soviet Union

**Weight** 34 tons (30.9 tonnes)

**Engine** Kharkiv Model V-2-34 diesel, 500 hp

**Main armament** 122 mm M-30S L/23 howitzer

Classified as a medium assault gun, the SU-122 was built on the T-34 chassis. It mounted a direct fire weapon mainly intended for use against fortifications. Its firepower and armor made the SU-122 a popular infantry support weapon. Around 1,100 were built. The upgraded SU-85 tank destroyer used the same design armed with an 85 mm D-5S gun.

**3 in** main gun

**Gun** points to rear

**Serial** number

**◁ Valentine Archer**

**Date** 1943 **Country** UK

**Weight** 17.9 tons (16.3 tonnes)

**Engine** General Motors
6-71M diesel, 192 hp

**Main armament** QF
17-pounder gun

In 1943, the Valentine was the only available tank chassis that could be fitted with the powerful 17-pounder for use as a tank destroyer. However, the gun's size meant that the only way it could be made to fit was by pointing it to the rear. Despite this, Archers were reliable and effective.

**▷ M18 Hellcat**

**Date** 1943 **Country** USA

**Weight** 19.6 tons (17.8 tonnes)

**Engine** Wright Continental R-975
gasoline, 400 hp

**Main armament** 76 mm M1A2 L/52 gun

One of the fastest ever armored vehicles, the M18 was well suited to US tank destroyer doctrine. However, its speed and mobility–enhanced by very thin armor and torsion bar suspension–proved to be of limited value, and its firepower was inadequate against the heaviest German tanks.

**Arctic** camouflage

**Heavily armored** mantlet

**Spare track links** on hull

**◁ ISU-152**

**Date** 1944 **Country** Soviet Union

**Weight** 52.1 tons (47.2 tonnes)

**Engine** Kharkiv Model V-2IS diesel, 520 hp

**Main armament** 152 mm ML-20S L/29 gun-howitzer

The chassis of Soviet heavy tanks formed the basis for a series of heavy assault guns. The SU-152 was built on the KV-1S, while the very similar ISU-152 used the later IS chassis. A shortage of 152 mm barrels led to another variation–the 122 mm-armed ISU-122. These vehicles were held in separate units to support attacks and breakthroughs. Their devastating firepower made them popular in urban fighting.

**▷ M36**

**Date** 1944 **Country** USA

**Weight** 31.9 tons (29 tonnes)

**Engine** Ford GAA V8 gasoline, 500 hp

**Main armament** 90 mm M3 L/53 gun

A development of the M10A1 with heavier firepower but similar armor and mobility, the M36 proved its worth in combat. It could knock out the heaviest German tanks at long range. High demand led to versions based on the diesel M10 and the unmodified M4A3 hull. Around 2,300 were built in total.

**90 mm** main gun

**External** fuel tank

**Commander's** cupola

**◁ SU-100**

**Date** 1944 **Country** Soviet Union

**Weight** 34.7 tons (31.5 tonnes)

**Engine** Kharkiv Model V-2-34 diesel, 500 hp

**Main armament** 100 mm D-10S L/53.5 gun

The design of SU-85 was upgraded to become the SU-100. Both vehicles provided long-range antitank support to formations, and were also held in reserve to defend against the heaviest German tanks. Around 1,200 were built during the war. Production and upgrades continued afterward, and the vehicle remained in service around the world for decades.

# M18 Hellcat

The M18 Hellcat was one of a series of fast, lightly armored, but powerfully armed US antitank vehicles. It was designed according to the American tank destroyer doctrine formulated before World War II: tanks supported an infantry attack, and if enemy tanks attacked, fast tank destroyers such as the Hellcat would rush to the breakthrough to destroy the enemy tanks, using speed to avoid enemy fire.

THE HELLCAT was designed by Buick and was equipped with the powerful Wright R-975 radial engine. This, combined with its thin armor and open-topped turret (standard on all American tank destroyers), meant it weighed less than 20 tons (18 tonnes) and was very fast, capable of up to 50 mph (80 km/h) on a road. It carried the 76 mm high-velocity gun that was also mounted on the later model Sherman tanks.

**REAR VIEW**

The Hellcat saw combat service in Europe after D-Day, but struggled to defeat the thicker front armor of later German tanks such as the Panther. High Velocity Armor Piercing (HVAP) ammunition gave a better chance of penetration, but was in short supply. A muzzle brake was added to the gun to help reduce dust from its blast; this was fixed to the last 700 of the 1,857 Hellcats built as tank destroyers. Another 650 unarmed versions, the M39, were made or converted to act as ammunition or troop carriers. Some of these saw service in the Korean War.

| SPECIFICATIONS | |
|---|---|
| Name | M18 Hellcat |
| Date | 1942 |
| Origin | USA |
| Production | 1,857 |
| Engine | Wright Continental R-975 gasoline, 400 hp |
| Weight | 19.6 tons (17.8 tonnes) |
| Main armament | 76 mm M1 or M1A2 |
| Secondary armament | .50 Browning M2 machine gun |
| Crew | 5 |
| Armor thickness | 1 in (25 mm) max |

Co-driver

Commander

Gunner

Loader

Driver

**Transmission** front cover plate

**Torsion bar** suspension

**THREE-QUARTER VIEW**

**Rubber** tracks

**Tank destroyer**
The M18 Hellcat could easily be mistaken for a tank, but it was designed as a fast, thinly-armored carrier for an antitank gun. It relied on speed rather than armor to protect itself.

**"Seek... Strike... Destroy"**
This was the badge of the US Tank Destroyer forces. Over 100 tank destroyer battalions were formed during World War II.

**Bridging weight badge**
The Hellcat had a bridging weight of 20 tons (18 tonnes), indicated by this insignia. It was extremely light for such a heavily armed vehicle.

## EXTERIOR

Many American vehicles such as the Hellcat used common components, a feature that was noticed by German commander Erwin Rommel in Tunisia when he first encountered American forces. Interchangable parts such as headlights meant that fewer items were required in the supply chain, helping with the logistic burden of supplying an army in the field.

1. Allied recognition symbol  2. Klaxon  3. Headlamp
4. Fuel filler cover  5. Main gunsight aperture  6. Gunner's periscope  7. Commander's machine gun  8. Gun cleaning rods stowed on hull  9. Crewman's stowage  10. Machine gun tripod for ground use  11. Shovel stowed on hull  12. Return roller under top of track  13. Rear light  14. Engine bay

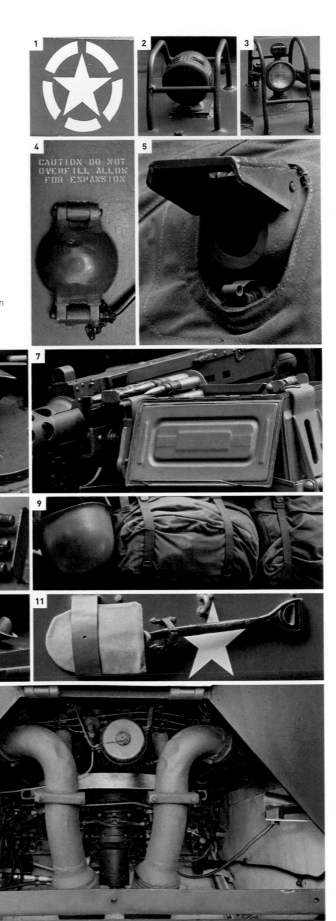

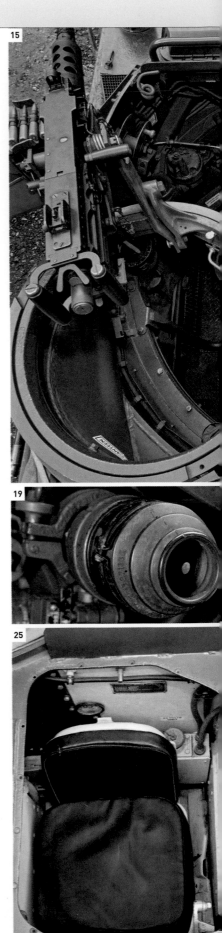

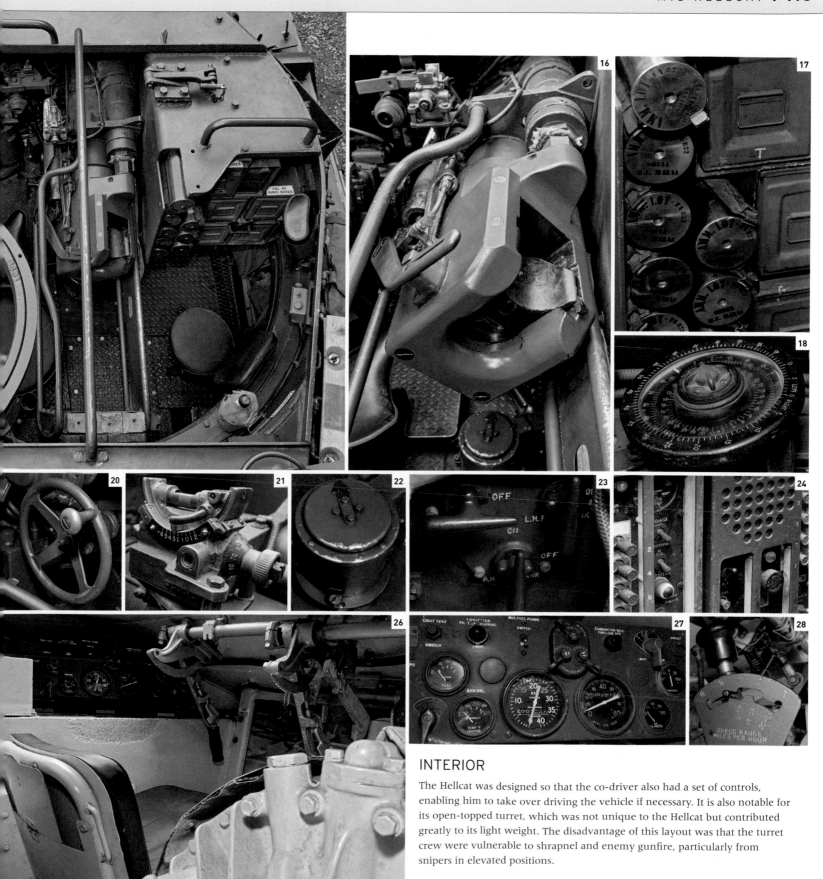

## INTERIOR

The Hellcat was designed so that the co-driver also had a set of controls, enabling him to take over driving the vehicle if necessary. It is also notable for its open-topped turret, which was not unique to the Hellcat but contributed greatly to its light weight. The disadvantage of this layout was that the turret crew were vulnerable to shrapnel and enemy gunfire, particularly from snipers in elevated positions.

**15.** Overhead view of fighting compartment   **16.** Main gun breech   **17.** Ammunition stowage
**18.** Azimuth indicator   **19.** Gunsight eyepiece   **20.** Gun elevation wheel   **21.** Clinometer
measures angle for indirect fire   **22.** Direction of travel indicator   **23.** Driver's controls
**24.** Radio and intercom equipment   **25.** Driver's seat   **26.** Driver's position   **27.** Driver's
instrument panel   **28.** Gear lever

# Engineering and Specialized Vehicles

After the failed Dieppe Raid of 1942 exposed the difficulty of landing vehicles during an amphibious invasion, Allied commanders knew that getting tanks across the beaches of France would be a challenge. The job of developing suitable vehicles was given to Percy Hobart, the commander of the British 79th Armoured Division. Known as "Hobart's Funnies," these vehicles were based on tank hulls, which gave them similar mobility and protection, and made logistics easier. They were used in northwest Europe, Italy, and the Far East.

**Turret** with searchlight

T16278

**Mine** housed in vehicle body

### △ Matilda CDL

| | |
|---|---|
| **Date** 1940 | **Country** UK |
| **Weight** 29.7 tons (26.9 tonnes) | |
| **Engine** 2 x AEC 6 cylinder diesel, 95 hp each | |
| **Main armament** None | |

The Canal Defence Light (CDL) was an attempt to dazzle the enemy during night fighting. The turret of the Matilda contained a 13-million candle power searchlight that flickered at a frequency that increased the blinding effect.

### ▷ Valentine Bridgelayer

| | |
|---|---|
| **Date** 1943 | **Country** UK |
| **Weight** 20 tons (19.9 tonnes) | |
| **Engine** AEC A189 gasoline, 135 hp | |
| **Main armament** None | |

The first bridgelaying tanks were developed at the end of World War I, but it was not until World War II that they were used. The Scissors Bridge shown here could span a 30 ft (9.2 m) gap and support 33 ton (30 tonne) vehicles.

### △ Goliath tracked mine

| | |
|---|---|
| **Date** 1943 | **Country** Germany |
| **Weight** 0.5 tons (0.4 tonnes) | |
| **Engine** Zundapp SZ7 gasoline, 12.5 hp | |
| **Main armament** 100 kg (220 lb) explosive | |

Just 5.3 ft (1.63 m) long and 2 ft (0.62 m) tall, the Goliath was effectively a small bomb. It was remotely controlled by a 2,130 ft (650 m)-long wire, which allowed its operator to remain in cover. It was intended to be used against fortifications or to clear minefields, but was vulnerable to small arms fire and rough terrain.

### ▽ Churchill Crocodile

| | |
|---|---|
| **Date** 1943 | **Country** UK |
| **Weight** 44.8 tons (40.6 tonnes) | |
| **Engine** Bedford Twin-Six gasoline, 350 hp | |
| **Main armament** Flamethrower, 75 mm QF gun | |

A flamethrower is extremely effective against fortifications, and mounting one onto a tank enables the latter to survive enemy fire as it closes in. The Churchill Crocodile was one such vehicle; a fully operational gun tank with a trailer for carrying fuel. Crocodiles attracted heavy enemy fire, but their presence often persuaded German forces to surrender.

**Trailer** for carrying fuel

**Turret** houses 290 mm mortar

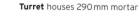

**Scissors Bridge**
folded on tank

HANNIBAL

**Hydraulic arm**
unfolds bridge

### △ Churchill AVRE

| | |
|---|---|
| **Date** 1943 | **Country** UK |
| **Weight** 43.7 tons (39.6 tonnes) | |
| **Engine** Bedford 12-cylinder gasoline, 350 hp | |
| **Main armament** 290 mm Petard Mortar | |

The Armoured Vehicle Royal Engineers (AVRE) was a highly versatile version of the Churchill developed after the Dieppe Landings to allow engineers to work under armor protection. It was armed with a short-range mortar to destroy fortifications.

**Chain flails**
detonate mines

### △ Sherman V Crab

| | |
|---|---|
| **Date** 1943 | **Country** USA |
| **Weight** 35.5 tons (32.2 tonnes) | |
| **Engine** Chrysler A57 Multibank gasoline, 425 hp | |
| **Main armament** 75 mm M3 L/40 gun | |

Clearing minefields was a dangerous job, both because of the mines and because they were usually protected by enemy fire. Flail tanks, such as this Sherman V Crab, had to move in a straight line at less than 2 mph (3.2 km/h), while the rotating chains beat the ground with enough force to set off any mines.

**Canvas screen**
provides buoyancy

**Dummy** gun

### △ Sherman III Duplex Drive

| | |
|---|---|
| **Date** 1943 | **Country** USA |
| **Weight** 35.5 tons (32.2 tonnes) | |
| **Engine** General Motors 6046 diesel, 375 hp | |
| **Main armament** 75 mm M3 L/40 gun | |

Fully combat capable, the Sherman III (an M4A2 in this case) was equipped with propellers and a canvas screen, allowing it to be driven in water. It was developed to support the infantry in the first waves of the D-Day invasion. The canvas screen provided buoyancy although they were vulnerable in the rough sea.

### △ Churchill Armored Recovery Vehicle (ARV)

| | |
|---|---|
| **Date** 1944 | **Country** UK |
| **Weight** 37 tons (33.5 tonnes) | |
| **Engine** Bedford Twin-Six gasoline, 350 hp | |
| **Main armament** None | |

The armored recovery vehicle allowed the mechanics of the Royal Electrical and Mechanical Engineers (REME) the mobility and protection to move around the battlefield and repair disabled vehicles. It carried a crane for removing engines, towing gear, and tools and equipment needed to repair damaged tank components.

# Experimental Vehicles

The pressures of war saw a large number of tank designs being developed, with many never seeing service. Some were rendered obsolete due to advances in technology, or canceled because the war ended before they could be developed. Others were abandoned because existing vehicles, while perhaps not as capable as the replacement, were good enough, and the delays to production that would be caused by introducing a new type of tank were seen as unacceptable.

### △ TOG II*

| | | | |
|---|---|---|---|
| **Date** 1941 | **Country** UK | | |
| **Weight** 89.6 tons (81.3 tonnes) | | | |
| **Engine** Paxman Ricardo 12-cylinder diesel, 600 hp | | | |
| **Main armament** QF 17-pounder gun | | | |

Created by the men responsible for the first tank in 1915, "The Old Gang" (TOG) was designed to operate on a World War I-style battlefield. It was large, heavy, and slow. Combat experience in World War II showed that the TOG was no longer suited to modern warfare.

**Firing** port

**Vertical volute** suspension

### △ M7

| | |
|---|---|
| **Date** 1942 | **Country** USA |
| **Weight** 26.9 tons (24.4 tonnes) | |
| **Engine** Wright Continental R-975 gasoline, 400 hp | |
| **Main armament** 75 mm M3 L/40 gun | |

Originally designed as a 14 ton (12.7 tonne) light tank, the M7 grew significantly in size during development. It was reclassified as a medium tank, but this placed it in competition with the M4 Sherman (see pp.86–89). The M4 was a superior vehicle and was already in production, so the M7 was abandoned after only seven were built.

**Lifting** lug

**Armored** mantlet

### △ T14

| | |
|---|---|
| **Date** 1943 | **Country** USA |
| **Weight** 42 tons (38.1 tonnes) | |
| **Engine** Ford GAZ V8 gasoline, 520 hp | |
| **Main armament** 75 mm M3 L/40 gun | |

Intended as a heavy Infantry or assault tank for both American and British forces, the T14 used many Sherman components. Two pilot models were built. Testing showed they were too heavy for practical battlefield use, and did not offer sufficient improvement over the Sherman and Churchill to be worth pursuing.

**Fixed mantlet** instead of turret

**Spare** track links

**Tow** cable

P1 PE3530

▷ **Valiant**

**Date** 1944 **Country** UK

**Weight** 30.8 tons (27.4 tonnes)

**Engine** General Motors 6-71M diesel, 210 hp

**Main armament** QF 75 mm gun

The Valiant was developed as an infantry assault tank for the Far East, but trials of the single prototype revealed that it was too slow, with poor ground clearance that damaged the suspension. Moreover, the driver's compartment was too cramped, which aggravated the risk of injury from its controls. It is considered to be one of the worst tanks ever built.

**Driver's** compartment

**Light armor** to keep weight down

**Drive sprocket** at rear

**Individually sprung** wheel suspension

▽ **Tortoise**

**Date** 1945 **Country** UK

**Weight** 87.4 tons (79.3 tonnes)

**Engine** Rolls-Royce Meteor Mark 5 gasoline, 600 hp

**Main armament** QF 32-pounder gun

Heavily armed and armored, the Tortoise could both outgun and outlast the heaviest German vehicles. It was originally intended to be used as an assault vehicle against German fortifications. It sacrificed mobility, with a top speed of just 19.3 km/h (12 mph) on road. Six were built before the end of the war.

**Muzzle** brake

**105 mm** main gun

**32-pounder** main gun

▽ **Black Prince**

**Date** 1945 **Country** UK

**Weight** 56 tons (50.8 tonnes)

**Engine** Bedford Type 120 gasoline, 350 hp

**Main armament** QF 17-pounder gun

The Black Prince was a larger and heavier version of the Churchill that could mount the 17-pounder gun. The thickness of the armor remained unchanged, as did the engine, which led to a reduced top speed. Wider tracks and an improved suspension restored some mobility.

**Small** road wheels

**Ring mount** for external machine gun

**Torsion bar** suspension

△ **T28**

**Date** 1945 **Country** USA

**Weight** 95 tons (86.2 tonnes)

**Engine** Ford GAF V8 gasoline, 500 hp

**Main armament** 105 mm T5E1 L/65 gun

Designed to attack the strong defenses of the German Siegfried Line, the T28 was the heaviest tank ever built in the US. It used the same Horizontal Volute Suspension System (HVSS) as later Shermans in a twin track arrangement. Only two were built, before the end of the war left them without a role.

# The tank in peace and war

Like all weapons, the tank can be viewed in many different ways. All too often it is seen as a symbol of oppression, invasion, and menace—for many, however, precisely the opposite is true. Here, for example, on the ruined streets of Flers, Normandy, soon after the D-Day landings of June 1944, the tank is a bringer of liberation; the flags are out and the population is welcoming the troops.

Such differing views of the tank were already clear in World War I, almost as soon as the tank was invented. On the British home front, toys, teapots, a handbag, all kinds of souvenirs and even a dance paid homage to the vehicle that had turned the tide on Germany. At last, Britain was ahead of the country that had been the first to use airpower when it bombed London and the first to use poison gas on the battlefield. Subsequently, the tank became a huge success in raising money for the war effort and many were sent on tour around Britain. For the Germans, on the other hand, by late 1918 the appearance of a tank on the battlefield simply gave exhausted and demoralized soldiers an excuse to surrender. As Hindenburg said: "that they could cross our undamaged trenches and obstacles did not fail to have a marked effect on our troops."

**A British-crewed Sherman tank** makes its way through the ruins of Flers, Normandy, in 1944. A bulldozer clears rubble in the background.

# Armored Cars and Troop Carriers

World War II saw the widespread use of armored vehicles in a variety of roles. Scout Cars, Light Reconnaissance cars, and Armored Cars were used for reconnaissance and to provide armored support to infantry. Some carried light firepower, while other variants were as well armed as contemporary tanks. Their main role was to find the enemy and survive to report back, so binoculars, a radio, and good tactics were their main weapons.

### ▷ Sd Kfz 231 Schwerer Panzerspahwagen, 8-rad

**Date** 1936 **Country** Germany

**Weight** 9.3 tons (8.4 tonnes)

**Engine** Bussing-NAG L8V gasoline, 155 hp

**Main armament** 2 cm KwK 30 L/55 cannon

The prewar 6x4 Panzerspahwagens lacked suffcient cross-country mobility, and were replaced by these eight-wheeled vehicles. Their roles and armament remained the same, and they kept the rear driver's position. Some variants carried the large "bedstead" radio aerial, while others were upgraded with a 7.5 cm KwK 37 gun.

**External** frontal armor

**Driver's** compartment

**Interleaved** road wheels

### ◁ Sd Kfz 251/8 Mittlere Krankenpanzerwagen Ausf C

**Date** 1939 **Country** Germany

**Weight** 8.7 tons (7.9 tonnes)

**Engine** Maybach HL42 TUKRM gasoline, 100 hp

**Main armament** None

Designed as an armored personnel carrier for German Panzergrenadiers to accompany the tanks, this vehicle had a capacity to carry 10 infantrymen. It was well armored, but open-topped, and its half-track design gave it good cross-country mobility. More than 15,000 of these were built, including around 2,500 in postwar Czechoslovakia.

### ▷ Universal Carrier, Mark II

**Date** 1939 **Country** UK

**Weight** 4.4 tons (4 tonnes)

**Engine** Ford flathead V8 gasoline, 85 hp

**Main armament** .303 Bren machine gun

One of the most-produced armored vehicles in history, the Universal Carrier descended from the Carden-Loyd (see pp.46–47). A number of different carriers were developed and amalgamated into one "universal" design. Highly versatile, it was used to carry machine guns, mortars, infantrymen, supplies and artillery observation equipment, among other roles. Carriers were popular with the infantry and in high demand.

**Front-mounted** idler wheel

Body armored on sides only

◁ **M3A1**

| | |
|---|---|
| **Date** 1940 | **Country** USA |

**Weight** 4.5 tons (4.1 tonnes)

**Engine** Hercules JXD gasoline, 87 hp

**Main armament** None

The M3 was a durable and reliable four-wheel scout car with an open-topped, armored body. It was widely used by the Americans, British, and Soviets to ferry troops, as well as other roles such as ambulance, command, and forward observation. The roller at the front of the vehicle helped prevent it from ditching.

Armored vision port

Fuel cans

▷ **Daimler Mark II**

| | |
|---|---|
| **Date** 1940 | **Country** UK |

**Weight** 3.4 tons (3 tonnes)

**Engine** Daimler 6HV gasoline, 55 hp

**Main armament** None

Popularly known as the Dingo, this scout car was a small, two-man vehicle with very high mobility due to its transmission design, which it shared with the Daimler Armored Car. Early Dingos had four-wheel steering and a sliding armored roof, but both features were later removed. The solid rubber tires, however, were retained. Around 6,600 were built and they were very popular.

Armored body offered only limited protection

Driver's vision port

Pneumatic tires

◁ **Humber Scout Car**

| | |
|---|---|
| **Date** 1942 | **Country** UK |

**Weight** 3.8 tons (3.5 tonnes)

**Engine** Humber 5-cylinder gasoline, 87 hp

**Main armament** .303 Bren machine gun

Although the Dingo was the standard British Scout Car, wartime demand meant that other companies were tasked with producing similar vehicles. Although Humber's offering did not include all the Dingo's advanced automotive features, it could accommodate a third crewman. Later in the war, many Humbers were allocated to armored units, while Dingos were mainly used by the infantry.

Turret houses 7.62 mm machine gun

▷ **BA-64**

| | |
|---|---|
| **Date** 1942 | **Country** Soviet Union |

**Weight** 2.6 tons (2.3 tonnes)

**Engine** GAZ-MM 4-cylinder gasoline, 50 hp

**Main armament** 7.62 mm DT machine gun

A light, two-man, 4x4 armored car, the BA-64 was used by the Soviet forces for reconnaissance, liaison, and communication, and supporting the infantry. Unlike most Allied armored cars, only a few BA-64 had a radio. The angles and placement of the armor offered greater protection than its thickness would suggest.

# Armored Cars and Troop Carriers (cont.)

Armored half-tracks were used by Allied and Axis nations to carry infantry across country and under fire. Being versatile, they were used for different roles, including as platforms for antitank or antiaircraft guns, towing vehicles for artillery, ambulances, maintenance workshops, and command vehicles. Fully tracked support vehicles were less common, but the popular Universal Carrier saw extensive use. Toward the end of the war, the Ram Kangaroo pioneered the concept of the fully tracked armored personnel carrier.

**Angled** crew compartment

**Machine gun** tripod stowed on hull

USA 604325-S

### △ Praying Mantis

| | | | |
|---|---|---|---|
| **Date** 1943 | **Country** UK | | |
| **Weight** 5.8 tons (5.3 tonnes) | | | |
| **Engine** Ford flathead V8 gasoline, 85 hp | | | |
| **Main armament** 2 x .303 Bren machine guns | | | |

The Praying Mantis was a failed attempt to produce a very low-profile weapon carrier. The two-man crew lay prone inside the body, which could be elevated by hydraulics to see and fire over cover. Although innovative, it was difficult to operate and made the crew sick.

### ◁ M8 Greyhound

| | |
|---|---|
| **Date** 1943 | **Country** USA |
| **Weight** 8.2 tons (7.4 tonnes) | |
| **Engine** Hercules JXD gasoline, 110 hp | |
| **Main armament** 37 mm M6 L/56.6 gun | |

The M8 was originally designed as a wheeled tank destroyer, but it soon became a reconnaissance vehicle because of its light armament. Its six-wheel drive gave it a high speed on roads, but its suspension limited it across country. The M8 was open-topped and thinly armored.

### ▽ M5 half-track

| | |
|---|---|
| **Date** 1943 | **Country** USA |
| **Weight** 10.9 tons (9.9 tonnes) | |
| **Engine** IHC RED-450-B gasoline, 141 hp | |
| **Main armament** .50 Browning M2 machine gun | |

The Allies used the M2 and M9 as artillery tractors, and the M3 and M5 as armored personnel carriers. Both were put to a wide range of other uses during the war, including recovery, command, and ambulance. Israel used these vehicles for decades after 1945.

**.50** Browning machine gun

DIXIE CLIPPER

**Continuous** track at rear

Rear-mounted engine

2-pounder main gun

◁ **Marmon-Herrington, Mark IV**

| | | | |
|---|---|---|---|
| **Date** 1943 | **Country** South Africa | | |
| **Weight** 7.4 tons (6.7 tonnes) | | | |
| **Engine** Ford V8 gasoline, 95 hp | | | |
| **Main armament** QF 2-pounder gun | | | |

The Mark IV bore little resemblance to earlier Marmon-Herringtons. Its engine was now at the rear, and it had no separate chassis. It was more heavily armed, with a 2-pounder. By 1943, the North African Campaign had ended, so the Mark IV was used in Italy instead. It saw combat one final time in 1974, during the Turkish invasion of Cyprus.

Pneumatic tires

Canvas canopy

Aerial mount

△ **Fox Armored Car**

| | |
|---|---|
| **Date** 1943 | **Country** Canada |
| **Weight** 9 tons (8.1 tonnes) | |
| **Engine** General Motors 270 gasoline, 97 hp | |
| **Main armament** .50 Browning M2 machine gun | |

The Fox was a Canadian-built version of the British Humber Armored Car, based on the standard Canadian Military Pattern truck chassis and armed with more easily obtainable American machine guns. Around 1, 500 were built, and they were used in Italy and India.

△ **CT15TA Armored Truck**

| | |
|---|---|
| **Date** 1943 | **Country** Canada |
| **Weight** 5 tons (4.6 tonnes) | |
| **Engine** General Motors 270 gasoline, 100 hp | |
| **Main armament** None | |

Like the Fox Armored Car, the CT15TA was based on the Canadian Military Pattern truck chassis. It was used as a troop carrier and an ambulance, as well as a load carrier, but was not intended as a frontline vehicle.

◁ **Sd Kfz 234/3 Schwerer Panzerspahwagen, 8-rad**

| | |
|---|---|
| **Date** 1944 | **Country** Germany |
| **Weight** 12.9 tons (11.7 tonnes) | |
| **Engine** Tatra 103 diesel, 220 hp | |
| **Main armament** 7.5 cm Kwk 51 L/24 gun | |

The Sd Kfz 234 replaced the Sd Kfz 231 in 1944. It had more advanced suspension and steering, giving greater mobility, as well as a more powerful engine and thicker armor. There were four variants, with different armament. This version was used against fortifications and area targets to support other variants, which were armed with dedicated antitank guns.

7.5 cm main gun

External kit stowage

Pneumatic tires at front

△ **Ram Kangaroo**

| | |
|---|---|
| **Date** 1944 | **Country** Canada |
| **Weight** 27.4 tons (24.9 tonnes) | |
| **Engine** Wright-Continental R-975 gasoline, 400 hp | |
| **Main armament** .30 Browning M1919 machine gun | |

Kangaroo was the name given to a number of different tanks converted to carry infantry. Most were based on the Ram. They were used in Italy and northwest Europe. Each could carry 11 soldiers. The development of the Kangaroo was driven by the Canadian forces.

# 1945-1991
# THE COLD WAR

# THE COLD WAR

**After World War II** it was clear that the tank had a dominant, but not invincible, place on the battlefield. Shaped-charge warheads fired from cheap, lightweight weapons presented a major threat even to the heaviest tanks, and this prompted many manufacturers to stress mobility over armor as the best form of protection. The tanks of the Cold War adversaries first faced each other during the Korean War, but that conflict saw few tank battles, with armored vehicles being used mainly as infantry support. Likewise, both the American forces in Vietnam and the Soviet forces in Afghanistan deployed large numbers of armored vehicles, but they rarely faced enemy tanks. Indeed, the largest tank battles of the Cold War did not involve the superpowers at all. Some battles of the Indo-Pakistani War of 1965, for instance, involved hundreds of tanks on each side.

The Israeli experience of the Six Day War of 1967 and the Yom Kippur War of 1973 spurred critical developments in tank design. High Israeli losses to antitank missiles accelerated work on new methods to protect against shaped charges, including Explosive Reactive Armor, which was developed by the Soviet Union and Israel, and British Chobham armor, made of layers of different materials. During the 1980s, a new generation of tanks incorporating this armor, and systems such as computerized fire control and thermal night sights took to the field. Many of these tanks proved themselves in the first Gulf War in 1991, where their superiority over older Soviet vehicles was clearly demonstrated.

△ **Vietnamese pride**
A nationalist poster celebrates the victory of Vietnam over its former colonial masters with an image showing tanks leading the country to freedom.

## Key events

▷ **1945** The Soviet IS-3 Heavy Tank takes part in the Allied Victory Parade in Berlin, alarming Western observers.

▷ **1950** The outbreak of the Korean War generates a "tank panic" in the US, accelerating the development of new vehicles.

▷ **1956** Soviet tanks are involved in street fighting during the crushing of the Hungarian Revolution. Several are destroyed with improvised weapons.

▷ **1965** India stops a Pakistani invasion at the Battle of Asal Uttar. Pakistan loses 99 of over 250 tanks; India loses 10.

△ **M48 Patton in Vietnam**
Vietnamese rangers are covered by a US M48 Patton in a battle in the Cholon district of Saigon during the Vietnam War.

▷ **1972** Centurion AVREs demolish IRA barricades during Operation Motorman, the largest operation during the Troubles in Northern Ireland.

▷ **1973** On the Golan Heights, a force of just 170 Israeli Centurions stall an invasion of over 1,200 Syrian tanks.

▷ **1980** The American M1 Abrams enters service, the first tank to be fitted with Chobham armor.

▷ **1982** During the Lebanon War, the Israelis make the first use of Explosive Reactive Armor.

▷ **1991** At the Battle of 73 Easting, during the first Gulf War, US tanks destroy some of Iraq's most capable forces, despite being vastly outnumbered.

"**Victory** is no longer a **truth**. It is only a **word** to **describe** who is **left alive** in the **ruins.**"

LYNDON B. JOHNSON, PRESIDENT OF THE UNITED STATES

◁ **A Soviet propaganda poster** depicts Stalin (left) standing over an army led by columns of invincible-seeming tanks.

# Tanks of the Communist Bloc

Soon after the end of World War II, the Soviet Union introduced the T-54. This was the first of a series of tanks that were produced in massive numbers and exported to the Warsaw Pact and Communist client states around the world. Soviet doctrine envisaged using tanks, supported by artillery and infantry, to break through frontline defenses and to make long advances into the enemy's rear positions. This influenced their design, which emphasized mobility and low height so that the tanks would be harder to hit. As a result, their crews usually found them cramped and uncomfortable.

### △ T-54

| | |
|---|---|
| **Date** 1947 | **Country** Soviet Union |
| **Weight** 39.6 tons (36 tonnes) | |
| **Engine** V-54 V12 diesel, 520 hp | |
| **Main armament** 100 mm D-10T L/53.5 rifled gun | |

The T-54 is one of the most produced armored vehicles in history. It moved away from Christie suspension, opting for torsion bars instead, and was armed with the 100 mm gun that proved its worth on the SU-100. The T-54 saw combat in Africa, the Middle East, Asia, and Europe.

### ▷ PT-76

| | |
|---|---|
| **Date** 1951 | **Country** Soviet Union |
| **Weight** 16.1 tons (14.6 tonnes) | |
| **Engine** Model V-6 diesel, 240 hp | |
| **Main armament** 76.2 mm 2A16 L/42 rifled gun | |

A light tank, the PT-76 was able to swim with the help of two water jets. This made it highly mobile and versatile, but its buoyancy requirements resulted in a large hull and thin armor that could barely protect the tank against heavy machine guns.

**Commander and loader** stations in turret

**Light armor** gives vehicle buoyancy

**Extractor** prevents propellant gases from entering the tank

**100 mm** L/53.5 rifled gun

**Elongated** hull

**Spare** track links

### △ T-10M

| | |
|---|---|
| **Date** 1952 | **Country** Soviet Union |
| **Weight** 57.3 tons (52 tonnes) | |
| **Engine** Kharkiv Model V-2-IS diesel, 700 hp | |
| **Main armament** 122 mm M-62-T2 L/46 rifled gun | |

The last of the KV and IS line of heavy tanks, the T-10 had a short career, made obsolete by the development of the main battle tank. The Soviets used heavy tanks in independent battalions that were attached to larger units to provide extra combat power where needed. The last T-10s were withdrawn by the late 1960s, and replaced with the T-64.

### ▷ T-55

| | |
|---|---|
| **Date** 1958 | **Country** Soviet Union |
| **Weight** 39.6 tons (36 tonnes) | |
| **Engine** V-55 V12 diesel, 580 hp | |
| **Main armament** 100 mm D-10T2S L/53.5 rifled gun | |

Unlike the T-54, the T-55 had a Nuclear, Biological, Chemical (NBC) warfare protection system and a more powerful engine. Its production continued until 1981, with upgrades incorporating more modern systems, such as laser range finders and new sights. Many countries developed their own upgrades to keep it viable into the 21st century.

▷ **Type 59**

**Date** 1959 **Country** China

**Weight** 39.6 tons (36 tonnes)

**Engine** 12150L V12 diesel, 520 hp

**Main armament** 105 mm L7 rifled gun

Originally based on the T-54, the Type 59's development has diverged significantly, incorporating Chinese and Western systems. This version, a Type 59-II, has a British-designed gun, NBC protection, and a gun stabilization system.

**Smoothbore** main gun

**Exhaust** capable of making a smoke screen

◁ **T-62**

**Date** 1962 **Country** Soviet Union

**Weight** 41.9 tons (38 tonnes)

**Engine** V-55-5 V12 diesel, 580 hp

**Main armament** 115 mm 2A20 L/49.5 smoothbore gun

The T-55 evolved into the T-62, which had a larger hull and more powerful 115 mm gun. It was the first smoothbore gun to enter service and to fire Armor Piercing Fin Stabilized, Discarding Sabot (APFSDS) projectiles. Intended as a stopgap, the T-62 became the mainstay of the Soviet Army into the 1970s.

**Fighting compartment** at front of tank

**Radio** antenna

**Stowage** boxes

**Hull** capable of withstanding a tactical nuclear blast at 330 yards (300m)

△ **Type 62**

**Date** 1962 **Country** China

**Weight** 23.2 tons (21 tonnes)

**Engine** 12150L-3 V12 diesel, 430 hp

**Main armament** 85 mm Type 62-85TC rifled gun

As capable as it was, the Type 59 was simply too large and heavy for some areas of China. The Type 62 was essentially a scaled down version issued to units based in such areas. As a result, its firepower and protection were weaker, but the tank did have improved ground pressure and mobility.

**Low** turret profile

**Sprocket wheel** at rear of tank

**Wheel arrangement** with characteristic gap between the first and second pairs

# Tanks of the Communist Bloc (cont.)

The combat record of Soviet tanks, particularly as used by client states in the Middle East, suggests that they were inferior to Western tanks in one-on-one encounters. However, the truth is that these states rarely used tanks in accordance with the doctrine for which they were designed. Indeed, Soviet tanks were generally quite sophisticated, especially later in the Cold War, featuring gas turbine engines, Kontakt Explosive Reactive Armor, and the Drozd Active Protection System.

**Watertight** hull

△ **Type 63**

**Date** 1963 **Country** China

**Weight** 20.3 tons (18.4 tonnes)

**Engine** Model 12150-I diesel, 400 hp

**Main armament** 85 mm Type 62-85TC rifled gun

Although similar in concept to the PT-76, the Type 63 is a largely indigenous design. It is powered by two water jets that give it a speed of 7.5 mph (6.5 knots). The Type 63 can swim over long distances, a feature that enables it to cross wide rivers and paddy fields, as well as play a role in amphibious operations.

**Smoothbore** gun with guided missile capability

▷ **T-64B**

**Date** 1966 **Country** Soviet Union

**Weight** 43 tons (39 tonnes)

**Engine** 5DTF diesel, 700hp

**Main armament** 125mm 2A46M2 L/48 smoothbore gun

An advanced but complex design, the T-64 introduced many new features, notably an autoloader for the gun, which could also fire guided missiles. It was intended for independent tank battalions—the spearhead of the Soviet Army—and was never exported. The breakup of the Soviet Union left the T-64 factory in Ukraine, which has developed the tank further.

**Kontakt** reactive armor

**Ceramic** composite armor

**125mm** smoothbore gun

**Composite** armour protection

**Twelve wheels** powered by a V-46 diesel engine

△ **T-72M1**

**Date** 1973 **Country** Soviet Union

**Weight** 45.7 tons (41.5 tonnes)

**Engine** V-46.6 diesel, 780 hp

**Main armament** 125 mm 2A46 L/48 smoothbore gun

Designed as a simpler and cheaper alternative to the T-64, the T-72 has received extensive upgrades over its long career. The latest models are equipped with distinctive Explosive Reactive Armor (ERA) panels and thermal hunter-killer sights. Versions exported by the Soviets generally have less sophisticated systems and thinner armor.

**Smoke grenade** launchers

**Explosive** Reactive Armor on glacis plate

▷ **T-80**

**Date** 1976 **Country** Soviet Union

**Weight** 50.7 tons (46 tonnes)

**Engine** GTD-1250 gas-turbine, 1,250 hp

**Main armament** 125mm 2A46M1 L/48 smoothbore gun

Developed from the T-64, the T-80 was powered by a gas turbine engine. It was seen on the streets of Moscow during the attempted coup of 1991, and saw combat in Chechnya in 1995. This T-80U upgrade has a more powerful turbine and a new turret that is protected by ERA panels.

**12.7 mm** air-defense machine gun

▷ **Type 88C**

**Date** 1981 **Country** China

**Weight** 45.2 tons (41 tonnes)

**Engine** VR36 V12 diesel, 790 hp

**Main armament** 125 mm smoothbore gun

**125 mm** smoothbore gun

During the Cold War, two generations of Chinese tanks shared the basic T-54 design. This began to change in the late 1980s. The culmination of a series of prototypes and export models, the Type 88C had a new road-wheel arrangement and a new turret fitted with an autoloader.

**100 mm** main gun muzzle

**Infrared** searchlight

**Rounded** turret

**Headlight** cage

◁ **Type 69**

**Date** 1983 **Country** China

**Weight** 40.4 tons (36.7 tonnes)

**Engine** 12150L-7BW V12 diesel, 580 hp

**Main armament** 100 mm rifled gun

A heavily upgraded Type 59, the Type 69 was developed by Chinese companies without Soviet support. This later version, the Type 69-II, had a laser range finder mounted over the barrel and an infrared searchlight next to the gun. It was not widely used by the Chinese, but was a significant export success.

**Road wheels** follow pattern of Soviet tanks

**100 mm** rifled gun

▷ **T-55AD**

**Date** 1989 **Country** Soviet Union

**Weight** 39.6 tons (36 tonnes)

**Engine** V-55 V12 diesel, 580 hp

**Main armament** 100 mm D-10T2S L/53.5 rifled gun

Popularly known as Enigma, this Iraqi T-55 has extra armor attached to its turret, side skirts, and glacis plate. It contains layers of steel, rubber, and aluminum to defeat High Explosive Anti Tank (HEAT) warheads. This is an example of the kind of upgrades applied by many countries to keep older tanks viable on the battlefield. A disadvantage is the extra weight, which can affect the tank's mobility.

# T-72

The T-72 was a Soviet tank designed for use if the Cold War had escalated into open conflict. Simple to manufacture and maintain, it followed the T-64 (see p.132), a more expensive and complex tank. The T-72 entered service with the Red Army in the 1970s and is still used by over 40 countries. Versions of the T-72, often with lower standards of protection, were built in the Soviet Union for exportation, while Poland and Czechoslovakia also manufactured T-72s.

**THE T-72 INCLUDED FEATURES** from earlier Soviet tank designs—a low profile, a frying pan-shaped turret, and a reliable diesel engine. At just over 45 tons (41 tonnes), it was relatively light compared to contemporary Western tanks. It was also considered less effective than its Western rivals in one-on-one encounters, as with many Soviet tanks of the Cold War. However, it was fit for purpose: Soviet commanders intended to use it in huge massed attacks to swamp western defenses.

The T-72 was equipped with an autoloader system for the main gun, with 22 rounds housed in a circular, horizontal carousel; 17 extra rounds were stored in the hull. This allowed a maximum rate of fire of up to three shots in 13 seconds. It also meant that a three-man crew could be used (commander, gunner, and driver), reducing the need for crew space and enabling a smaller, lighter design. This was so effective that official guidelines specified a maximum height of 5 ft 9 in (175 cm) for crewmen, to ensure they could fit into the T-72's cramped interior.

**REAR VIEW**

| SPECIFICATIONS | |
|---|---|
| **Name** | T-72M1 |
| **Date** | 1973 |
| **Origin** | Soviet Union |
| **Production** | Over 25,000 |
| **Engine** | V46.6 V-12 diesel, 780 hp |
| **Weight** | 45.7 tons (41.5 tonnes) |
| **Main armament** | 125 mm 2A46M smoothbore |
| **Secondary armament** | 12.7 mm NSVT machine gun |
| **Crew** | 3 |
| **Armor thickness** | Max 11 in (280 mm) |

Commander

Driver

Gunner

**Smoothbore barrel**, strong enough to ram through walls

**Wading snorkel** on rear of turret

**125 mm gun**, larger than contemporary Western equivalents

**Sloped armor** on front of hull

**Metal tracks** with wide footprint

**THREE-QUARTER VIEW**

**"Gill" armor** helps to protect against hollow charge rounds

### Stealth and mobility

The front view of the T-72 reveals one of its major tactical assets—its low profile. At just over 6 ft (2 m) in height, it presents a difficult target for an enemy. The autoloader allows a reduction in height since there is no need for a standing crew member in the turret.

## EXTERIOR

Tanks often feature improvements and additions, and this T-72 from Polish service shows added "gill" armor along the sides. These rubber squares can be angled forward to detonate or disrupt hollow charge rounds before they meet the main body of the tank. The external machine-gun bracket was originally mounted wth an antiaircraft 12.7 mm NSVT, and the turret also housed a 7.62 mm PKT coaxial machine gun.

1. Polish national emblem  2. Station keeping/convoy light  3. Main gunsight
4. Headlight  5. Infrared light  6. Machine-gun bracket  7. Commander's hatch (closed)
8. Gunner's hatch (closed)  9. Deep wading snorkel (stowed)  10. Machine-gun ammunition boxes  11. Engine exhaust  12. Additional "gill" armor  13. Fuel-drum brackets
14. Spare track links on hull  15. Rear reflector

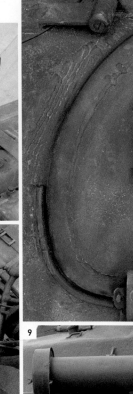

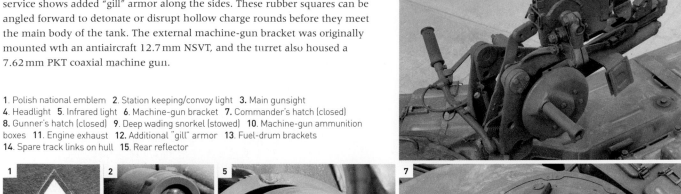

## INTERIOR

Housing just three crew, the interior of the T-72 was cramped and made few concessions to human comfort. Its crew compartment offered nuclear, biological, and chemical (NBC) protection, and the gunner had access to gunsights and a laser range finder for use in the day, as well as infrared sights for use at night.

16. Looking down into commander's position
17. Commander's sight  18. Looking down into gunner's position  19. Gunner's sight  20. Commander's seat back and pistol case  21. Gun elevation handwheel
22. Main gun breech and autoloader  23. Looking down into driver's position  24. Driver's periscope  25. Gearshift
26. Driver's instrument panel  27. Left-hand steering lever

# Berlin brinkmanship

Berlin was a constant battleground during the Cold War. When East German border guards stopped an American diplomat in October 1961 and insisted on seeing his passport, American authorities in West Berlin reacted by escorting their diplomats into the eastern part of the city with troops in Jeeps. The alarmed American government sent General Lucius D. Clay to Berlin to ensure that no further encroachments were made by the Soviets into the Four Party Agreement made at the end of World War II. Clay was determined not to back down to any form of Soviet posturing, so on October 27 he sent M48 tanks to Checkpoint Charlie, the manned gateway between East and West Berlin. The tanks stood 246 ft (75 m) from the border, guns forward and

engines revving. In response, the Russian leader Nikita Khrushchev ordered Russian T-55 tanks to meet the Americans. The two sides faced each other for 16 hours while President Kennedy had a separate conversation with the Kremlin. Eventually, first one T-55 was withdrawn and then an M48 backed away—and this continued until normalcy resumed.

The Russians honored the earlier Four Party Agreement over free movement in Berlin, but General Clay was told that such brinkmanship was too dangerous a policy to pursue in the future.

**Russian and American tanks face each other** from either side of Checkpoint Charlie–a crossing-point between East and West Berlin–in 1961.

The sign reads: YOU ARE LEAVING THE AMERICAN SECTOR / ВЫ ВЫЕЗЖАЕТЕ ИЗ АМЕРИКАНСКОГО СЕКТОРА / VOUS SORTEZ DU SECTEUR AMERICAIN / SIE VERLASSEN DEN AMERIKANISCHEN SEKTOR

The Ulan infantry fighting vehicle, on maneuvers

# Key Manufacturers
# General Dynamics

General Dynamics is one of a new breed of highly adaptable military-industrial conglomerates. Following the end of the Cold War, its future looked bleak, but by concentrating on armored vehicles, warships, and military information systems, it was able to rise to prominence again.

IN 1982, GENERAL DYNAMICS, until then a major force in submarine construction and military aviation, took a decision to move into the manufacturing of fighting vehicles, and a new division, Land Systems, was created to acquire the Chrysler Corporation's defense interests. Its main asset was the M60 Patton Main Battle Tank, over 15,000 of which were produced between 1961 and 1987. These equipped the US Army and US Marine Corps' armored divisions throughout much of the Cold War, and saw active service (by now in its third generation) with the USMC in the 1991 Gulf War.

American fighting vehicles are often named after historic senior commanders, and the Patton's successor, the M1 Abrams, was no exception. After a lengthy design process, it entered service in 1980 and soon demonstrated its superiority. Successive upgrades enabled it to remain active for many decades. Its original composite armor was progressively improved, most significantly by adding depleted uranium or "reactive" (explosive) plates to the most vulnerable areas (see pp.238–39), while the original rifled 105 mm gun, the M68A1, deemed inadequate for the modern battlefield, was soon

**Flyer Advanced Light Strike Vehicle**
Developed for Special Forces, the Flyer carries up to nine men at up to 100 mph (160 km/h). It can be armed with a machine gun, a cannon, or a 40 mm grenade launcher.

replaced by the smoothbore 120 mm M256A1, designed in Germany. This 44-caliber cannon could fire a variety of projectiles, including the M829 APFSDS (Armor Piercing Fin Stabilized Discarding Sabot) "dart"—made of depleted uranium, and capable of penetrating 22 in (570 mm) of steel armor at 2,200 yds (2,000 m)—as well as high-explosive (shaped charge) and antipersonnel cartridges containing over a thousand $\frac{3}{8}$ in (9.5 mm) tungsten balls.

General Dynamics had divested itself of all of its military aviation interests by the end of the 20th century, but Land Systems soon expanded further, with acquisitions from Europe as well as at home. First came Santa Bárbara Sistemas, acquired from the Spanish Government, which produced not only vehicles but also small arms, munitions, and missiles. Next, in 2003, Land Systems acquired General Motors' defense interests, and then Steyr Daimler Puch Spezialfahrzeug (SDPS) from an Austrian investment house. The latter brought with it the Swiss MOWAG company, which had been producing specialized military and civilian vehicles with a degree of success since 1950. These new European interests soon became an important part of the parent company's armored vehicle development effort, with Santa Bárbara and Steyr working together (as ASCOD—Austrian-Spanish Cooperation Development) to produce the Pizarro Infantry Fighting Vehicle (known as the Ulan in Austrian service) and the Scout SV (Specialist Vehicle). The Pizzaro/Ulan was a limited success, adopted by Austria and Spain only, but the Scout

SV was a different story. In preference to BAE Systems' CV90, it was adopted by the British Army as the Ajax family, to replace its aging Combat Vehicle Reconniassance (Tracked) family of vehicles.

SDPS independently developed the (wheeled) Pandur Armored Fighting Vehicle from a design produced by another Spanish concern, Pegaso, while MOWAG produced the Eagle, a light tactical vehicle, the DURO, an off-road tactical transport, and, most successfully, the Piranha family of wheeled multirole APC/IFVs. The Piranha entered service in 1972, and was soon available in four distinct versions, from four- to 10-wheeled, some of them equipped with twin propellers and rudders to give them a limited "smooth-water" amphibious capability. The Piranha was to become the basis for the eight-wheeled LAV-25 and Bison, used by US and Canadian units, and the latter's six-wheeled AVGPs (Armored Vehicle General Purpose), known in their various forms as Cougar, Grizzly, and Husky, as well as the eight-wheeled LAV III known as the Kodiak. Later variants of the Piranha formed the basis of the US Army's Stryker family of armored fighting vehicles, almost 4,500 of which had entered service when

**Abrams production**
Production of Abrams MBTs began at Detroit and the Lima plant at Ohio. When the Detroit plant closed in 1996, Lima took over refurbishment duties. The Lima plant had previously built tanks such as the Sherman.

# "...if you want to **get somebody's attention**, just put an **M1A1 tank** on the ground."

## GENERAL LON E. MAGGART, COMMANDING GENERAL, THE ARMOR CENTER, FORT KNOX

**Ocelot**
Unlike mine-protected vehicles based on existing chassis, Ocelot is modular. Its design integrates V-hull, blast-protection technology with a demountable protected crew pod.

production ceased in 2014. There were also numerous sub-types of all these vehicles. The Kodiak, for example, was equipped with a turret-mounted 25mm chain gun, while Swiss versions of the Piranha could mount TOW antitank missiles and the M1128 Mobile Gun System version of the Stryker could even support a 105mm M68 cannon.

Another US-based specialist, Force Protection Inc., was added to the portfolio in 2011. Its most important product line was the Cougar MRAP

(Mine-Resistant, Ambush Protected), available in both a 4x4 and a 6x6 wheel configuration. It was produced to a specification issued by the US Marine Corps, which was dissatisfied with the fragility of the Humvee in hostile territory, but went on to be adopted by the armed services of over a dozen nations under a variety of names and forms. Force Protection later produced a lighter mine-resistant vehicle named Ocelot, which was adopted by the British Army as the Foxhound, to replace its unsatisfactory and unpopular Snatch Land Rovers.

**Ajax armored fighting vehicle**
The British Army's new family of infantry fighting vehicles was designed in Austria and Spain. This version's turret is German, while its 40mm cannon was developed in France.

**M1 Abrams MBT**
The world's heaviest Main Battle Tank, the Abrams first saw combat in the 1991 Gulf War and proved itself outstanding. Over 10,000 were built, in three versions, with a fourth to follow.

# Centurion

The Centurion is one of the classic postwar tanks. It started life as a heavy cruiser tank designed to take the highly effective 17-pounder gun used in World War II. By 1947 the gun's makers, the Royal Ordnance Factory, had designed a new weapon, the 20-pounder. This was capable of much better performance, and was adopted for a new Centurion model, the Mark 3, which also featured an improved version of the Rolls-Royce Meteor engine.

PRODUCTION BEGAN in 1945 at the Royal Ordnance Factory near Leeds, and the Vickers-Armstrong plant at Newcastle-upon-Tyne in the north of England; around 2,800 Mark 3 tanks were completed by 1956. In 1959, the 20-pounder guns were again replaced with the Royal Ordnance Factories' new L7 105mm gun. This main gun fired a range of ammunition types, including Armor Piercing Discarding Sabot (APDS), Armor Piercing Fin Stabilized Discarding Sabot (APFSDS), and High Explosive Squash Head (HESH) rounds.

REAR VIEW

The Centurion's combat history began in the Korean War in 1950, where one regiment of Centurions was deployed with great success. The tank also saw action in Vietnam, the India–Pakistan conflict of 1965, and a number of Middle East conflicts.

Many features remained consistent throughout the tank's variants, including the welded, boat-shaped hull, Horstmann suspension, and Meteor engine. The latter was regarded as underpowered, limiting the tank's speed and agility, and it had a short operational range. In British service, the Centurion ran until the Mark 13—the version shown here—but other countries continued to improve their models until 2003.

| SPECIFICATIONS | |
|---|---|
| **Name** | Centurion Mark 13 FV4017 |
| **Date** | 1945-62 |
| **Origin** | UK |
| **Production** | More than 13,750 |
| **Engine** | Rolls Royce Meteor Mark 4B gasoline, 650 hp |
| **Weight** | 58 tons (52.6 tonnes) |
| **Main armament** | 105 mm L7A2 |
| **Secondary armament** | .30 Browning M1919, .50 Browning M2 |
| **Crew** | 4 |
| **Armor thickness** | 6 in (152 mm) max |

Loader

Commander

Gunner

Driver

**105 mm** L7 gun

**Aerial** mount

**Infrared** headlight

**THREE-QUARTER VIEW**

**Metal track**—later "Hush
Puppy" rubber-blocked
track was used

**Horstmann**
suspension

09 BB 33

**Royal Tank Regiment badge**
A tank could serve with a number
of Regiments in its service life.
The Royal Tank Regiment were the
successors to the Tank Corps of
World War I.

**Night fighting**
The Mark 13 can be distinguished by the large
spotlight attached to the turret. This could
provide conventional white light or an infrared
beam for night fighting. It was adopted as a result
of British experience in Korea, and that of the
Americans and Australians in Vietnam. Infrared
filters were also installed for night driving and
these can be seen here as the outermost
headlights each side, on the front of the tank.

## EXTERIOR

The Centurion was memorably described by a former crewman as a tank "with a soul": for many crewmen, it was remembered with affection and considered the last generation of tank that the crew could repair themselves with standard tools. The ability of broken-down or knocked-out tanks to be recovered and repaired ready for a following day's battle was one of the reasons the Israeli Army thought very highly of the vehicle. The commander's cupola can counter-rotate against the position of the turret to allow him to keep eyes on a target while the turret moves.

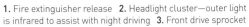

1. Fire extinguisher release   2. Headlight cluster—outer light is infrared to assist with night driving   3. Front drive sprocket
4. Covers for driver's periscopes   5. Gunner's sight aperture
6. Infrared /white light searchlight   7. Loader's periscope
8. Commander's cupola with hatch closed   9. Smoke grenade launchers   10. Infantry telephone box   11. Fishtail exhaust

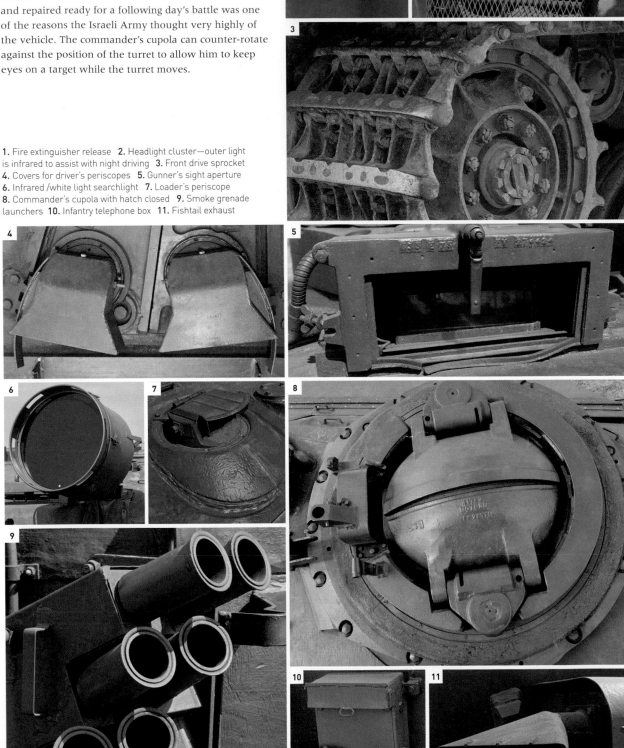

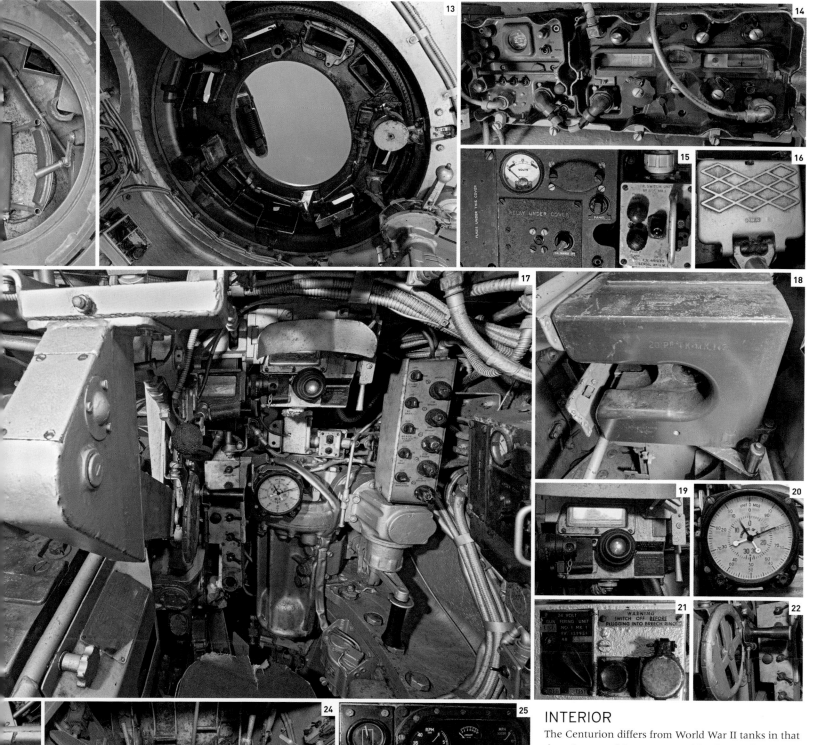

## INTERIOR

The Centurion differs from World War II tanks in that there is no co-driver—ammunition is stored next to the driver in the place a co-driver would normally have sat. The gunner and commander's gun sights are mechanically linked.

**12.** Looking down into commander's position
**13.** Commander's cupola interior  **14.** Larkspur radio set  **15.** Fuses (left) and control box (right) for searchlight
**16.** Commander's foot rest  **17.** Gunner's position  **18.** Main gun breech  **19.** Gunner's sight  **20.** Traverse indicator
**21.** Emergency main gun firing panel  **22.** Elevation handwheel
**23.** .50-cal ranging machine gun  **24.** Driver's compartment
**25.** Driver's instrument panel  **26.** Driver's switchboard

# Tanks of the NATO Alliance

Without an equivalent to Soviet domination, NATO nations were free to produce a wide range of tanks. All were intended to defend Western Europe against a Soviet threat, but differing national doctrines led to a variety of different designs. The German Leopards, for example, emphasized mobility and had very light armor, whereas the British Chieftain was far more heavily armored but much less mobile. Many of these tanks were exported to other NATO members and Western allies across the world.

**20-pounder** main gun

**Commander's** cupola

**Gun** mantlet

**Headlight**

### △ Centurion Mark I

**Date** 1945 **Country** UK

**Weight** 51 tons (46.2 tonnes)

**Engine** Rolls-Royce Meteor Mark IVA gasoline, 640 hp

**Main armament** Ordnance QF 17-pounder gun

The design of the Centurion began in 1943. It used the engine and transmission of the Comet, in a vehicle large enough to take the 17-pounder gun. Six prototypes were sent to Europe just weeks after the end of the war in 1945. The Mark I, which entered service in 1946, had a 20 mm Polsten cannon in a separate mount.

### △ M41A1 Walker Bulldog

**Date** 1951 **Country** USA

**Weight** 25.5 tons (23.2 tonnes)

**Engine** Continental AOS-895-3 gasoline, 500 hp

**Main armament** 76 mm M32 L/64 gun

The replacement for the M24 Chaffee, the M41 was designed to have significantly heavier firepower, but still be light enough to be transported by air. It was widely exported around the world and saw combat with the Americans and the South Vietnamese. A number of nations still use it.

**Drive** sprocket

### ▽ M47 Patton

**Date** 1952 **Country** USA

**Weight** 48 tons (43.6 tonnes)

**Engine** Continental AV1790-5A gasoline, 810 hp

**Main armament** 90 mm M36 L/50 rifled gun

The M47 was an interim vehicle using the hull of the M46 and a new turret. Although the Americans had replaced it with the M48 by the end of the 1950s, more than 9,000 M47s were built. It was widely exported to American allies under the Military Assistance Program. Many of these countries operated it for decades and several used it in combat.

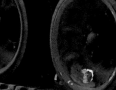

**Road** wheels

▷ **M48 Patton**

**Date** 1952 **Country** USA

**Weight** 49.3 tons (44.7 tonnes)

**Engine** Continental AV-1790-5B gasoline, 810 hp

**Main armament** 90 mm M41 L/50 rifled gun

The M48 was being developed even before M47 production began. It had an improved hull, design, and suspension. Almost 12,000 tanks were built and used by 26 nations, seeing service in several wars. An AVDS-1790 diesel engine and 105 mm gun were added to later versions.

▽ **AMX-13**

**Date** 1953 **Country** France

**Weight** 16.5 tons (15 tonnes)

**Engine** Sofam Model 8Gxb gasoline, 250 hp

**Main armament** 75 mm SA 50 rifled gun

This lightly-armored tank incorporated several innovative features to keep its weight down. The engine was located at the front, the gun had an autoloader, and the turret had an oscillating design, where the entire upper section moved with the gun. A great success, the AMX-13 received many upgrades, including 90 mm and 105 mm guns.

**.50 Browning M2** machine gun

▷ **M103A2**

**Date** 1953 **Country** USA

**Weight** 64 tons (58 tonnes)

**Engine** Continental AVDS-1790-2 diesel, 750 hp

**Main armament** 120 mm M58 L/63.2 rifled gun

The M103 was developed from the late 1940s to support medium tanks and counter Soviet IS-3 and T-10 heavy tanks. The size and weight of the separate-loading 120 mm ammunition required two loaders. It was popular with the US Marine Corps, where 220 tanks served from 1959 to 1972.

**Fume** extractor

◁ **M60A1 RISE**

**Date** 1960 **Country** USA

**Weight** 58 tons (52.6 tonnes)

**Engine** Continental AVDS-1790-2A diesel, 750 hp

**Main armament** 105 mm M68 L/52 rifled gun

To save development time and money, the M60 was based on the M48. The 105 mm gun and its fire-control system gave the tank greater firepower. It also featured a diesel engine and thicker armor. The improved M60A1 was introduced in 1963. It served more than 20 countries for decades, receiving numerous upgrades.

▽ **Chieftain Mark 11**

**Date** 1966 **Country** UK

**Weight** 60.6 tons (55 tonnes)

**Engine** Leyland L60 multifuel, 750 hp

**Main armament** 120 mm L11A5 L/55 rifled gun

The Chieftain had heavy armor and powerful firepower, with mobility as a lower priority, for its anticipated role in defending against a Soviet attack. It replaced both Conqueror and Centurion in 1966. This was the first tank where the driver drove semireclined, reducing its overall height.

**Drive** sprocket

# Tanks of the NATO Alliance (cont.)

NATO nations standardized many aspects of their militaries so that they could fight effectively together, including ammunition, fuel, and command procedures. However, despite several failed multinational projects, the alliance never produced a NATO standard tank. From the late 1950s, however, the British-designed L7 105 mm gun was widely—although not exclusively—adopted for use in tanks across the nations of the alliance.

**120 mm** smoothbore gun

**105 mm** main gun

### ▷ AMX-30B2

**Date** 1963 **Country** France

**Weight** 40.8 tons (37 tonnes)

**Engine** Hispano-Suiza HS110 multifuel, 720 hp

**Main armament** 105 mm Modele F1 L/56 rifled gun

The lightweight AMX-30 was the result of French tank design in the 1950s, emphasizing mobility and firepower. The tank's low height and speed of up to 40mph (64km/h) provided extra protection. After serving the French Army throughout the Cold War, the upgraded AMX-30B2 saw combat in the Gulf War of 1991.

**Road** wheels

**Fume** extractor

### ▷ Leopard 1

**Date** 1965 **Country** West Germany

**Weight** 46.7 tons (42.4 tonnes)

**Engine** MTU MB838 multifuel, 830 hp

**Main armament** 105 mm L7A3 L/52 gun

Unlike Germany's wartime tanks, the Leopard was fast with thin armor. Around 5,000 of these were produced and they served over a dozen nations. In more than 30 years of service, it received upgrades in armor protection, sights, and fire control system. Two turret variants were produced—this one was cast, the other, with an angular shape, was welded.

**Skirt** covers treads

**Stowage** basket

**Camouflage** netting

### ▽ M60A2

**Date** 1972 **Country** USA

**Weight** 58 tons (52.6 tonnes)

**Engine** Continental AVOS-1790-2A diesel, 750 hp

**Main armament** 152 mm M162 gun/missile launcher

The M60A2 had a radically redesigned turret armed with a 152 mm gun that could also fire the MGM-51 Shillelagh anti-tank missile. Unsuccessful, it was withdrawn in 1980. Instead, the M60A3 was developed, which kept the 105 mm gun and added a laser rangefinder, sophisticated fire-control system, and a thermal sight often rated better than that on early M1 Abrams.

**152mm** main gun

### △ Centurion Mark 13

**Date** 1966 **Country** UK

**Weight** 58 tons (52.6 tonnes)

**Engine** Rolls-Royce Meteor Mark IVB gasoline, 650 hp

**Main armament** 105 mm L7 L/52 rifled gun

The 105mm L7 gun was developed after the British analyzed the Soviet T-54 tank. It was attached to the Centurion in 1959. Subsequent Centurions were equipped with ranging machine guns for accurate gunnery, an infrared searchlight for night fighting, and thicker armor. Upgraded Israeli versions of the Centurion saw heavy combat and earned a stellar reputation.

**Vertical** turret armor

### △ Leopard 2A4

**Date** 1979 **Country** West Germany

**Weight** 60.8 tons (55.2 tonnes)

**Engine** MTU MB 873 Ka-501 diesel, 1,500 hp

**Main armament** 120 mm Rheinmetall 120 L/44 gun

The Leopard 2 introduced the 120 mm smoothbore gun, which soon became the Western standard. Almost 3,000 were produced, with the 2A4 version being the most common. The turret incorporated composite armor made from different materials, which meant it did not have to be sloped to be effective.

**Coaxial** machine gun

**Stowage** on turret

**Rubber** tracks

### ◁ M1 Abrams

**Date** 1980 **Country** USA

**Weight** 60 tons (54.5 tonnes)

**Engine** Textron Lycoming AGT1500 gas turbine, 1,500 hp

**Main armament** 105 mm M68 L/52 rifled gun

The M1 was adopted to replace the aging M60. It featured an advanced Chobham armor, a gas-turbine engine, and a computerized fire-control system. The gas turbine gave it unmatched speed, but at the cost of very high fuel consumption. Later models improved the armor, and the M1A1 replaced its gun with the 120 mm smoothbore.

### ▽ Challenger 1

**Date** 1984 **Country** UK

**Weight** 68.3 tons (62 tonnes)

**Engine** Perkins CV12 V-12 diesel, 1,200 hp

**Main armament** 120 mm L11A5 L/55 rifled gun

The Challenger was not intended for the British Army. It was designed for Iran but was cancelled after the revolution in 1979. Internally, it was very similar to a late model of Chieftain, but had a much more reliable engine and hydrogas suspension. It was protected by advanced, top-secret Chobham composite armor. Challenger 1 first saw combat in the Gulf War.

**7.62 mm** machine gun

**Toolbox** on hull

**Composite** armor

# Leopard 1

The German Leopard, in all its many forms, is undoubtedly one of the most successful postwar tank designs. When the West German Army was re-formed in 1955, it was initially equipped with American tanks, but two years later a Franco-German tank development program began. However, this partnership ended in 1962, and France went its own way to build the rival AMX-30 design.

**GERMANY CONTINUED** the wartime practice of ordering prototypes from different companies (or, in this case, groups of companies) and then selecting the best model. In 1963, Krauss-Maffei of Munich was awarded the contract for the new Standard Panzer, the tank that became known as Leopard 1. In contrast to late-World War II German tank design, the Leopard emphasized mobility over protection. However, in terms of firepower, the Germans selected the best weapon available at that time—the British 105 mm L7 gun, as used in the Centurion (see pp.142–45).

**REAR VIEW**

Although it began life as a relatively simple tank, new technologies, increased armor protection, and individual countries' requirements led to the Leopard developing many subvariants. This version is the Leopard 1A1A2, which has a gun stabilization system, additional layers of armor around the turret, and improved gunsights and observation equipment.

## SPECIFICATIONS

| | |
|---|---|
| **Name** | Leopard 1A1A2 |
| **Date** | 1965 |
| **Origin** | West Germany |
| **Production** | 6,486 |
| **Engine** | MTU MB838 10-cylinder multifuel, 830 hp |
| **Weight** | 46.7 tons (42.4 tonnes) |
| **Main armament** | 105 mm L7A3 |
| **Secondary armament** | 2 x 7.62 mm MG3 |
| **Crew** | 4 |
| **Armor thickness** | 0.39–2.76 in (10–70 mm) |

Loader

Engine

Driver

Commander | Gunner

**105 mm L7** main gun

**Torsion-bar** suspension

**THREE-QUARTER VIEW**

**Grousers,** to be attached to tracks in icy conditions

**Double-pin** tracks

## Enduring appeal

The Leopard was a great export success, with variants being operated by 15 countries. Many were then taken out of service, refurbished, and sold in modified forms, including engineer-vehicle and recovery models.

## EXTERIOR

With its emphasis on lightness and mobility, the Leopard 1 had minimal armor protection. To compensate for this, the front-most part of the tank, known as the glacis plate, is sloped at 60 degrees to the vertical. This helps deflect enemy projectiles, and effectively thickens the hull by forcing projectiles to take a diagonal route through its surface.

**1.** National recognition symbol  **2.** Headlight  **3.** Ice grousers  **4.** Driver's periscopes  **5.** Commander's TRP 2A panoramic sight-head  **6.** Commander's cupola (closed)  **7.** Range-finder aperture  **8.** Smoke launchers  **9.** Rear stowage box  **10.** Holder for engine deck lifting tool (tool missing)  **11.** Gun cleaning rods  **12.** Drive sprocket  **13.** Spare-track link  **14.** Gun cradle above Leitkreuz blackout light

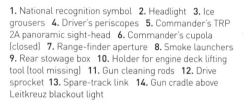

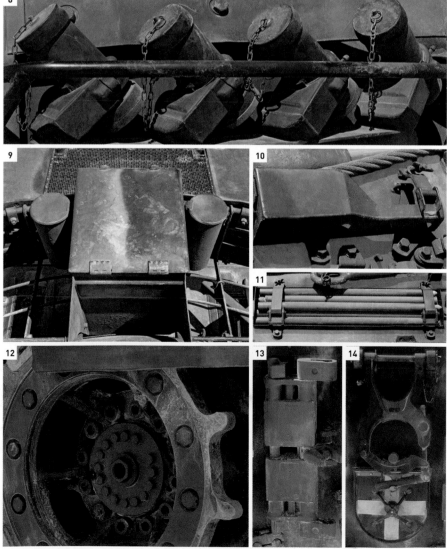

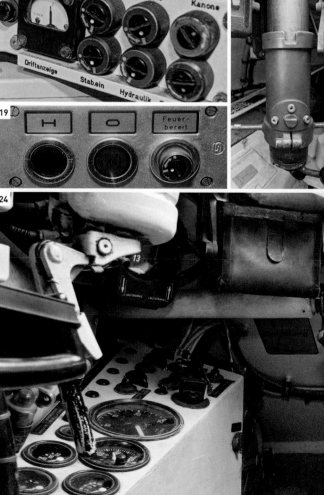

# INTERIOR

The interior is divided into two compartments, with a fire wall in between. The engine is situated in the rear compartment, while the crew are in the front: the commander in the turret, with the gunner in front of him and loader to his left, and the driver positioned forward and to the right.

**15.** Looking down into commander's cupola  **16.** Gunner's position  **17.** Commander's TRP 2A panoramic sight eyepiece  **18.** Gun stabilization system drift compensation box  **19.** Loader's safety switch  **20.** Commander's hydraulic hatch controls  **21.** 105mm gun breech  **22.** Gunner's azimuth indicator dial  **23.** Driver's position  **24.** Driver's controls  **25.** Driver's instrument panel  **26.** Gearshift  **27.** Fire-extinguisher system  **28.** Intercom control panel

# Tanks of the Nonaligned World

Many nations attempted to steer between the two Cold War powers. Some, such as Yugoslavia in the 1950s, purchased equipment from both sides; others, such as the Swiss, continued designing and building their own weapons. Many countries purchased Western tanks, using them for decades and upgrading them with their own systems.

**Variety** of Sherman hulls converted

◁ **Sherman M-50**

| | |
|---|---|
| **Date** 1956 | **Country** Israel |

**Weight** 37.5 tons (34 tonnes)

**Engine** Cummins V8 diesel, 460 hp

**Main armament** 75 mm CN75-50 rifled gun

Developed to keep around 300 older Israeli M4 Shermans viable, the M-50 was equipped with a more powerful engine, HVSS suspension, and the French 75 mm gun also used on the AMX-13. It saw service in the Six Day War of 1967.

△ **Sho't**

| | |
|---|---|
| **Date** 1958 | **Country** Israel |

**Weight** 57.1 tons (51.8 tonnes)

**Engine** Continental AVDS-1790-2A diesel, 750 hp

**Main armament** 105 mm L7 L/52 rifled gun

At first, the Centurion was unpopular in Israel, with poor reliability. Upgrades including a diesel engine and improved crew training soon changed this perception. Its combat record in 1967 and 1973 proved stellar, especially the defense of the Golan Heights in 1973.

▷ **Strv 74**

| | |
|---|---|
| **Date** 1958 | **Country** Sweden |

**Weight** 24.8 tons (22.5 tonnes)

**Engine** 2 x Scania-Vabis 603/1 diesels, 170 hp each

**Main armament** 75 mm Strv 74 rifled gun

The Strv 74 was an upgrade of the 1940s vintage m/42; the most obvious difference was the new, more powerful gun in a large but thinly armored turret. The 225 conversions supplemented the Centurion in Swedish tank units until the late 1960s.

**External** machine gun

**Thin** turret armor

**105 mm** rifled gun

**Commander's** cupola

**Barrel** clamp

**Muzzle** brake

◁ **Type 61**

| | |
|---|---|
| **Date** 1961 | **Country** Japan |

**Weight** 38.5 tons (35 tonnes)

**Engine** Mitsubishi 12HM21WT diesel, 570 hp

**Armament Main** 90 mm L/52 rifled gun

The first post-World War II Japanese tank, the Type 61 was developed instead of buying American vehicles, since they were assessed as being too large and heavy for the Japanese crewmen and the country's geography. A total of 560 were built. None were exported and it never saw combat.

**Towing** hitch

**Stowage** bins

**Aerial** mount

**M4A1**
**Sherman** hull

### △ Panzer 61

**Date** 1961 **Country** Switzerland

**Weight** 42.6 tons (38.6 tonnes)

**Engine** MTU MB837 Ba-500 diesel, 630 hp

**Main armament** 105 mm L7 L/52 rifled gun

The Panzer 61 was developed for Swiss terrain–steep mountains and narrow train tunnels. It replaced the Centurion, with 150 built. The original coaxial 20 mm cannon was later replaced with a more conventional 7.5 mm machine gun. It served until the 1990s.

### △ Sherman M-51

**Date** 1965 **Country** Israel

**Weight** 43 tons (39 tonnes)

**Engine** Cummins V8 diesel, 460 hp

**Main armament** 105 mm Modele F1 L/44 rifled gun

The M-51 upgrade was applied to 76 mm-armed M4A1 Shermans. In addition to the modified French gun, the transmission, ammunition racks, and rear of the turret were all replaced. M-51s fought in 1967, and were pressed back into service in the Yom Kippur War of 1973.

### ▷ Vijayanta

**Date** 1965 **Country** India

**Weight** 43 tons (39 tonnes)

**Engine** Leyland L60 diesel, 535 hp

**Main armament** 105 mm L7A2 L/52 rifled gun

The Vijayanta was based on the British Vickers Mark 1, which was privately developed for export. Use of components common to the Centurion, already used in India, made maintenance and training simpler. Around 2,200 were built.

**Stowage** bins

**Vision** port

### ▽ Strv 103C (S-Tank)

**Date** 1967 **Country** Sweden

**Weight** 43.7 tons (39.6 tonnes)

**Engine** Rolls-Royce K60 multifuel, 240 hp and Caterpillar 553 gas turbine, 490 hp

**Main armament** 105 mm Bofors L/62 rifled gun

The Strv 103 was intended to fight defensively, ambushing the enemy then escaping; its low profile and second, rear-facing driver made it very effective in this role. The autoloading gun was aimed by steering and adjusting the height of the hydropneumatic suspension.

**Wide tracks** for winter conditions

# Tanks of the Nonaligned World (cont.)

Some nations used both domestic and upgraded foreign vehicles—South Korea and Israel both moved from upgrades to indigenous vehicles as their economies developed. In addition to being a symbol of industrial and military power, a domestically-designed tank could be optimized for the conditions a country expected to face on the battlefield. The unique designs of the Israeli Merkava and Swedish Strv 103 illustrate this most clearly.

**Geometric** camouflage

**105 mm** main gun

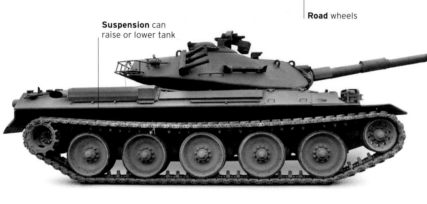

**Widened** tracks

**Periscope**

**Road** wheels

◁ **Panzer 68**

| | | | |
|---|---|---|---|
| **Date** 1971 | **Country** Switzerland | | |
| **Weight** 45 tons (40.8 tonnes) | | | |
| **Engine** MTU V8 diesel, 660 hp | | | |
| **Main armament** 105 mm L7 L/52 rifled gun | | | |

Based on the Panzer 61, the Panzer 68 featured wider tracks with rubber pads to improve mobility, especially over snow, and a gun stabilization system that enabled more accurate firing on the move. The final version, Panzer 68/88, served until the early 2000s.

**Suspension** can raise or lower tank

△ **Type 74**

| | |
|---|---|
| **Date** 1975 | **Country** Japan |
| **Weight** 41.9 tons (38 tonnes) | |
| **Engine** Mitsubishi 10ZF diesel, 720 hp | |
| **Main armament** 105 mm L7 L/52 rifled gun | |

Developed in response to the Soviet T-62, the Type 74 suffered from a long development period and slow entry into service; 893 were built, the last in 1989. Its hydropneumatic suspension could raise, lower, or incline the vehicle to suit terrain. Upgrades included a laser range finder and improved night-vision systems.

**Gun sight** aperture

**7.62 mm** machine gun

**105 mm** main gun

▷ **Merkava 1**

| | |
|---|---|
| **Date** 1979 | **Country** Israel |
| **Weight** 66.1 tons (59.9 tonnes) | |
| **Engine** Continental AVDS-1790-6A diesel, 900 hp | |
| **Main armament** 105 mm M68 L/52 rifled gun | |

The Merkava incorporated lessons from Israeli combat experience, meaning crew protection was highly emphasized. The engine was placed at the front and a door in the rear hull allowed protected ammunition resupply and casualty evacuation under fire. The Mark 1 was first used in Lebanon in 1982. The Mark 2 and 3 vehicles were significant redesigns; in addition, all three received further upgrades.

**Nonslip coating** on composite armor

**Skirt**

Muzzle cover

◁ **Khalid**

**Date** 1981 **Country** UK

**Weight** 64 tons (58 tonnes)

**Engine** Perkins CV12 V-12 diesel, 1,200 hp

**Main armament** 120 mm L11A5 L/55 rifled gun

Originally developed for Iran as the Shir 1, the Khalid was an evolution of the Chieftain. The larger engine required the distinctive sloped rear hull. It also incorporated an improved fire control system, better suspension, and extra fuel capacity. The Iranian Revolution resulted in the order being canceled in 1979, but Jordan stepped in and ordered 274.

◁ **Strv 104**

**Date** 1985 **Country** Sweden

**Weight** 59.5 tons (54 tonnes)

**Engine** Continental AVDS-1790-2DC diesel, 750 hp

**Main armament** 105 mm L7 L/52 rifled gun

Around 600 Centurions were bought by the Swedish Army during the 1950s and upgraded over the next 30 years: the 80 Strv 104s were the most advanced. The tank had a more powerful engine, ERA, modernized suspension, and improved sights and night vision. Drawdowns after the end of the Cold War led to its retirement in 2003.

Coaxial machine gun

One of three external machine guns

Aerial

△ **K1**

**Date** 1987 **Country** South Korea

**Weight** 56.3 tons (51.1 tonnes)

**Engine** MTU MB 871 Ka-501 diesel, 1,200 hp

**Main armament** 105 mm M68 L/52 rifled gun

The K1 design came from the XM1 Abrams prototype, modified for Korean specifications, including hydropneumatic suspension. Over 1,000 K1s were built, followed by almost 500 K1A1s, with several improvements including a 120 mm smoothbore gun.

△ **Magach 7C**

**Date** 1985 **Country** Israel

**Weight** 55 tons (49.9 tonnes)

**Engine** Continental AVDS-1790-5A diesel, 908 hp

**Main armament** 105 mm M68 L/52 rifled gun

The first Magachs in the 1960s were modified M48s, while later vehicles, such as this one, were based on the M60. The add-on armor protected against tank rounds—unlike earlier ERA which only protected against missiles. The fire control system and tracks were also upgraded.

# Tank Destroyers

Tracked tank destroyers as used in World War II became less common as the Cold War progressed. By the 1970s, the development of lightweight antitank missiles meant that a heavy, gun-armed vehicle was no longer needed to destroy a tank. Many countries adapted their standard Armored Personnel Carriers (APCs) for the job. Some countries retained the gun-armed vehicles for specific conditions such as close support to infantry or airborne forces, where the ability to fire high-explosive shells remained important.

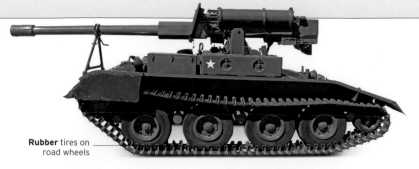

**Rubber** tires on road wheels

### △ M56 Scorpion

| | |
|---|---|
| **Date** 1953 | **Country** US |
| **Weight** 8 tons (7.2 tonnes) | |
| **Engine** Continental AOI-402-5 gasoline, 200 hp | |
| **Armament Main** 90 mm M54 L/53 rifled gun | |

Unarmored except for a gun shield, the lightweight Scorpion was designed to be airdropped. Unusually, the road wheels had rubber tires. It saw limited use in Vietnam, with 325 built. Its light weight meant that the gun's recoil was strong enough to lift the front wheels off the ground.

**Smoke grenade** dischargers

### △ Charioteer

| | |
|---|---|
| **Date** 1954 | **Country** UK |
| **Weight** 34.7 tons (31.5 tonnes) | |
| **Engine** Rolls-Royce Meteor Mark IB gasoline, 600 hp | |
| **Main armament** QF 20-pounder gun | |

An attempt to quickly field more vehicles armed with the highly capable 20-pounder gun, the Charioteer was based on the wartime Cromwell hull. The large gun required a large turret, which was very lightly armored to keep the weight down. A total of 442 Charioteers were built, with almost half being exported.

### ▷ M50 Ontos

| | |
|---|---|
| **Date** 1955 | **Country** USA |
| **Weight** 9.5 tons (8.6 tonnes) | |
| **Engine** General Motors Model 302 gasoline, 145 hp | |
| **Main armament** 6 x 106 mm M40A1 recoilless rifles | |

Originally intended for US airborne forces, the Ontos was instead adopted by the Marine Corps. In Vietnam, it was used to support infantry. Although its ammunition capacity was limited and the crew had to dismount to reload, its mobility made it popular and its heavy firepower proved invaluable in the urban combat in Hue in 1968.

**Armed** with six recoilless rifles

**76 mm** main gun

### ▷ Saladin

| | |
|---|---|
| **Date** 1958 | **Country** UK |
| **Weight** 12.4 tons (11.3 tonnes) | |
| **Engine** Rolls-Royce B80 Mark 6A gasoline, 160 hp | |
| **Main armament** 76 mm L5A1 rifled gun | |

Designed to replace the wartime Daimler and AEC armored cars, the Saladin had heavier firepower and six-wheel drive, giving it excellent cross-country mobility. It was developed alongside the Saracen (see pp.180–81), with which it shared many components. Highly successful, almost 1,200 Saladins were built. It was exported to more than 20 countries, and saw combat with several, including Oman and Kuwait.

## ▷ ASU-85

**Date** 1960 **Country** Soviet Union

**Weight** 17.1 tons (15.5 tonnes)

**Engine** Model V-6 diesel, 240 hp

**Main armament** 85 mm 2A15
rifled gun

A replacement for the open-topped ASU-57, the
ASU-85 was a fully enclosed assault gun for Soviet
Airborne Forces (VDV). Lightly armored, it could
be carried by the heaviest Soviet helicopters or
dropped by a parachute. Its main role was to
provide fire support to the paratroopers,
rather than attacking tanks.

**Road** wheels

**Headlamp**

**Stowage** bin

## ◁ Panhard AML

**Date** 1961 **Country** France

**Weight** 6.2 tons (5.6 tonnes)

**Engine** Panhard 4 HD gasoline,
90 hp

**Main armament** 60 mm Brandt
LR gun-mortar

French experience in colonial conflicts
showed the need for a lightweight
armored car with heavy firepower.
The AML fulfilled this, being armed
with either a 90 mm gun or a 60 mm
mortar. Highly successful, it was sold
to around 50 countries. More than
4,800 vehicles were built.

**Armored**
windshield cover

## ▷ Hornet

**Date** 1962 **Country** UK

**Weight** 6.4 tons (5.8 tonnes)

**Engine** Rolls-Royce B60 Mark 5A gasoline,
120 hp

**Main armament** Malkara antitank missile

Based on the Humber 1-Ton APC, the
Hornet was designed to be airdropped
and was the first British missile-armed
tank destroyer. It was armed with two
Malkara antitank missiles, which were
wire guided and controlled manually
by the gunner using a joystick.

**Glacis plate**
armor

**Rear** light

**Torsion bar**
suspension

## △ Kanonenjagdpanzer

**Date** 1966 **Country** West Germany

**Weight** 30.4 tons (27.5 tonnes)

**Engine** Mercedes Benz MB837 diesel, 500 hp

**Main armament** 90 mm Rheinmetall BK90
L/40 rifled gun

**Drive sprocket**
at rear

**Pneumatic** tires

Armed with reused guns from the outdated M47, this vehicle
was used to provide antitank support to infantry formations.
Its low height and speed made it well suited for the mobile
defensive tactics these units would use. As the gun became
obsolete, several were rearmed with the TOW missile.

# Tank Destroyers (cont.)

Large guns continued to be widely used on wheeled vehicles. These vehicles still offered greater speed and lighter weight than a tracked vehicle, giving them superior mobility over long distances or poor infrastructure. Their guns were increasingly obsolete against the latest main battle tanks, but they still offered sufficient firepower to destroy older vehicles or fortifications. Many were used for reconnaissance or in areas such as Africa, where this was all they were likely to face.

▷ **EE-9 Cascavel**

**Date** 1974 **Country** Brazil

**Weight** 14.6 tons (13.2 tonnes)

**Engine** Mercedes-Benz OM 352 diesel, 190 hp

**Main armament** 90 mm EC-90 rifled gun

The EE-9 and the EE-11 Urutu APC were developed together. Both used the unique Boomerang suspension system on the rear wheels, ensuring that both wheels remained on the ground over a larger range of motion. The Cascavel has seen combat with Libyan, Iraqi, and Zimbabwean forces.

**90 mm** main gun

▷ **Ikv-91**

**Date** 1975 **Country** Sweden

**Weight** 17.9 tons (16.3 tonnes)

**Engine** Volvo-Penta TD 120A diesel, 330 hp

**Main armament** 90 mm KV90S73 L/54 rifled gun

The Ikv-91 was used by Swedish infantry units for fire-support and antitank warfare. It was lightly armored and its light weight made it highly mobile and amphibious, enabling it to cross difficult terrain and outmaneuver enemy tanks. Sweden operated 212 Ikv-91s until 2002.

**Torsion bar** suspension

▷ **AMX-10RC**

**Date** 1981 **Country** France

**Weight** 17.5 tons (15.9 tonnes)

**Engine** Renault HS 115 diesel, 260 hp

**Main armament** 105 mm F2 L/48 rifled gun

Intended for reconnaissance and fire support, the AMX-10RC has seen combat in Chad and Afghanistan. Extensive upgrades have been applied during its service, especially to the sights and fire-control systems. Unusually for a wheeled vehicle, it uses skid steering rather than a conventional mechanism.

**Barrel** sleeve

**Wing** mirror

△ **Cougar**

**Date** 1979 **Country** Canada

**Weight** 11.8 tons (10.7 tonnes)

**Engine** Detroit Diesel 6V53T diesel, 275 hp

**Main armament** 76 mm L23A1 rifled gun

The Cougar was the fire support variant of the Canadian Armored Vehicle General Purpose (AVGP) family, which also included an APC named Grizzly and an Armored Recovery Vehicle (ARV) named Husky. Their design was based on the MOWAG Piranha I and they saw service in peacekeeping operations in the Balkans and Somalia.

**Welded** hull armor

▷ **Wiesel**

| | | | |
|---|---|---|---|
| **Date** 1989 | **Country** West Germany |
| **Weight** 2.9 tons (2.6 tonnes) |
| **Engine** Audi 5 cylinder turbo-diesel, 87 hp |
| **Main armament** 20 mm Rheinmetall Rh 202 DM6 cannon |

The Wiesel was developed to provide lightweight fire support for West German paratroopers. Of 343 purchased, 133 had the 20 mm cannon, and 210 were armed with the TOW antitank missile. It could be airlifted by helicopters or airdropped. The larger and heavier Wiesel 2 was later adopted by Germany as an air defense vehicle, ambulance, and command post.

**Vision** ports

▷ **B1 Centauro**

| | |
|---|---|
| **Date** 1991 | **Country** Italy |
| **Weight** 27.6 tons (25 tonnes) |
| **Engine** Iveco VTCA V-6 diesel, 520 hp |
| **Main armament** 105 mm OTO-Melara L/52 rifled gun |

Designed as a highly mobile tank destroyer, the Centauro has been mostly used in peacekeeping missions, for which its combination of armor, firepower, and wheels were well suited. It was used in the Balkans and Somalia, and saw combat in Iraq. It has been exported to Spain, Jordan, and Oman.

◁ **Rooikat**

| | |
|---|---|
| **Date** 1990 | **Country** South Africa |
| **Weight** 30.9 tons (28 tonnes) |
| **Engine** V10 diesel, 563 hp |
| **Main armament** 76 mm GT4 L/62 rifled gun |

Rooikat incorporated lessons from the South African Border War. It emphasized mine protection and high speed, resulting in a wheeled design. The Rooikat had sufficient firepower to destroy buildings and older armored vehicles. Its armor was resistant to the very common 23 mm antiaircraft gun.

**Sloping** hull armor

**Smoke grenade** launchers

**Engine** ventilation

# Cougar

The Canadian-built Cougar Fire Support Vehicle is a light, wheeled vehicle that can trace its lineage back to the 1970s' Swiss-built Mowag Piranha–a multirole family of vehicles that had 4x4, 6x6, 8x8, and 10x10 wheel configurations. Cheaper to build and easier to transport than a tracked vehicle, the Cougar is also less aggressive looking, making it ideal for peacekeeping and peace-enforcement roles.

**THE COUGAR** was ordered for the Canadian Armed Forces in 1977 as part of a family of three Armored Vehicle General Purpose (AVGP) fighting vehicles—the other two being the Grizzly armored personnel carrier, and the Husky wheeled maintenance and recovery vehicle. Rather than being built from scratch, it was developed from the proven design of the Mowag Piranha I, which first saw service in 1974. The Cougar was intended to equip armored units that were not issued with Leopard tanks (see pp.150–53), and it was used in Canada for training in a reconnaissance and later a fire support role. The vehicle had the basic 6x6 hull, with the driver at the front, next to the Detroit Diesel engine, and two more crew members, the commander and the gunner, in the turret. It was equipped with the British Scorpion light tank turret (see pp.192–95), complete with a 76 mm gun, a coaxial machine gun, and eight smoke launchers. Ten rounds for the main gun were carried in the turret and another 30 rounds were stored in the hull. The rear compartment also had room for two more troops.

**REAR VIEW**

The Cougar saw peacekeeping service in Bosnia with IFOR—or the Implementation Force that was sent to ensure peace in the region after the signing of the Dayton Peace Accords in 1995. The vehicle has now been withdrawn from service, along with the other two AVGP vehicles.

| SPECIFICATIONS | |
| --- | --- |
| Name | Cougar AVGP |
| Date | 1976 |
| Origin | Canada |
| Production | 496 |
| Engine | Detroit Diesel 6V53T 2-cycle turbocharged, 275 hp |
| Weight | 11.80 tons (10.70 tonnes) |
| Main armament | 76 mm L2A1 |
| Secondary armament | 7.62 mm C6 machine gun |
| Crew | 3 |
| Armor thickness | 0.4 in (10 mm) |

Gunner
Commander
Driver

**76 mm** main armament

**Klaxon**

**Radio** aerial

**Engine** hatch

**THREE-QUARTER VIEW**

**Pneumatic** tires

**Flag of Canada**
The maple leaf has long been a symbol of Canada, and took pride of place on the Canadian flag in 1965. Here it features on the side of the Canadian-built Cougar.

**Versatile machine**
The Cougar is one of the many wheeled armored vehicles based on a 6x6 or 8x8 chassis that came into service at the end of the 20th century. Faster, lighter, and cheaper, these vehicles have taken on a number of roles that were previously performed by tanks.

## EXTERIOR

The Cougar's boat-shaped hull helps direct blasts away from its underside—a vital defense against mines, which can easily overturn a flat-hulled vehicle. Its multiple driven wheels are another defense, enabling it to survive the loss of any single wheel—a mine would otherwise completely incapacitate the vehicle.

**1.** Tactical number  **2.** Headlight  **3.** Sidelight and indicator  **4.** Driver's periscopes and hatch  **5.** Stowed wire cutter and textured surface for grip  **6.** Smoke launchers  **7.** Exhaust outlets  **8.** Gunner's periscope with wiper blade  **9.** Suspension bracket  **10.** Hull vision port  **11.** Rear-light cluster

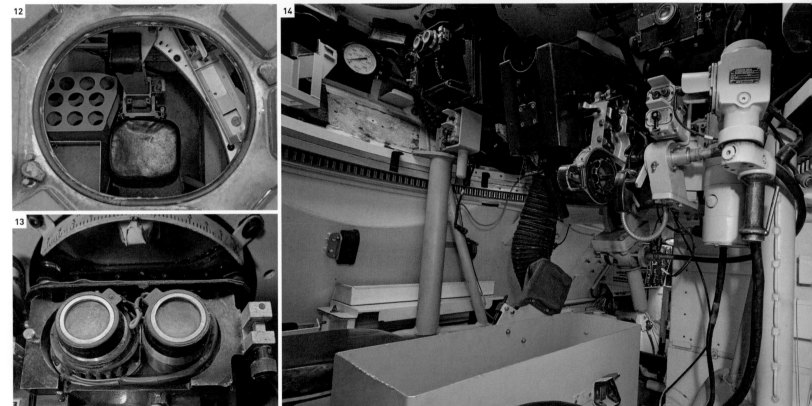

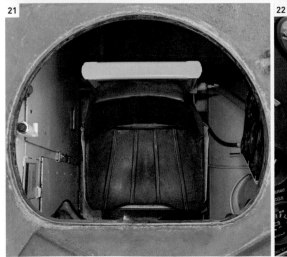

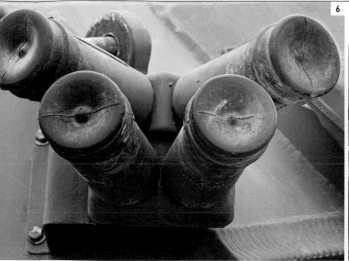

## INTERIOR

The interior is divided into two compartments. The front compartment houses the driver with the commander and gunner in the turret above. The rear one, which has two vertical doors at the back, contains a bench and space for a small number of troops, plus a store of projectiles for the 76 mm main gun.

**12.** Looking down into gunner's seat **13.** Commander's sight **14.** Main gun position showing turret interior **15.** Main gun breech ring **16.** Monocular gunner's sight **17.** Turret ancillaries control box **18.** Traverse handwheel **19.** Selector for coaxial machine gun or main gun **20.** Quadrant fire control gear **21.** Driver's seat **22.** Driver's position with instruments and periscopes **23.** Driver's controls **24.** Steering wheel **25.** Gear lever **26.** Handbrake **27.** Rear compartment with passenger seats and ammunition stowage

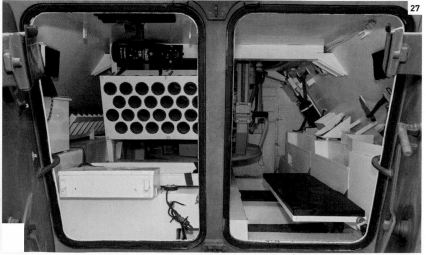

# Flame-throwing tanks

Flame weapons have been in use since ancient times, and were used effectively as man-portable weapons in World War I. They often had a major psychological impact—sometimes their very presence caused surrender. However, they were limited by their short range, the amount of fuel that could be carried, and their vulnerability. Some of these issues, however, could be overcome by mounting a flame-thrower on a vehicle.

## ADAPTED VEHICLES

The Italian army produced a flame-throwing tankette in 1935, the L3 Lf, which saw extensive service before and during the early period of World War II, as did a flame-thrower mounted on the Russian T-26 tank. The German army mounted flame-throwers on half-tracks and on Panzer III tanks, particularly with urban operations in mind, where they could be used to clear bunkers and houses. In Britain, flame-throwers were attached to Universal Carriers to form the Wasp, or to Churchill tanks to make the Crocodile, which towed an armored trailer of fuel and could fire up to 80 one-second bursts. Flame-throwing tanks continued to be used into the 21st century.

**A US Marine Corps M67 "Zippo" tank**, one of 109 converted M48 Pattons, flames a village near Binh Son in the Quang Ngai Province, 1969.

# Armored Reconnaissance Vehicles

Reconnaissance vehicles were not intended to fight, but to find enemy forces and report back. This role drove their design, which emphasized mobility over protection to the point that many were light enough to float across rivers. They were armed with machine guns or light cannon designed for self-defense only—their main weapon was still the radio. Wheeled vehicles allowed for a faster and quieter mobility, although their limitations on rough terrain led to several countries using tracked vehicles instead.

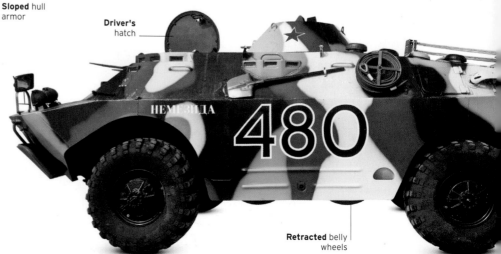

**.30 Browning** machine gun

**Painted** in UN colours

**Spare** wheel

### ▷ FV701(E) Ferret Mark 2/5

**Date** 1952 **Country** UK

**Weight** 4.8 tons (4.4 tonnes)

**Engine** Rolls-Royce B60 Mark 6A gasoline, 129 hp

**Main armament** .30 Browning M1919 machine gun

The development of Ferret began in 1947 as a replacement for the successful Dingo. The Mark I had an open top like the Dingo, but most had a machine gun turret, as here. Its main roles were reconnaissance and liaison, but some variants carried antitank missiles. A total of 4,409 were built, finding service in more than 30 countries.

**Watertight** hull

### △ BRDM 1

**Date** 1957 **Country** Soviet Union

**Weight** 6.2 tons (5.6 tonnes)

**Engine** GAZ-40P gasoline, 90 hp

**Main armament** 7.62 mm SGMB machine gun

The BRDM 1 was fully amphibious. It was powered by a water jet, had four-wheel drive, and had four extra wheels under the belly that could be lowered on rough ground. Its variants included Nuclear, Biological, Chemical (NBC) reconnaissance and command vehicles, and a variety of antitank missile launchers. The BRDM 1 was exported to around 50 countries.

**20 mm** cannon

**Sloped** hull armor

### △ Schutzenpanzer (SPz) 11.2

**Date** 1958 **Country** France, West Germany

**Weight** 9.1 tons (8.2 tonnes)

**Engine** Hotchkiss 6-cylinder gasoline, 164 hp

**Main armament** 20 mm Hispano-Suiza HS.820 cannon

A French design, only adopted by West Germany, the SPz 11.2 was mainly used for reconnaissance, with variants employed as mortar carriers, artillery forward observation and command vehicles, and ambulances. More than 2,300 were built, serving until 1982.

### ▽ BRDM 2

**Date** 1962 **Country** Soviet Union

**Weight** 7.7 tons (7 tonnes)

**Engine** GAZ-41 V8 gasoline, 140 hp

**Main armament** 14.5 mm KPVT machine gun

Many limitations of the BRDM-1 were corrected in its successor, the BRDM 2. This featured an NBC protection system, better sights, and an armored turret housing its machine gun. It retained the BRDM-1's belly wheels and its amphibious capability.

**Driver's** hatch

**Retracted** belly wheels

▷ **Lynx Command and Reconnaissance Vehicle**

**Date** 1968 **Country** USA

**Weight** 9.6 tons (8.7 tonnes)

**Engine** Detroit Diesel 6V-53 diesel, 215 hp

**Main armament** .50 Browning M2 machine gun

The Lynx, which shared many components with the M113 Armored Personnel Carrier, was bought by Canada and the Netherlands. The two countries configured their vehicles slightly differently. Both versions had a three-man crew and a .50 Browning M2 machine gun, which the Dutch later replaced with the 25 mm cannon.

Engine ventilation

Stowage bin

▽ **FV721 Fox Combat Reconnaissance (Wheeled)**

**Date** 1973 **Country** UK

**Weight** 6.7 tons (6.1 tonnes)

**Engine** Jaguar XK gasoline, 195 hp

**Main armament** 30 mm L21A1 Rarden cannon

Developed from the Ferret, the Fox was the wheeled counterpart of the tracked CVR(T). It was mainly used by infantry units. Less successful than Ferret and CVR(T), the Fox was found to be unstable under certain driving conditions and was withdrawn from service in 1994. Its turret was mated with the retired Scorpion hull to produce the Sabre vehicle.

**20 mm** MK 20 Rh202 cannon

Smoke grenade launchers

▽ **Panhard Véhicule Blindé Léger (VBL)**

**Date** 1990 **Country** France

**Weight** 4 tons (3.6 tonnes)

**Engine** Peugeot XD 3T diesel, 105 hp

**Main armament** Varies

The Panhard VBL was designed as a lightweight armored vehicle to be used for reconnaissance and antitank warfare. It has been widely exported, particularly to Africa and Asia, and today the French also use a longer version as a command vehicle. It has seen service in the Balkans, Somalia, Lebanon, Afghanistan, Ivory Coast, Nigeria, and Mali.

△ **Spahpanzer 2 Luchs**

**Date** 1975 **Country** West Germany

**Weight** 21.8 tons (19.8 tonnes)

**Engine** Daimler Benz type OM 403VA multifuel, 390 hp

**Main armament** 20 mm Rheinmetall MK 20 Rh202 cannon

The replacement for the Spz 11.2, the Luchs was a significant departure from its predecessor, being wheeled, amphibious, and much bigger. Each of its four axles could be steered, and it had a driver at each end, enabling easy escape from dangerous situations. It was also extremely quiet−a major advantage in a reconnaissance vehicle.

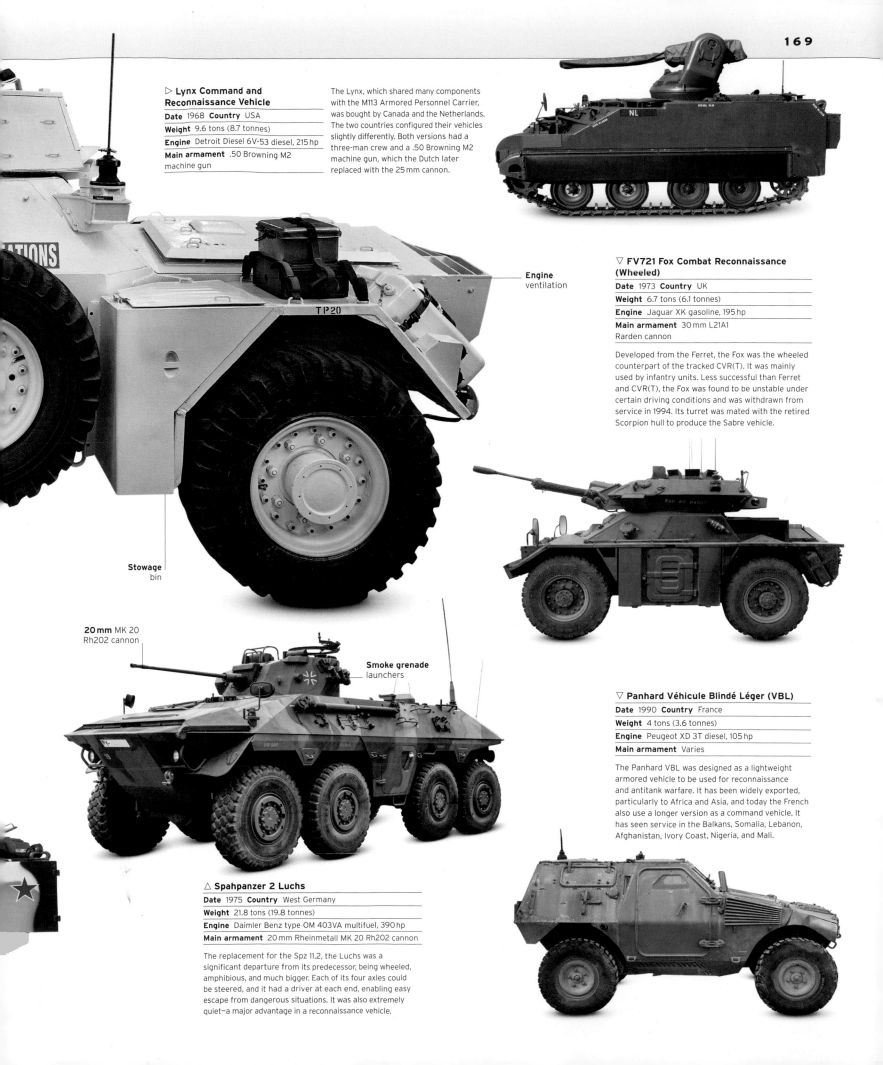

# Tracked Armored Personnel Carriers

A fully tracked, fully armored vehicle that could carry infantry into battle alongside tanks has been sought since the latter's invention, and indeed the first, the Mark IX (see p.32), was ready in late 1918. It was not until the 1950s, however, that they began to become widespread. Many early designs resembled boxes on tracks, having only light armor and firepower that rarely extended beyond a machine gun. Few had the mobility to keep up with tanks over rough terrain.

### △ M75

**Date** 1952 **Country** USA

**Weight** 20.7 tons (18.8 tonnes)

**Engine** Continental AO-895-4 gasoline, 295 hp

**Main armament** .50 Browning M2 machine gun

The M75 could carry a standard US infantry squad of 11 men, who accessed the vehicle through double doors at the rear. Its running gear was based on the M41 light tank, but overall it was too heavy, tall, and expensive, and its production ended after 1,729 had been built. Belgium was gifted 600, which they operated until the 1980s.

**Spare** fuel drum

**Troop compartment** accommodates 20

**Trim vane** for fording water

**Rubber road wheels** aid buoyancy

**Room** for two crew and eleven passengers

### △ BTR-50P

**Date** 1954 **Country** Soviet Union

**Weight** 15.7 tons (14.2 tonnes)

**Engine** Model V-6 diesel, 240 hp

**Main armament** 7.62 mm SGMB machine gun

The BTR-50P was based on the PT-76 light tank and shared its parent's amphibious capability. Originally open-topped, it could carry 20 infantrymen, who climbed in and out over the sides. Early vehicles also had ramps to allow a towed artillery piece to be carried on the engine deck. A wide range of variants were used by dozens of nations.

**Room** for two crew and ten passengers

**Room** for three crew and ten passengers

### △ M59

**Date** 1954 **Country** USA

**Weight** 21.3 tons (19.3 tonnes)

**Engine** 2 x General Motors Model 302 gasoline, 127 hp each

**Main armament** .50 Browning M2 machine gun

The lighter, lower, and cheaper replacement for the M75, the M59 added amphibious capability but was less well armored. Infantrymen now used a ramp to access the vehicle, which, along with folding seats, made it a more useful cargo carrier. Its twin engines were considered unreliable, and by the mid-1960s it was being retired.

### △ AMX VCI

**Date** 1957 **Country** France

**Weight** 16.6 tons (15 tonnes)

**Engine** Detroit Diesel 6V-53T diesel, 280 hp

**Main armament** .50 Browning M2 machine gun

The VCI chassis was based on the AMX-13 tank. Ten infantrymen entered through the two rear doors; firing ports were mounted on each of these and the hull. The machine gun was replaced with a 20 mm cannon on some vehicles. Variants included a radar carrier, engineer vehicle, mortar carrier, and ambulance.

### ◁ Type SU 60

**Date** 1960 **Country** Japan

**Weight** 14.6 tons (13.2 tonnes)

**Engine** Mitsubishi 8HA21 WT diesel, 220 hp

**Main armament** .50 Browning M2 machine gun

By the late 1950s, Japan's economy had recovered enough for the country to be able to build its own military equipment. The Type SU 60 was one of its first vehicles. It had a crew of four and space for six infantrymen. Unusually for a postwar vehicle, it was armed with a 7.62 mm bow machine gun.

### ▽ M113A1

**Date** 1960 **Country** USA

**Weight** 12.1 tons (11 tonnes)

**Engine** Detroit Diesel 6V-53 diesel, 212 hp

**Main armament** .50 Browning M2 machine gun

Highly successful, more than 80,000 M113s were built in over 40 variants for at least 44 countries. Early vehicles had a gasoline engine, but this was soon replaced by a diesel equivalent. Many users developed their own upgrades to keep the vehicles viable in the 21st century, and gave them nicknames that included "bathtub" and "elephant shoe."

**Smoke launchers**

**Side skirts** protect tracks

**Armor** includes kevlar plates to protect against IEDs

### ▷ FV432 Bulldog

**Date** 1963 **Country** UK

**Weight** 16.8 tons (15.2 tonnes)

**Engine** Rolls-Royce K60 No4 Mk 4F multifuel, 240 hp

**Main armament** 7.62 mm L7 machine gun

The standard British APC for almost 30 years, the FV432 remains in use in the 21st century. The latest Bulldog variant was developed for service in Iraq and features a new engine and transmission, extra armor, and improved systems. It is part of the FV430 family, which also includes mortar, ambulance, command, communications, and recovery vehicles.

# Tracked Armored Personnel Carriers (cont.)

Infantry generally used APCs as transportation, dismounting to fight on foot when they encountered enemy forces. In certain circumstances, however, they were used for mounted combat. In particular, American and South Vietnamese forces in Vietnam appreciated the mobility offered by their M113s, which they modified with extra machine guns and armor for this role. In both Vietnam and Afghanistan the threat of mines saw many infantrymen opting to ride on top of the vehicle.

## ▷ Bv202

| | |
|---|---|
| **Date** 1964 | **Country** Sweden |
| **Weight** 3.5 tons (3.2 tonnes) | |
| **Engine** Volvo B20B gasoline, 97 hp | |
| **Main armament** None | |

Designed for high mobility over the snow and bogs of northern Sweden, the Bv202 had extremely low ground pressure and was steered by hydraulic rams located between its two cabs. The rear cab could carry eight infantry. It was sold to the UK and neighboring Norway, who expected to deploy it in the Arctic.

**Front cab** contains crew of two

## ▽ YW701A

| | |
|---|---|
| **Date** 1964 | **Country** China |
| **Weight** 14.1 tons (12.8 tonnes) | |
| **Engine** BF8L 413F diesel, 320 hp | |
| **Main armament** 12.7 mm Type 54 machine gun | |

The YW701A command vehicle was a high-roofed variant of the Type 63 or YW531 APC. This was the first Chinese armored vehicle designed with no input from the Soviet Union. It could carry up to 13 infantrymen, plus two crew. The Type 63 and its variants were widely exported and were used in combat by Vietnam and Iraq.

**Machine gun** mounting with 360-degree traverse

**Steel hull** protects against small-arms fire

**Trim vane** used when fording rivers

## ◁ Pbv 302

| | |
|---|---|
| **Date** 1966 | **Country** Sweden |
| **Weight** 14.9 tons (13.5 tonnes) | |
| **Engine** Volvo-Penta Model THD 100B diesel, 280 hp | |
| **Main armament** 20 mm Hispano-Suiza HS.404 cannon | |

The Pbv 302 had a crew of three and carried eight infantrymen, who entered the vehicle through its twin doors at the rear. It was used exclusively by Sweden, and its variants included command, observation post, and radio relay. Vehicles used on UN missions received extra armor and improved automotive systems.

## ▷ AAV7A1

**Date** 1971 **Country** USA
**Weight** 27.9 tons (25.3 tonnes)
**Engine** Cummins VT400 diesel, 400 hp
**Main armament** .50 Browning M2 machine gun, 40mm MK 19 Automatic Grenade Launcher

Originally called the LVTP-7, this vehicle was built for the US Marine Corps as their latest amphibious tractor, or "amtrac." Around 1,500 have been built and sold around the world, and it has received numerous upgrades, the latest incorporating M2 Bradley automotive components. It can carry up to 25 marines.

**Light armor** aids buoyancy

**Infrared** driving lights

## ◁ Type 73

**Date** 1973 **Country** Japan
**Weight** 14.7 tons (13.3 tonnes)
**Engine** Mitsubishi 4ZF diesel, 300 hp
**Main armament** .50 Browning M2 machine gun

The successor to the Type SU60, the Type 73 also had a bow machine gun. It could carry nine infantrymen, with one generally acting as the machine gunner, and had a three-man crew. As is the case with other Japanese-designed military equipment, it has never been exported nor seen combat.

**Room for six** in the front cabin

**Room for 11** in the rear cabin

## ▷ Bv206

**Date** 1980 **Country** Sweden
**Weight** 7.3 tons (6.6 tonnes)
**Engine** Ford V6 gasoline, 136 hp
**Main armament** None

Larger and more capable than the Bv202, the Bv206 was sold to more than 20 countries and many civilian groups, including search-and-rescue units. An armored version called the Bv206S has also been introduced and widely sold. Both have high mobility and are light enough to be lifted by larger helicopters.

**All four tracks** are driven

**12.7 mm** Type 54 machine gun

**Stowage** boxes

**Tracks** propel vehicle in water

## ▷ YW 534

**Date** 1990 **Country** China
**Weight** 16 tons (14.5 tonnes)
**Engine** Deutz BF8L413F diesel, 320 hp
**Main armament** 12.7 mm Type 54 machine gun

Also known as the Type 89, this APC was developed from the very similar YW 531H, or Type 85, which also carries 13 infantry. In addition to the standard variants (ambulance, command post, and engineer vehicles), the YW 534's chassis has been used for rocket launchers, antitank guided missiles, and self-propelled artillery.

# The Soviet endgame

The Cold War saw the buildup of thousands of tanks in Europe. Countries of the North Atlantic Treaty Organization (NATO) manufactured tanks that tended to have a technological edge over the more numerous, but simpler, Soviet bloc tanks. The performance of Soviet-built tanks in conflicts in the Middle East and other regions gave the West and NATO a comforting sense of the superiority of their equipment: individually, the tanks of the West often beat the technical specifications of the Eastern bloc vehicles. However, Soviet high command's operational plan was based on many thousands of tanks from the Red Army and satellite countries—such as these Hungarian T-72s—sweeping West in vast numbers, with air and infantry support.

To face this threat, Western powers looked for examples of a smaller, highly trained, and technically superior force holding off a larger but less sophisticated force. As a result, NATO commanders visited the World War II battlefields of Normandy, France, on "staff rides" to try and learn lessons on how the smaller German tank forces held off the Allies' armor. Fortunately, the Cold War never became "hot," and the lessons from Normandy were not put to the test.

**Hungarian tank crewmen** operate Soviet T-72s during maneuvers in Tata, northwest Hungary, in 1990.

# Tracked Infantry Fighting Vehicles

Armored Personnel Carriers (APCs) allowed infantry to operate alongside tanks, but their thinner armor, lighter firepower, and limited mobility left them vulnerable to attack. To rectify this, designers turned their attention to developing vehicles that could not only fight alongside tanks, but freed their infantry to engage the enemy without leaving the vehicle. These new infantry fighting vehicles (IFVs) greatly sped up operations, and gave the crew greater protection against conventional threats and the atmospheric contamination expected on a nuclear battlefield.

## ▽ BMP-1

**Date** 1966  **Country** Soviet Union

**Weight** 14.9 tons (13.5 tonnes)

**Engine** UTD 20 diesel, 300 hp

**Main armament** 73 mm 2A28 smoothbore gun

The appearance of the BMP-1, the first true IFV, caused great concern in the West. Its firepower, protection, and capacity for eight infantrymen were unprecedented. However, it had flaws: it was cramped, vulnerable to mines, and its fuel tanks were located between the infantry's seats.

**Individual suspension** on first and sixth wheels

## △ Schützenpanzer Lang HS.30

**Date** 1958  **Country** West Germany

**Weight** 16.1 tons (14.6 tonnes)

**Engine** Rolls-Royce B81 Mark 80F gasoline, 220 hp

**Main armament** 20 mm Hispano-Suiza HS.820 cannon

According to West German military doctrine, tanks, infantry, and infantry carriers were to fight alongside each other. Accordingly, the Schützenpanzer Lang was more heavily armed and armored than contemporary APCs, and had a lower profile. It had a capacity for five infantry, who entered and left via roof hatches. Unreliable at first, it improved after costly modification.

**Characteristically** low profile

**73 mm** 2A28 smoothbore gun

**Light armor** suitable for airdropping

## ▷ BMD-1

**Date** 1969  **Country** Soviet Union

**Weight** 8.3 tons (7.5 tonnes)

**Engine** 5D-20 diesel, 240 hp

**Main armament** 73 mm 2A28 smoothbore gun

A lightly armored IFV for Soviet Airborne Troops, the BMD-1 could be dropped by parachute. It used the same turret as the BMP-1 and served alongside the turretless BTR-D APC, which carried 10 infantry. The BMP-1 carried four infantry and had a four-man crew, including a bow gunner.

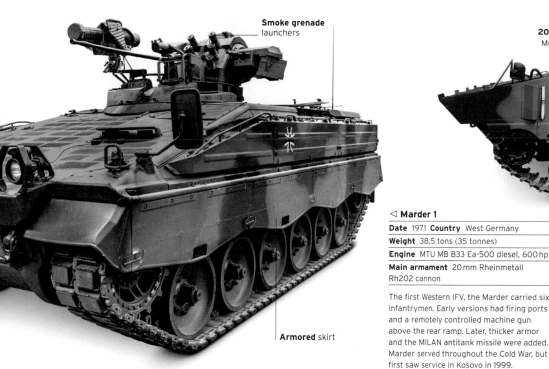

**Smoke grenade** launchers

**Armored** skirt

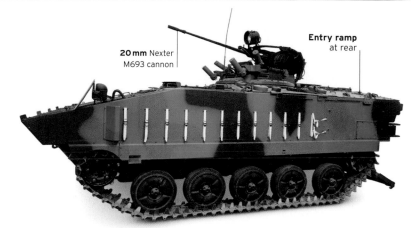

**20 mm** Nexter M693 cannon

**Entry ramp** at rear

◁ **Marder 1**

**Date** 1971 **Country** West Germany

**Weight** 38.5 tons (35 tonnes)

**Engine** MTU MB 833 Ea-500 diesel, 600 hp

**Main armament** 20 mm Rheinmetall Rh202 cannon

The first Western IFV, the Marder carried six infantrymen. Early versions had firing ports and a remotely controlled machine gun above the rear ramp. Later, thicker armor and the MILAN antitank missile were added. Marder served throughout the Cold War, but first saw service in Kosovo in 1999.

△ **AMX 10P**

**Date** 1973 **Country** France

**Weight** 16 tons (14.5 tonnes)

**Engine** Hispano-Suiza HS 115 diesel, 260 hp

**Main armament** 20 mm Nexter M693 cannon

The first French IFV carried eight infantrymen and a crew of three who entered and exited through a ramp at the rear. The AMX 10P was sold to various countries, including Saudi Arabia, Singapore, and Indonesia, the latter receiving a variant with a 90 mm gun designed for its marine corps.

▷ **AIFV (Armored Infantry Fighting Vehicle)**

**Date** 1977 **Country** USA

**Weight** 15.1 tons (13.7 tonnes)

**Engine** Detroit Diesel 6V-53T diesel, 267 hp

**Main armament** 25 mm Oerlikon KBA-B02 cannon

The AIFV was based on the M113 APC, but had firing ports, a turret, thicker armor, and an infantry capacity of seven. Its largest user was the Netherlands, which operated over 2,000 vehicles in several variants (naming it YPR-765), some of which saw action in Afghanistan.

**Welded** rolled steel armor

**Ground clearance** of 37 cm (15 in)

**Stowage** bin

**Variant** armed with .50 Browning M2

**Turret** for commander and gunner

**Hull** firing ports

**Engine compartment** forward right

▷ **BMP-2**

**Date** 1980 **Country** Soviet Union

**Weight** 15.8 tons (14.3 tonnes)

**Engine** UTD 20/3 diesel, 300 hp

**Main armament** 30 mm 2A42 cannon

Shortcomings in the BMP-1 led to the development of the BMP-2. Its cannon had a much higher rate of fire and elevation, and its two-man turret gave the commander a better view. It carried seven infantry and served in Chechnya and Afghanistan. Like the BMP-1, it was widely exported.

**Driver's position** forward left

# Tracked Infantry Fighting Vehicles (cont.)

The Soviet BMP-1 set the template for IFV design. The infantry it carried could fire their own weapons from inside the vehicle, while it had a powerful main gun and an antitank missile launcher of its own. It also had much thicker armor than an APC. Western nations followed the Soviet example, although firing ports were less common: firing from them was deemed impractical, and many users eventually covered them with extra armor.

**One of five** firing ports

**30 mm** 2A42 cannon

### △ BMD-2

| | |
|---|---|
| **Date** 1985 | **Country** Soviet Union |
| **Weight** 9.1 tons (8.2 tonnes) | |
| **Engine** 5D-20 diesel, 240 hp | |
| **Main armament** 30 mm 2A42 cannon | |

A Soviet Airborne Troops IFV, the BMD-2 is an improved version of the BMD-1. It has a slightly modified hull and a new turret, with high elevation for the cannon. However, its armor is still thin—protection against little more than machine-gun bullets and shrapnel.

### △ M2 Bradley

| | |
|---|---|
| **Date** 1983 | **Country** USA |
| **Weight** 35.4 tons (32.1 tonnes) | |
| **Engine** Cummins VTA-903T diesel, 600 hp | |
| **Main armament** 25 mm M242 cannon | |

The M2 Bradley suffered from a troubled and protracted development, but proved itself in combat. Its TOW antitank missile launcher is particularly popular with its three crew and six infantrymen. Upgrades have improved its armor, sights, and electronic systems, and added space for a seventh infantryman.

**Trim vane** for fording rivers

**Radio** antenna

**30mm** L21A1 RARDEN cannon

**Roadside** bomb protection device

### ▷ Warrior

| | |
|---|---|
| **Date** 1986 | **Country** UK |
| **Weight** 30.9 tons (28 tonnes) | |
| **Engine** Perkins CV-8 TCA diesel, 550 hp | |
| **Main armament** 30 mm L21A1 RARDEN cannon | |

The Warrior IFV (FV510) originally carried seven infantry. In the upgraded version seen here this was reduced to six, although the seats provided better protection against mine blasts. Suspension and crew visibility were also improved. Extra armor and electronic countermeasures were added for service in the Gulf, the Balkans, and Afghanistan. Command post, repair, and recovery variants have since been developed.

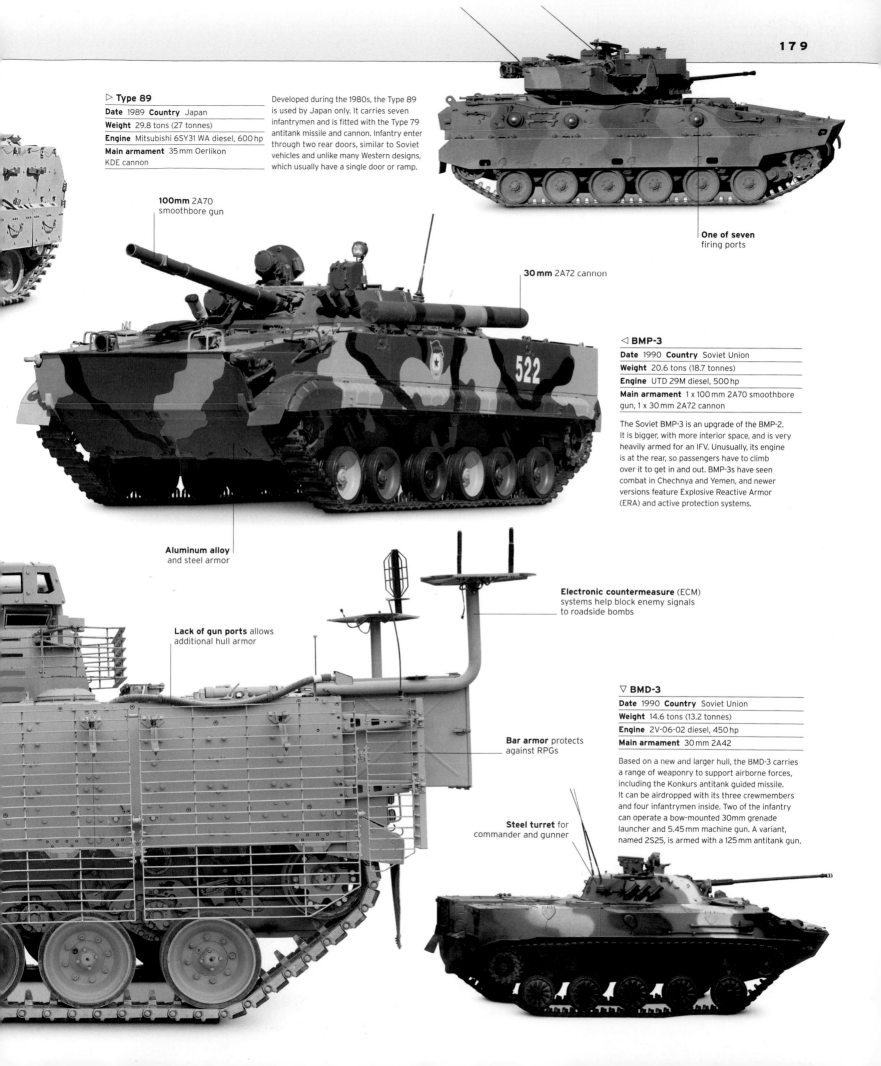

▷ **Type 89**

**Date** 1989 **Country** Japan

**Weight** 29.8 tons (27 tonnes)

**Engine** Mitsubishi 6SY31 WA diesel, 600 hp

**Main armament** 35 mm Oerlikon
KDE cannon

Developed during the 1980s, the Type 89
is used by Japan only. It carries seven
infantrymen and is fitted with the Type 79
antitank missile and cannon. Infantry enter
through two rear doors, similar to Soviet
vehicles and unlike many Western designs,
which usually have a single door or ramp.

**One of seven**
firing ports

**100mm** 2A70
smoothbore gun

**30 mm** 2A72 cannon

◁ **BMP-3**

**Date** 1990 **Country** Soviet Union

**Weight** 20.6 tons (18.7 tonnes)

**Engine** UTD 29M diesel, 500 hp

**Main armament** 1 x 100 mm 2A70 smoothbore
gun, 1 x 30 mm 2A72 cannon

The Soviet BMP-3 is an upgrade of the BMP-2.
It is bigger, with more interior space, and is very
heavily armed for an IFV. Unusually, its engine
is at the rear, so passengers have to climb
over it to get in and out. BMP-3s have seen
combat in Chechnya and Yemen, and newer
versions feature Explosive Reactive Armor
(ERA) and active protection systems.

**Aluminum alloy**
and steel armor

**Electronic countermeasure** (ECM)
systems help block enemy signals
to roadside bombs

**Lack of gun ports** allows
additional hull armor

**Bar armor** protects
against RPGs

▽ **BMD-3**

**Date** 1990 **Country** Soviet Union

**Weight** 14.6 tons (13.2 tonnes)

**Engine** 2V-06-02 diesel, 450 hp

**Main armament** 30 mm 2A42

Based on a new and larger hull, the BMD-3 carries
a range of weaponry to support airborne forces,
including the Konkurs antitank guided missile.
It can be airdropped with its three crewmembers
and four infantrymen inside. Two of the infantry
can operate a bow-mounted 30mm grenade
launcher and 5.45mm machine gun. A variant,
named 2S25, is armed with a 125mm antitank gun.

**Steel turret** for
commander and gunner

# Wheeled Troop Carriers

Wheeled personnel carriers remained in widespread use throughout the Cold War. They often shared automotive components with their more heavily armed counterparts, which made them easier and cheaper to build. However, few of them had the armor or firepower to operate on the front line. For this reason, some countries, such as the Soviet Union, West Germany, and the UK, split their fleets, equipping front-line forces with tracked infantry fighting vehicles (IFVs), and restricting wheeled vehicles to units tasked as reinforcements or for defensive operations.

▽ **BTR-152**

| | |
|---|---|
| **Date** 1950 **Country** Soviet Union | |
| **Weight** 11.1 tons (10.1 tonnes) | |
| **Engine** ZIS-123 gasoline, 110 hp | |
| **Main armament** 7.62 mm SGMB machine gun | |

Larger and more mobile than the BTR-40, the BTR-152 could carry 15 infantrymen. Later models had an armored roof and the first Soviet central tire pressure regulation system. Over 12,500 BTR-152s of all variants were built, and saw decades of service around the world.

**Soviet** insignia

UEZ 0256

**Armored** door to driver's compartment

**Sloped** front armor

141

△ **BTR-40**

| | |
|---|---|
| **Date** 1950 **Country** Soviet Union | |
| **Weight** 5.8 tons (5.3 tonnes) | |
| **Engine** GAZ-40 gasoline, 80 hp | |
| **Main armament** 7.62 mm SGMB machine gun | |

The first Soviet APC, the BTR-40 was a four-wheel drive, open-topped vehicle based on a light truck. It could carry eight infantrymen, or six in the later BTR-40B variant that had an armored roof. Sold around the world, it saw combat in Korea, Hungary, Vietnam, and the Middle East.

▽ **FV603 Saracen**

| | |
|---|---|
| **Date** 1952 **Country** UK | |
| **Weight** 11.2 tons (10.2 tonnes) | |
| **Engine** Rolls-Royce B80 Mk 6A gasoline, 160 hp | |
| **Main armament** .30 Browning M1919 machine gun | |

The British Army's standard APC during the 1950s, the Saracen had a drivetrain that gave excellent mobility. It had a capacity for 10 infantrymen, and its variants included a command vehicle, an ambulance, and an internal security version for use in Northern Ireland.

**Driver's** vision port

### △ BTR-60PA

**Date** 1963 **Country** Soviet Union

**Weight** 11 tons (10 tonnes)

**Engine** 2 x GAZ-49B gasoline, 90 hp each

**Main armament** 7.62 mm SGMB machine gun

The amphibious BTR-60PA, with its eight-wheel drive and water jet, was far more versatile than its predecessors. The first version was open topped, but later models had roof armor and an NBC system—albeit at the cost of reduced personnel capacity.

### △ OT-64 SKOT

**Date** 1964 **Country** Czechoslovakia, Poland

**Weight** 16 tons (14.5 tonnes)

**Engine** Tatra 928-18 diesel, 180 hp

**Main armament** 14.5 mm KPVT machine gun

Although the Warsaw Pact countries were tightly controlled by the Soviet Union, they were still able to design their own equipment. Poland and Czechoslovakia collaborated on the OT-64 instead of using the BTR-60. Its main advantages were better armor protection and doors at the rear.

**All-welded** steel body

**Tools** on hull

### △ YP-408

**Date** 1964 **Country** Netherlands

**Weight** 13.2 tons (12 tonnes)

**Engine** DAF DS 575 gasoline, 165 hp

**Main armament** .50 Browning M2 machine gun

The YP-408 had six-wheel drive, its second axle being unpowered. The basic APC version could carry 10 infantrymen. Mortar, command, ambulance, and antitank variants were developed, the Dutch using some as part of the UN force in Lebanon from 1979–85.

### ▽ Panhard M3

**Date** 1971 **Country** France

**Weight** 6.7 tons (6.1 tonnes)

**Engine** Panhard Defense Model 4HD gasoline, 90 hp

**Main armament** 7.62 mm machine gun

A private venture based on the successful AML armored car, the M3 was in production for 15 years, with around 1,500 sold to almost 30 countries, mainly in Africa. The APC version could carry 10 infantrymen, and variants included antiaircraft, repair, command, engineer, and ambulance models.

**Searchlight**

**Side doors** between middle wheels

### △ BTR-70

**Date** 1972 **Country** Soviet Union

**Weight** 12.9 tons (11.7 tonnes)

**Engine** 2 x GAZ-40P gasoline, 180 hp each

**Main armament** 14.5 mm KPVT machine gun

A faster, more mobile, and better protected version of the BTR-60, the BTR-70 was also more accessible, with doors placed between the second and third wheels. Unlike BTR-60, which fought in many conflicts, the BTR-70 only saw service in Afghanistan during the Cold War.

# Wheeled Troop Carriers (cont.)

Some nations assessed wheeled carriers as being better suited to their requirements than tracked vehicles. This included many African countries, who operated carriers over large areas of relatively smooth terrain. With generally lighter weight and lower ground pressure, wheeled vehicles could often move through areas that their heavier tracked counterparts could not, and rubber tires did less damage to local infrastructure than metal tracks. They also offered higher speeds, better reliability, and more protection against mines.

▷ **Véhicule de l'Avant Blindé**

| | |
|---|---|
| **Date** 1976 | **Country** France |
| **Weight** 14.3 tons (13 tonnes) | |
| **Engine** Renault MIDS 06-20-45 diesel, 220 hp | |
| **Main armament** .50 Browning M2 machine gun | |

The Véhicule de l'Avant Blindé (VAB) was intended as a counterpart to the tracked AMX-10P. Featuring amphibious capability and NBC protection, it can carry ten infantrymen. VABs have received hundreds of upgrades and continue in French service today. Its many variants include antiaircraft-missile launcher, radar carrier, and command-post models.

**Windscreen** can be covered by shutter

**Pneumatic** tires

**All-welded** armored steel

**Aluminum hull** protects against small-arms fire

△ **Transportpanzer 1 Fuchs**

| | |
|---|---|
| **Date** 1979 | **Country** West Germany |
| **Weight** 20.9 tons (19 tonnes) | |
| **Engine** Mercedes-Benz OM 402A diesel, 320 hp | |
| **Main armament** 7.62 mm MG3 machine gun | |

The basic Fuchs APC carried 10 infantrymen, and variants included radar vehicles, supply carriers, and electronic warfare platforms. The NBC reconnaissance vehicle was the most successful export version, its major buyers being the UK and the US.

**Rifle** ports

△ **Blindado Medio de Ruedas (BMR) 600**

| | |
|---|---|
| **Date** 1979 | **Country** Spain |
| **Weight** 15.5 tons (14 tonnes) | |
| **Engine** Pegaso 9157/8 diesel, 310 hp | |
| **Main armament** .50 Browning M2 machine gun | |

The BMR-600 and its many variants have seen service in the Balkans, Lebanon, and Iraq, as well as Afghanistan. It shares components with the VEC M1 armored car and both vehicles have received an upgrade to M1 standard, involving a new engine and additional armor.

**25 mm** cannon

△ **Ratel 20**

| | |
|---|---|
| **Date** 1979 | **Country** South Africa |
| **Weight** 20.9 tons (19 tonnes) | |
| **Engine** Bussing D 3256 BXTF diesel, 282 hp | |
| **Main armament** 20 mm M693 cannon | |

The arms embargo and the unique conditions facing South African forces during the 1970s and '80s forced them to design their own combat vehicles, using wheeled vehicles for their mobility and range. More heavily armed Ratels equipped with a 90 mm gun provided fire support for the 20 mm-armed vehicle.

◁ **LAV-25**

| | |
|---|---|
| **Date** 1983 | **Country** USA |
| **Weight** 14.2 tons (12.9 tonnes) | |
| **Engine** Detroit Diesel 6V53T diesel, 275 hp | |
| **Main armament** 25 mm M242 cannon | |

The US Marine Corps version of the MOWAG Piranha I, the LAV-25 is used mainly for reconnaissance. Its variants include antitank, command, and recovery vehicles. The fleet has undergone upgrades to armor, suspension, and sights over time, and in response to experiences in the Persian Gulf and Afghanistan.

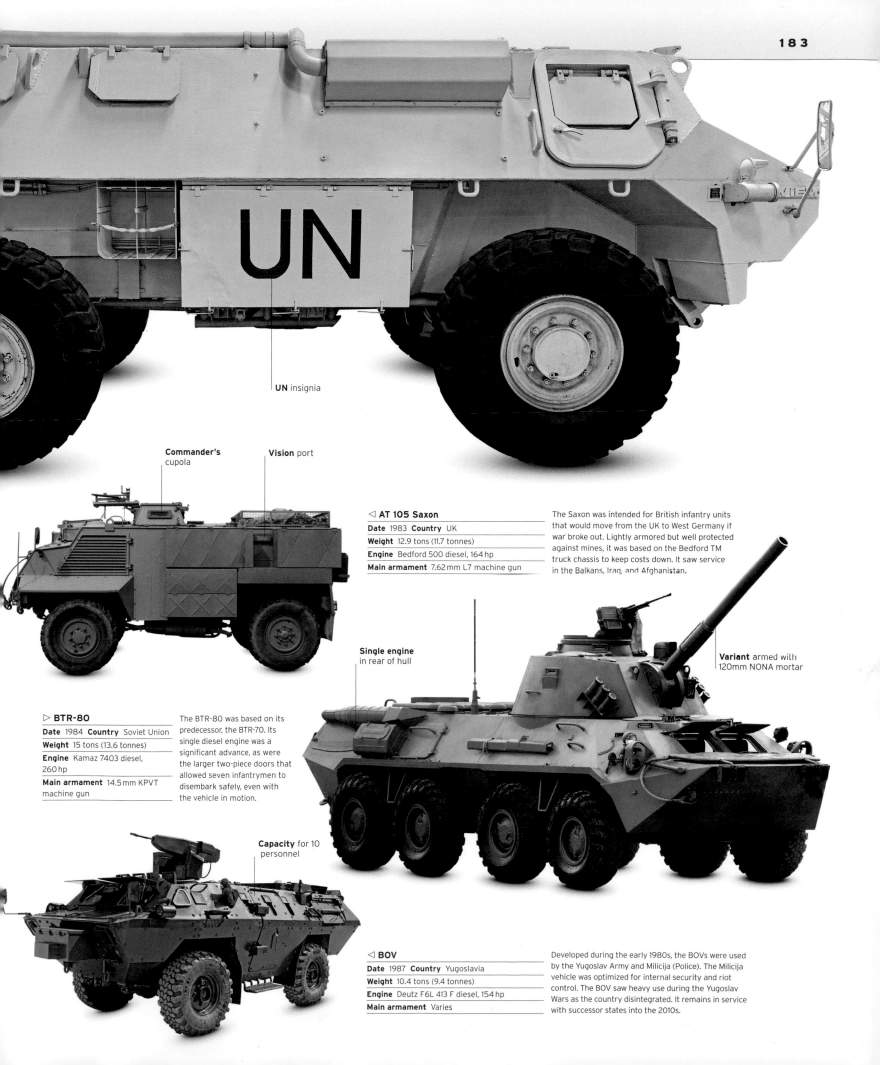

**UN** insignia

**Commander's** cupola

**Vision** port

◁ **AT 105 Saxon**

| Date 1983 | Country UK |
|---|---|
| **Weight** 12.9 tons (11.7 tonnes) | |
| **Engine** Bedford 500 diesel, 164 hp | |
| **Main armament** 7.62 mm L7 machine gun | |

The Saxon was intended for British infantry units that would move from the UK to West Germany if war broke out. Lightly armored but well protected against mines, it was based on the Bedford TM truck chassis to keep costs down. It saw service in the Balkans, Iraq, and Afghanistan.

**Single engine** in rear of hull

**Variant** armed with 120mm NONA mortar

▷ **BTR-80**

| Date 1984 | Country Soviet Union |
|---|---|
| **Weight** 15 tons (13.6 tonnes) | |
| **Engine** Kamaz 7403 diesel, 260 hp | |
| **Main armament** 14.5 mm KPVT machine gun | |

The BTR-80 was based on its predecessor, the BTR-70. Its single diesel engine was a significant advance, as were the larger two-piece doors that allowed seven infantrymen to disembark safely, even with the vehicle in motion.

**Capacity** for 10 personnel

◁ **BOV**

| Date 1987 | Country Yugoslavia |
|---|---|
| **Weight** 10.4 tons (9.4 tonnes) | |
| **Engine** Deutz F6L 413 F diesel, 154 hp | |
| **Main armament** Varies | |

Developed during the early 1980s, the BOVs were used by the Yugoslav Army and Milicija (Police). The Milicija vehicle was optimized for internal security and riot control. The BOV saw heavy use during the Yugoslav Wars as the country disintegrated. It remains in service with successor states into the 2010s.

# Antitank defenses

The German army quickly formulated antitank tactics after the first tank attack in September 1916. Artillery moved closer to the frontline: crews hid the guns and manhandled them into firing position should the enemy attack. The 77 mm field gun was converted to an antitank weapon by making the wheels smaller so the gun could be more easily hidden; trench mortars such as the 7.58 cm Minenwerfer were given new mounts to enable them to be more easily fired at tanks, and a new 13 mm antitank rifle was put into production. Engineers dug hidden pits deep enough to stop a tank, and trenches were widened—8 ft-wide (2.5 m) was thought to be wide enough for the purpose. Another simple tactic was to bury artillery shells—again on likely approach routes—and place a pressure fuse in the shell. The round would then have a board placed over it to increase the pressure area: a charge of around 27–55 lb (12–25 kg) was considered enough to destroy a tank.

## THE DOCTRINE OF MINES

Antitank mines in their hundreds of thousands were used in World War II. A mine didn't have to destroy a tank, only blow off or break a track: the crew would then have to either abandon the tank or try to repair it, making them vulnerable to machine gun fire and other weapons covering the minefield. Because of the threat of ditches, traps, and mines, various engineering vehicles were developed—such as these Combat Engineer Tractors—to overcome obstacles and allow an armored advance to continue.

**Combat Engineer Tractors** of the British 7th Armoured Brigade clear mines, January 7, 1991. Just over a week later they begin the liberation of Kuwait.

# Engineering and Specialized Vehicles

Hobart's Funnies (see pp.116–17) had proven their worth during World War II, and after the war the idea of building specialized vehicles based on a tank chassis became common. Armored Personnel Carriers (APCs) often received this treatment too, with a dizzying array of vehicles developed. These versatile vehicles have been used as mortar carriers, antitank missile launchers, signals vehicles, artillery observation posts, command posts, antiaircraft missile launchers, and many other roles.

▷ **Centurion BARV**

| | | |
|---|---|---|
| **Date** 1960 | **Country** UK | |

**Weight** 44.8 tons (40.6 tonnes)

**Engine** Rolls-Royce Meteor Mark IVB gasoline, 650 hp

**Main armament** None

Beach Armored Recovery Vehicles (BARVs) were used to pull vehicles out of the sea, or to push landing craft back in. The Centurion BARV could wade through 9½ft (2.9 m) of water, although at this depth the driver relied on the commander for guidance. One member of the four-man crew had to be a trained diver.

▽ **Centurion Armored Vehicle Royal Engineers (AVRE)**

| | |
|---|---|
| **Date** 1963 | **Country** UK |

**Weight** 56 tons (50.8 tonnes)

**Engine** Rolls-Royce Meteor Mark IVB gasoline, 650 hp

**Main armament** 165 mm L9 demolition gun

The AVRE carried a wide range of equipment to allow engineers to do their work, with similar armor protection and mobility to the standard tank. It was equipped with a dozer blade or a mine plough, and could carry a fascine or a roll of trackway. The AVRE was used in Northern Ireland in 1972 and the Gulf War in 1991.

**165 mm** main gun used for destroying obstacles

**Canvas** canopy

△ **M548**

| | |
|---|---|
| **Date** 1965 | **Country** USA |

**Weight** 14.8 tons (13.4 tonnes)

**Engine** General Motors Model 6V-53 diesel, 215 hp

**Main armament** .50 Browning M2 machine gun

An unarmored cargo carrier using the running gear of M113 APC, the M548 was originally intended to carry artillery ammunition and gunners. Its mobility and 6-ton (5.4-tonne) capacity meant it was adapted for a wide range of roles, including launchers for the Chaparral and Rapier surface-to-air missiles. It has seen service in Vietnam, the Yom Kippur War, and the Gulf War.

△ **MT-LB**

| | |
|---|---|
| **Date** 1970 | **Country** Soviet Union |

**Weight** 14.7 tons (13.3 tonnes)

**Engine** YaMZ 238 V diesel, 240 hp

**Main armament** 7.62 mm PKT machine gun

The amphibious MT-LB was developed as an armored, all-terrain artillery tractor. It was widely used as a command post vehicle, chemical warfare reconnaissance vehicle, electronic warfare vehicle, and missile carrier. It also saw service as an APC, especially in Arctic regions where its low ground pressure gave it better mobility than other vehicles.

▷ **Chieftain Armored Vehicle Launched Bridge (AVLB)**

**Date** 1974 **Country** UK

**Weight** 58.7 tons (53.3 tonnes)

**Engine** Leyland L60 multifuel, 750 hp

**Main armament** None

The Chieftain AVLB (shown here without a bridge) enabled armored forces to cross rivers or obstacles. Powered by hydraulics, the vehicle could launch or recover its bridge in just three minutes. The largest bridge launched by Chieftain, the Number 8, could span a 75 ft (23 m) gap.

**Folding** bridge

**Chieftain** chassis

**Headlight**

**Dozer** blade

◁ **Chieftain ARRV**

**Date** 1974 **Country** UK

**Weight** 59 tons (53.5 tonnes)

**Engine** Leyland L60 multifuel, 750 hp

**Main armament** None

The Chieftain Armoured Recovery and Repair Vehicle (ARRV) was based on the Chieftain Mk 5 hull and suspension, with the addition of an Atlas crane for lifting damaged vehicles, two winches, and a dozer blade. It saw service in the first Gulf War in 1991.

**Radar** dish

△ **FV432 Cymbeline Mortar Locating Radar**

**Date** 1975 **Country** UK

**Weight** 16.8 tons (15.2 tonnes)

**Engine** Rolls-Royce K60 No4 Mk 4F multifuel, 240 hp

**Main armament** None

The Cymbeline Radar was used to track mortar shells back to their launch point, allowing rapid counterattacks. The Mark 2 version was mounted on an FV432 APC. The large, open space inside these vehicles makes them suitable for a wide range of roles, while their mobility and protection enables them to operate farther forward than wheeled trucks.

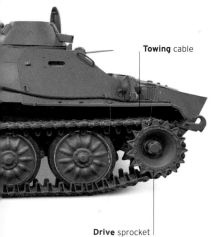

**Towing** cable

**Drive** sprocket

▷ **Challenger Armored Repair and Recovery Vehicle (CRARRV)**

**Date** 1991 **Country** UK

**Weight** 67.4 tons (61.2 tonnes)

**Engine** Perkins CV12 V-12 diesel, 1,200 hp

**Main armament** None

The CRARRV was based on the Challenger 1, although it has been upgraded to be compatible with the Challenger 2. It has a 55.1 ton (50 tonne) winch, 7.2 ton (6.5 tonne) crane, a three-man crew, and space for the crew of the recovered tank. This version is fitted with reactive armor, ECM, and underbelly protection.

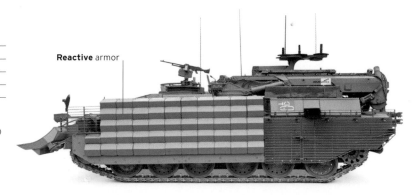

**Reactive** armor

# CVR(T) Family

Developed during the 1960s for the British Army, the Combat Vehicle Reconnaissance (Tracked) family was a range of lightweight vehicles that were constructed from common components for ease of manufacture. They were lightly armored and made of aluminum, and so could readily be moved by air. After decades of service with forces around the world, these vehicles were upgraded: the gasoline engine was replaced by a more powerful diesel one, while the Stormer was developed with a lengthened chassis.

**Road** wheels

▷ **FV101 Scorpion**

**Date** 1972 **Country** UK

**Weight** 8.9 tons (8.1 tonnes)

**Engine** Jaguar J60 No1 Mk100B gasoline, 190 hp

**Main armament** 76 mm L23A1 rifled gun

The world's fastest tank, at 51 mph (82 km/h), the Scorpion was a light reconnaissance vehicle with a three-man crew. It was by far the most widely exported CVR(T) vehicle, sold to around 20 countries. An upgraded variant with a 90 mm gun was later developed.

**Stowage** bin

◁ **FV107 Scimitar**

**Date** 1974 **Country** UK

**Weight** 8.6 tons (7.8 tonnes)

**Engine** Jaguar J60 No1 Mk100B gasoline, 190 hp

**Main armament** 30 mm L21A1 RARDEN cannon

A version of the Scorpion with a lighter, faster firing cannon, the Scimitar is intended for close reconnaissance. With their low ground pressure, Scimitars and Scorpions proved to be the only armored vehicles that could negotiate the soft, muddy terrain of the Falklands in 1982.

**Swingfire** missile launcher

**Commander's** cupola

▷ **FV102 Striker**

**Date** 1976 **Country** UK

**Weight** 9.2 tons (8.3 tonnes)

**Engine** Jaguar J60 No1 Mk100B gasoline, 190 hp

**Main armament** Swingfire antitank guided missile launcher

The Striker carried the Swingfire antitank guided missile in a five-round launcher box on the Armored Personnel Carrier (APC) hull. Swingfire was a wire-guided missile that could turn in flight to hide the launcher's location. It was used in the Persian Gulf in 1991 and 2003.

◁ **FV103 Spartan**

**Date** 1977 **Country** UK

**Weight** 9 tons (8.1 tonnes)

**Engine** Jaguar J60 No1 Mk100B gasoline, 190 hp

**Main armament** 7.62 mm L7 machine gun

An APC, the Spartan can carry five soldiers and two crew members. This capacity is too small for a standard British infantry section, so it is generally used to carry specialists such as antitank missile teams or mortar-fire controllers.

**Smoke grenade** launchers

◁ **FV105 Sultan**

**Date** 1977 **Country** UK

**Weight** 9.5 tons (8.6 tonnes)

**Engine** Jaguar J60 No1 Mk100B gasoline, 190 hp

**Main armament** 7.62 mm L7 machine gun

The Sultan is used by commanders at all levels, including in units that are not equipped with other CVR(T) variants. It provides enough room for a map board and desk, space for multiple radios, and has a tent that can be attached to the rear to provide more space for the commanders.

76mm main gun

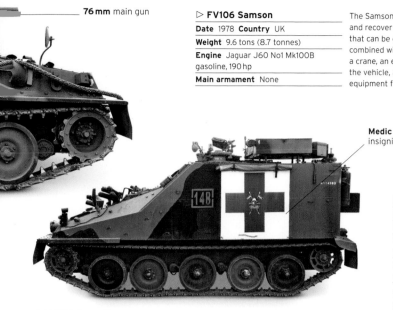

▷ **FV106 Samson**

| | |
|---|---|
| **Date** 1978 | **Country** UK |

**Weight** 9.6 tons (8.7 tonnes)

**Engine** Jaguar J60 No1 Mk100B gasoline, 190 hp

**Main armament** None

The Samson is designed to repair and recover CVR(T)s. It has a winch that can be configured for towing or combined with an A-frame for use as a crane, an earth anchor to secure the vehicle, and smaller tools and equipment for its crew of fitters.

Medic
insignia

△ **FV104 Samaritan**

| | |
|---|---|
| **Date** 1978 | **Country** UK |

**Weight** 9.5 tons (8.6 tonnes)

**Engine** Jaguar J60 No1 Mk100B gasoline, 190 hp

**Main armament** None

The Samaritan is an armored ambulance with a high-roofed hull, which gives the soldiers inside plenty of space to work. It also has a large rear door to enable easy access. The Samaritan can carry three stretchers or seated casualties, as well as medical personnel.

Starstreak surface-to-air missiles

Driver's hatch

▷ **FV4333 Stormer**

| | |
|---|---|
| **Date** 1991 | **Country** UK |

**Weight** 14.9 tons (13.5 tonnes)

**Engine** Cummins 6BTAA-T250A diesel, 250 hp

**Main armament** Starstreak surface-to-air missile launcher

The Stormer was developed as a larger version of the CVR(T) family. Its variants—APC, ambulance, and bridgelayer—were sold to Indonesia. The British Army adopted it as a carrier for the Starstreak surface-to-air missile, and also used a flatbed version fitted with the Shielder antitank mine-laying system.

▽ **FV107 Scimitar Mark 2**

| | |
|---|---|
| **Date** 2011 | **Country** UK |

**Weight** 13.4 tons (12.2 tonnes)

**Engine** Cummins BTA diesel, 235 hp

**Main armament** 30 mm L21A1 RARDEN cannon

The threat of mines and improvised explosive devices (IEDs) in Afghanistan led to a comprehensive upgrade for the Scimitar. The Mark 2 uses a remanufactured Spartan hull, a more powerful engine, upgraded suspension, add-on mine protection, and bar armor to defeat rocket-propelled grenade (RPG) warheads.

Commander's
periscope

Bar armor

Idler wheel

# Armor on wheels

The first AMX 10 RC (see p.160) was issued to the French Army in 1981. RC stands for "roues-canon," or wheeled gun, and the aluminum turret carries a 105 mm GIAT main gun—a tank-sized gun in a wheeled vehicle that is not a tank.

## WHEELS VERSUS TRACKS

The differences in the abilities of wheeled and tracked vehicles may merge over time, but currently a vehicle must have tracks to be considered a tank. As a general rule, tracks have less ground pressure and can travel over terrain that wheels cannot; however, they tend to be noisier and wear out more quickly. As a result, tracks are usually more expensive. Wheels tend to be

faster than tracks, and have been assessed as appearing less threatening: they are often used for peace enforcement roles ahead of a tracked vehicle. Since scouting and reconnaissance vehicles can be the first to discover mines, the ability of wheeled vehicles to remain mobile after mine strikes make them well suited to these roles. Multiwheeled armored vehicles can lose one or even two wheels and continue to be mobile. A vehicle with a broken track, on the other hand, can be classified as a "mobility kill," as two tracks are required for the vehicle to move.

**At the end of the Gulf War in 1991,** French crews parade before their AMX 10 RC wheeled reconnaissance vehicles.

# Scorpion CVR(T)

The design of the Scorpion dates to the 1960s, when both tracked and wheeled reconnaissance vehicles were required by the British Army. The Scorpion was created to meet the requirements of the Combat Vehicle Reconnaissance (Tracked)–CVR(T)–role.

**THE SCORPION** was part of a family of vehicles with the same engines and transmissions built by British manufacturer Alvis. One of the requirements of the design was air portability: it was clad in aluminum armor to save weight, and two Scorpions could fit in the hold of a C130 Hercules aircraft. Its lightweight design gave its tracks a low ground pressure—in fact, the ground pressure was less than that of a human foot. This lightness meant the Scorpion could travel across soft ground that would have been inaccessible to many other military vehicles, a trait that proved very useful in the British Army's Falklands campaign in 1982.

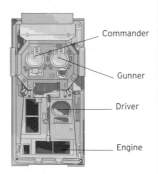

**REAR VIEW**

The Scorpion was initially equipped with the Jaguar J60 4.2-liter gasoline engine, similar to that of the manufacturer's famous E-type sports car. Like many British Army vehicles, these engines were later replaced by diesel variants, which were considered safer. The Scorpion was armed with a 76 mm low-velocity gun that could fire a range of projectiles including smoke, High Explosive, High Explosive Squash Head (HESH), and canister rounds. In theory, use of the HESH round gave the Scorpion a tank-killing capability, but its aluminum armor meant it was vulnerable to anything heavier than small-arms fire—it would have to rely on speed and maneuverability to survive engagements with heavier tanks.

## SPECIFICATIONS

| | |
|---|---|
| Name | Scorpion CVR(T) |
| Date | 1973 |
| Origin | UK |
| Production | Over 3,000 |
| Engine | Cummins BTA 5.9-liter diesel 190 hp |
| Weight | 9 tons (8.1 tonnes) |
| Main armament | 76 mm L23A1 |
| Secondary armament | 7.62 mm L34A1 |
| Crew | 3 |
| Armor thickness | 0.50 in (12.7 mm) |

Commander

Gunner

Driver

Engine

**76 mm L23A1** low-velocity gun

**Drive sprocket** positioned at front

**THREE-QUARTER VIEW**

**Hull bracket** for flotation screen

# RETALIATOR

**Vehicle name**
The Scorpion takes its name from its rear-mounted turret, which suggests a sting in the tail. Likewise, individual Scorpions have evocative names—such as "Retaliator," which indicates a swift response.

**Action Man's vehicle**
The Scorpion CVR(T) was so successful that it was chosen to be immortalized as the vehicle driven by the popular children's toy, Action Man.

## EXTERIOR

Scorpions were intended to perform tasks such as reconnaissance and screening (providing cover for a main force). Features of the exterior reveal this role. The cable drum on the side of the turret, for instance, allows an observer to take a communications handset away from the vehicle into an observation post. At 0.5 in (12.7 mm) thick, its light aluminum armor offers protection against small-arms fire and shrapnel, but nothing heavier.

1. Insignia   2. Maneuvering light   3. Driver's periscope
4. Engine bay   5. Smoke grenade dischargers   6. Infrared
light casing   7. Coaxial machine gun   8. Commander's
periscope with wiper blade   9. Tools stowed on hull
10. Fire extinguisher   11. Camouflage netting basket
12. Cable drum   13. Track and idler wheel   14. Exhaust

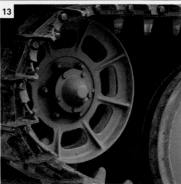

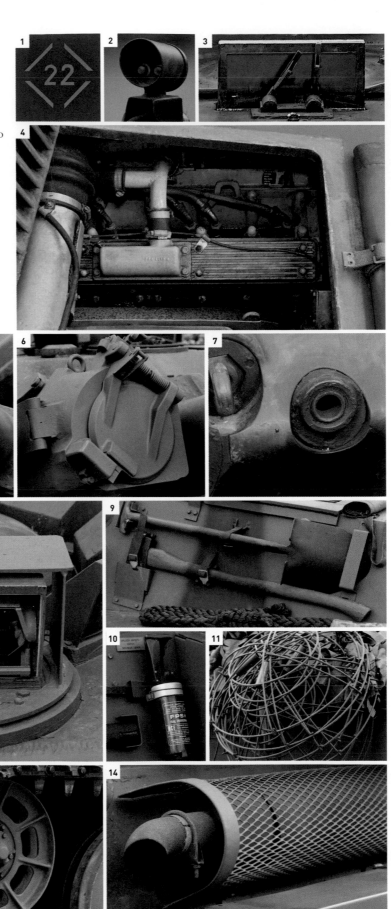

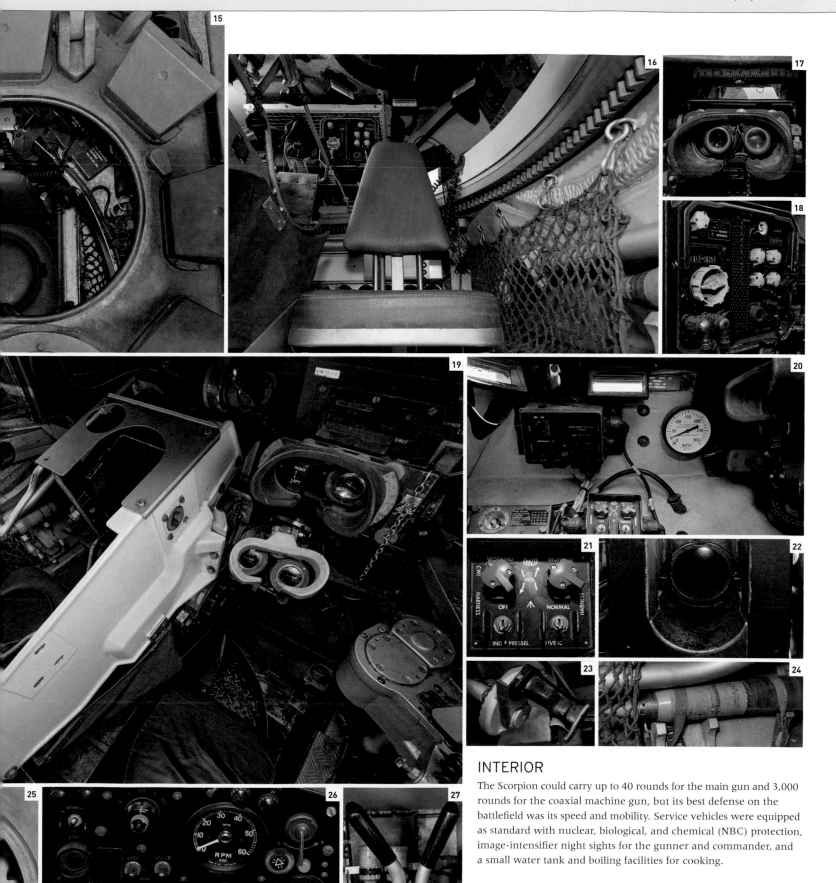

## INTERIOR

The Scorpion could carry up to 40 rounds for the main gun and 3,000 rounds for the coaxial machine gun, but its best defense on the battlefield was its speed and mobility. Service vehicles were equipped as standard with nuclear, biological, and chemical (NBC) protection, image-intensifier night sights for the gunner and commander, and a small water tank and boiling facilities for cooking.

15. Looking down into commander's position  16. Looking back at gunner's position  17. Commander's binocular gunsight  18. Radio  19. Turret interior from commander's position  20. Gunner's position with instruments and periscopes  21. Communication system control panel  22. Main gun breech  23. Turret traverse wheel with electronic control  24. Ammunition stowed by gunner's position  25. Looking down into driver's position  26. Driver's instrument panel  27. Steering levers

# After 1991
# POST-COLD WAR

# POST-COLD WAR

**The Berlin Wall fell** in November 1989. By 1991, the Soviet Union had ceased to exist and the Cold War was over. The end of this era of international tension resulted in large scale reductions in military forces, with thousands of tanks and armored vehicles scrapped or sold. Many nations retired large fleets of outmoded tanks, some dating back to the 1950s, and purchased modern, secondhand vehicles at a discount. The former communist nations of Eastern Europe also began restructuring their militaries along Western lines, with many joining NATO.

Armored vehicles found a new role in conflicts in the former Yugoslavia. United Nations and NATO peacekeepers used their presence to protect civilians, and to intimidate and keep apart warring factions.

Outside Europe, where security threats were ongoing, tank development continued, with nations such as Israel, South Korea, Japan, China, Turkey, India, and Pakistan developing new vehicles. Older tanks have continued to prove their usefulness in conflicts across the world, especially against irregular forces.

Advanced technology has begun to play a larger role in armored vehicles. Developments in cameras, thermal sights, and networked communications have increased situational awareness for crews, both around their vehicles and across the battlefield. Increasingly powerful antitank weapons, especially in urban environments such as Chechnya and Syria, have spurred improvements in protection, including Active Protection Systems. Some of these can automatically shoot back at incoming projectiles, while others can interrupt guidance systems or "hide" the tank. These suggest that, although its place on the battlefield is again threatened, the tank will endure.

△ **Second Gulf War magazine covers**
Tank combat in the invasion of Iraq was often characterized by US M1 Abrams defeating Iraqi forces in older Soviet armor.

> " **Tanks** being **deployed far forward** is an indication of **offensive action**; tanks in depth is an indication of **defensive action**."
>
> NORMAN SCHWARZKOPF, FORMER US ARMY GENERAL

◁ **A Merkava IV** of the Israel Defense Forces maneuvers with a mine-clearing device attached to the front of its hull.

## Key events

▷ **July 17, 1992** The CFE Treaty limits the amount of military equipment NATO and the Warsaw Pact may possess.

▷ **April 29, 1994** Operation Bøllebank is launched by Danish forces in Bosnia, the first use of the Leopard 1 in combat.

▷ **December 31, 1994** Russia attempts to capture Grozny, Chechnya using armored units, with heavy casualties.

▷ **March 2003** American and British armored forces invade Iraq.

△ **Iraq War at night, 2004**
A Bradley M2A2 infantry fighting vehicle opens fire in Samarra, Iraq.

▷ **July 2006** In the Israeli-Hezbollah War, Israeli weaknesses in armored warfare are exposed by Hezbollah's sophisticated tactics and equipment.

▷ **September 2006** NATO first deploys tanks, Canadian Leopard C2s, to Afghanistan. Danish Leopard 2A5s and USMC M1A1 Abrams also fight there.

▷ **2011–present** The Syrian Civil War sees intense urban fighting between Syrian Army armored units and rebels.

▷ **August 2014** Modern Russian tanks are observed in fighting in Eastern Ukraine between the government and Russian-backed separatists.

▷ **2015** In the Saudi-led intervention in Yemen, Houthi rebels use modern ATGMs to destroy Saudi tanks.

▷ **May 2015** A World War II-era T-34/85 and SU-100 are seen in use in Yemen.

# Counterinsurgency Vehicles

Conventional vehicles are generally low to the ground with lightly armored undersides, leaving them vulnerable to landmines. During the 1970s, the increasing use of such weapons by insurgents and terrorist organizations led to the development of armored vehicles specifically designed to protect against mines. Rhodesia (modern-day Zimbabwe) was the first to encounter this problem; its solution was to protect the crew compartment by raising it higher and angling the underside to deflect the blast—so the vehicle might lose a wheel, but the crew would survive.

### △ Humber "Pig"

| | |
|---|---|
| **Date** 1958 | **Country** UK |
| **Weight** 6.4 tons (5.8 tonnes) | |
| **Engine** Rolls-Royce B60 Mk 5A gasoline, 120 hp | |
| **Main armament** None | |

Designed as an eight-man armored personnel carrier, the Pig was hastily given extra armor and brought back into service as the conflict in Northern Ireland worsened. Some Pigs were modified for specialist roles, and the vehicle was used into the 1990s.

### ▷ Shorland Mark 1

| | |
|---|---|
| **Date** 1965 | **Country** UK |
| **Weight** 3.5 tons (3.1 tonnes) | |
| **Engine** Rover 4 cylinder gasoline, 67 hp | |
| **Main armament** 7.62 mm machine gun | |

Used by the Royal Ulster Constabulary and Ulster Defence Regiment, the Shorland Mark 1 was based on the Land Rover Series IIA chassis. The armored body was topped with a machine-gun turret. Successive upgrades improved the armor and engine power, with the final versions being based on the more modern Land Rover Defender's chassis.

Windshield armor

Water tanks

Water pump

Headlight

### △ Saracen Special Water Dispenser

| | |
|---|---|
| **Date** 1972 | **Country** UK |
| **Weight** 15 tons (13.7 tonnes) | |
| **Engine** Rolls-Royce B80 Mk 6A gasoline, 160 hp | |
| **Main armament** Water cannon | |

The Saracen was equipped with a water cannon originally intended for riot control. Tests showed that the water cannon was powerful enough to seriously injure people hit by it, so it was instead used for Explosive Ordnance Disposal (EOD). The water was powerful enough to break up bombs without detonating them.

### ▷ Casspir

| | |
|---|---|
| **Date** 1979 | **Country** South Africa |
| **Weight** 12 tons (10.9 tonnes) | |
| **Engine** Mercedes-Benz OM-352A diesel, 166 hp | |
| **Main armament** None | |

Designed for the South African Police, who were involved in both riot control and fighting in the Border War, the Casspir had an enclosed armored body and windows. It could carry 12 passengers. This versatile vehicle was put to a range of uses including mine clearance, recovery, mortar carrier, and tanker.

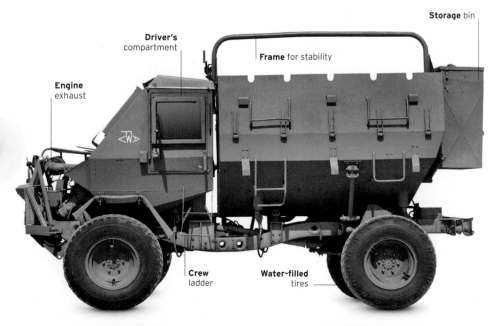

Driver's compartment

Frame for stability

Engine exhaust

Storage bin

### ◁ Buffel

| | |
|---|---|
| **Date** 1978 | **Country** South Africa |
| **Weight** 6.7 tons (6.1 tonnes) | |
| **Engine** Mercedes-Benz OM-352 diesel, 125 hp | |
| **Main armament** None | |

The Buffel's chassis and engine came from the Unimog truck, and the mine-resistant crew pod was open-topped, giving the 10 passengers an excellent field of view. The V-shaped floor deflected the blast away from the passengers, and the water-filled tires helped dissipate it further. Buffels were used by the South African Army until the 1990s.

Crew ladder

Water-filled tires

△ **Snatch Land Rover**

**Date** 1992 **Country** UK

**Weight** 4.5 tons (4.1 tonnes)

**Engine** Land Rover 300Tdi diesel, 111 hp

**Main armament** None

The British Army used a range of armored Land Rovers in Northern Ireland. The Series III "Piglets", equipped with Vehicle Protection Kits, gave way to the Glover-Webb armored patrol vehicle (APV) and then the Snatch. The Snatch was deployed in Iraq and Afghanistan, where high casualties among its crews led to its replacement.

**Accommodates** a driver, a commander, and nine troops

△ **Mamba**

**Date** 1995 **Country** South Africa

**Weight** 7.5 tons (6.8 tonnes)

**Engine** Daimler-Benz OM352A diesel, 123 hp

**Main armament** None

The South African Army's replacement for the Buffel, the Mamba added a roof and armored windows. The Mark I was two-wheel drive and carried five troops, but later models were four-wheel drive and carried nine passengers. The Mark II and its RG-31 variant proved popular for their high protection combined with a nonthreatening appearance. Its development has continued into the 21st century.

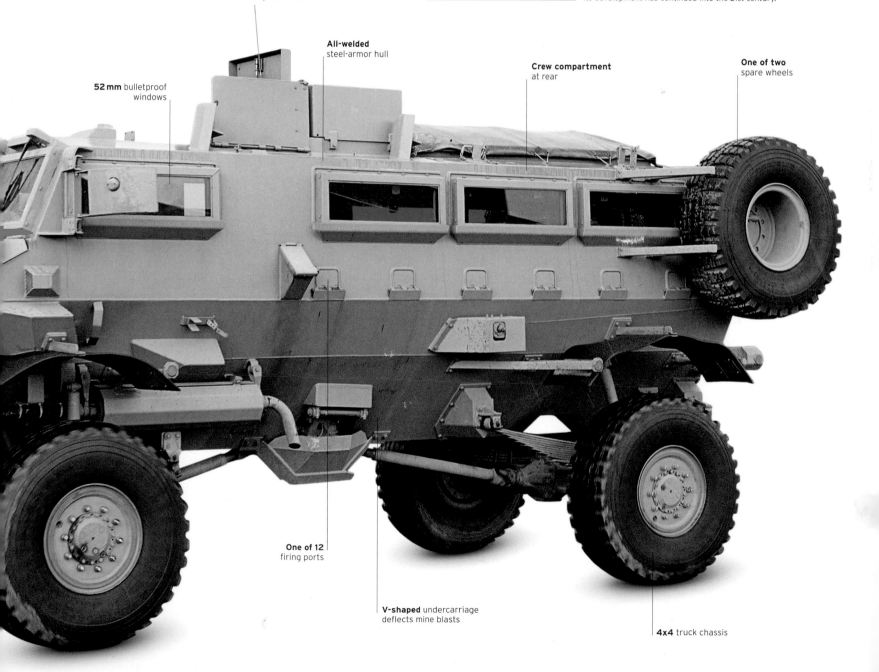

**52 mm** bulletproof windows

**All-welded** steel-armor hull

**Crew compartment** at rear

**One of two** spare wheels

**One of 12** firing ports

**V-shaped** undercarriage deflects mine blasts

**4x4** truck chassis

# Counterinsurgency Vehicles (cont.)

Political considerations often restricted the types of vehicles that could be used in counterinsurgency operations to lighter wheeled vehicles, which were often equipped with extra armor. The South African Border War of the 1980s saw the development of vehicles that protected against both mines and direct fire. When the Improvised Explosive Device (IED) threat began to arise in Iraq and Afghanistan during the 21st century, these designs formed the starting point for the American Mine-Resistant Ambush Protected (MRAP) vehicle program.

### △ Buffalo

| | |
|---|---|
| **Date** 2002 | **Country** USA |
| **Weight** 38.1 tons (34.5 tonnes) | |
| **Engine** Caterpillar C13 Diesel, 440 hp | |
| **Main armament** None | |

Designed to carry EOD personnel, the Buffalo is significantly longer and taller than other MRAPs. It is equipped with a 33 ft (10 m) articulated manipulator arm that can be used to uncover and disable IEDs. The Buffalo is also used by British, Canadian, French, Italian, and Pakistani forces.

**Cameras** provide situational awareness

**Armor** protects gunner

**6x6** chassis

### △ Mastiff

| | |
|---|---|
| **Date** 2002 | **Country** UK |
| **Weight** 26 tons (23.6 tonnes) | |
| **Engine** Caterpillar C7 diesel, 330 hp | |
| **Main armament** .50 Browning M2 machine gun | |

The Mastiff is the British Army's version of the Force Protection Cougar MRAP, which saved thousands of lives in Iraq and Afghanistan. Unlike Cougar, the Mastiff has armor plate instead of armored side windows, and is equipped with bar armor.

### ▷ Bushmaster

| | |
|---|---|
| **Date** 2003 | **Country** Australia |
| **Weight** 17 tons (15.4 tonnes) | |
| **Engine** Caterpillar 3126E diesel, 300 hp | |
| **Main armament** Varies | |

The Bushmaster was designed to provide protected mobility for a nine-man infantry section over long distances. Its armor and mine protection made it popular in Iraq and Afghanistan. Australia has ordered over 1,000 variants, including command, mortar, ambulance, air defense, and route clearance.

**Remote weapons** station

**Armored**
door

## △ Husky

**Date** 2009 **Country** UK

**Weight** 7.6 tons (6.9 tonnes)

**Engine** MaxxForce D6.0L diesel, 340 hp

**Main armament** 7.62Z mm L7 machine gun

The British adopted the International MXT truck as the Husky Tactical Support Vehicle (Medium). The TSV programme provided load-carrying vehicles with equivalent protection to combat vehicles, allowing them to operate alongside each other.

## △ MaxxPro

**Date** 2007 **Country** USA

**Weight** 14.8 tons (13.4 tonnes)

**Engine** MaxxForce D9.316 diesel, 330 hp

**Main armament** Varies

Navistar International manufactured a range of MaxxPro MRAPS for US forces in Afghanistan and Iraq. They are the most widely used MRAP design with over 7,000 built to date. Although the MaxxPro affords its crew of seven excellent protection, concerns have been raised about its poor off-road performance and its tendency to roll over.

**Objective Gunner Protection Kit** manned turret

**Bar** armor

## △ M-ATV

**Date** 2009 **Country** USA

**Weight** 16.1 tons (14.6 tonnes)

**Engine** Caterpillar C7 diesel, 370 hp

**Main armament** Varies

Concerns over the poor off-road maneuverability of MRAPs, especially in Afghanistan, led to the development of the M-ATV. This vehicle has the blast and armor protection of larger MRAPs, but is far more mobile, using the chassis of the USMC standard-issue truck.

**Electronic** mine-detection system

**Each wheel** functions independently

## ▷ Foxhound

**Date** 2012 **Country** UK

**Weight** 8.3 tons (7.5 tonnes)

**Engine** Steyr-Daimler-Puch M160036-A diesel, 214 hp

**Main armament** Varies

Designed as a replacement for Snatch, the Foxhound provides unmatched maneuverability and blast protection. It achieves this by using advanced composite materials instead of metal in many areas, which reduces weight. It carries a crew of six.

# Buffel

Named after the Afrikaans word for "buffalo," the Buffel was the first purpose-built mine-protected Armored Personnel Carrier. It was built in South Africa during the South African Border War, a series of conflicts that took place in South West Africa (now Namibia), Angola, and Zambia from 1966 to 1990.

**WHILE MANY VEHICLES** had used V- or boat-shaped hulls to deflect mine blasts away from their undersides—for example, the Saracen APC (see p.180)—the Buffel was the first vehicle to have the survivability of the driver and mounted infantry as the priority in the design brief. Its design led to the Mine-Resistant Ambush Protected concept (MRAP) in the 2000s, which resulted in tens of thousands of vehicles being built for use in Iraq and Afghanistan.

The Buffel was a development of the earlier Bosvark vehicle—a Mercedes Benz Unimog truck modifed with a basic level of mine protection. The Buffel took the design further using the same Mercedes Benz U416-162 Unimog chassis, but with a driver's position set high off the ground behind the front axle, and with bulletproof windows to the front and sides. The open-topped rear troop compartment could carry ten infantrymen, each with a four-point seat belt harness, back to back. Entry to the vehicle was over the sides of the compartment, which were hinged to allow the armor to be dropped down.

**REAR VIEW**

| SPECIFICATIONS | |
|---|---|
| Name | Buffel Armoured Personnel Carrier |
| Date | 1978 |
| Origin | South Africa |
| Production | Approx 2,400 |
| Engine | Mercedes-Benz OM-352 diesel, 125 hp |
| Weight | 6.7 tons (6.1 tonnes) |
| Main armament | None |
| Secondary armament | None |
| Crew | 1 + 10 |
| Armor thickness | Hull: unknown; windshield: 1.6 in (40 mm) armored glass |

Infantry seats

Driver

Engine

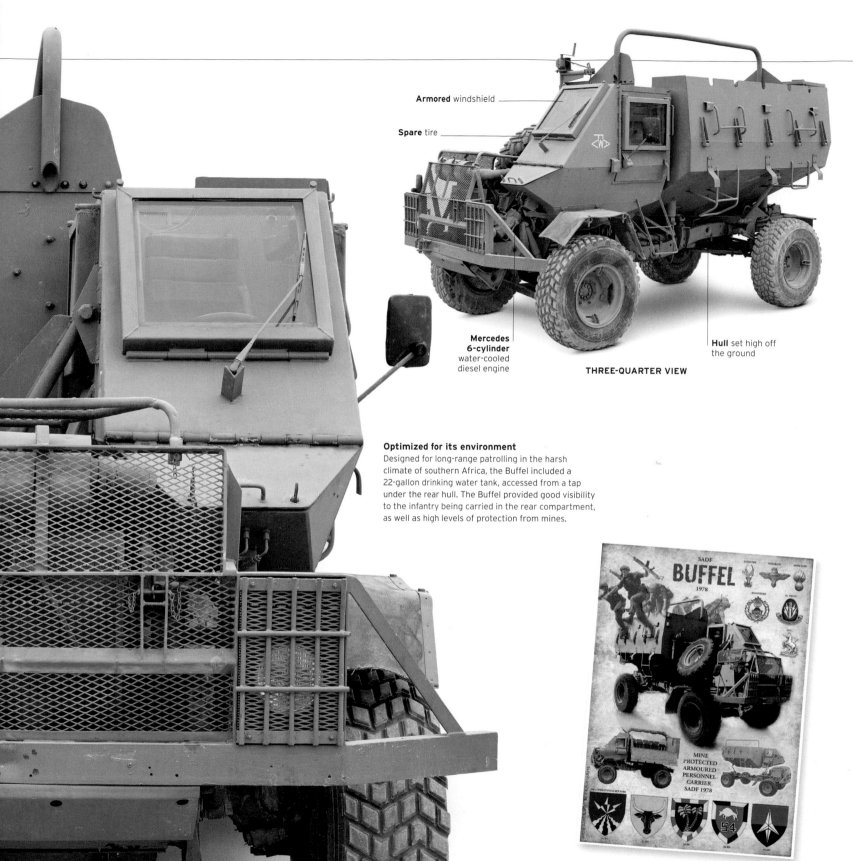

**Armored** windshield

**Spare** tire

**Mercedes 6-cylinder** water-cooled diesel engine

**THREE-QUARTER VIEW**

**Hull** set high off the ground

### Optimized for its environment

Designed for long-range patrolling in the harsh climate of southern Africa, the Buffel included a 22-gallon drinking water tank, accessed from a tap under the rear hull. The Buffel provided good visibility to the infantry being carried in the rear compartment, as well as high levels of protection from mines.

### Deploying from the Buffel

This poster shows infantrymen disembarking from the Buffel, and also illustrates an armoured side panel in the lowered position. The badges belong to some of the South African Defence Force units that used the vehicle.

## EXTERIOR

The Buffel was a relatively simple vehicle based on the running gear of the very successful Unimog truck, 12,000 of which were bought by the South African Defence Forces for a variety of roles. In addition to blast protection from mines, its hull shielded passengers from small arms fire. The Buffel was also buit in variants with closed infantry compartments and windows.

**1.** Headlight grille  **2.** Front tow point  **3.** Cab nose flap, open  **4.** Bulletproof glass windshield  **5.** Winch for raising items, including tires.  **6.** Main engine  **7.** Main engine detail  **8.** Main chassis frame  **9.** Access steps  **10.** Suspension arms  **11.** Vertical-spring suspension  **12.** 12.50 x 20 tires, often filled with water to absorb blasts  **13.** Drinking water tap  **14.** Rear light  **15.** Rear tow hook

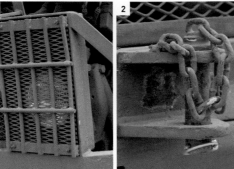

## INTERIOR

The South African experience in counterinsurgency warfare led to a number of countries studying their tactics and equipment. The Buffel was sold to Sri Lanka, but more importantly, its novel design characteristics were emulated in later MRAP vehicles.

**16.** Looking down into driver's compartment **17.** Driver's seat **18.** Instrument panel **19.** Warning indicator lights **20.** Driver's panel switches **21.** Gear and direction levers **22.** Choke lever **23.** Hand and foot holds with bolt to release side panel **24.** Safety harness **25.** Infantry seats

# The logistics of tank deployment

The movement of tanks can be divided into three categories; strategic, operational and tactical, and battlefield. At the strategic level, there is the movement of tanks from barracks or stores to the area of operations, which can mean transportation to a different continent. Two Abrams tanks, for example, can be transported in a C5 Galaxy aircraft, but the usual way is by road transporter or by train to a port and a roll-on roll-off ship. Indeed, the use of railroads to move tanks has had a considerable influence on tank design. In Europe, the Berne International Load Gauge deemed that a maximum width of 3.5 m could safely be carried on most European railroads—but in Britain, the rail loading gauge was narrower at 2.67 m.

At the operational level, i.e. in areas where combat may occur, problems may include road and bridge restrictions, the risk of damage to urban areas, and the distance a tank may have to drive —the greater the distance, the greater both the fuel requirement and the likelihood of breakdown. On the battlefield, the immediate ground will influence a tank's mobility, and may limit the way it can operate. Speed may help a tank become a harder target to hit—or thicker armor may make it less vulnerable—and so it can choose its route across a battlefield with impunity.

**M1A2 Abrams tanks and M2A3 Bradley IFVs** arrive at Busan in South Korea from Texas to boost South Korean defenses in February 2014.

# Tracked Troop Carriers

The end of the Cold War slowed down the development of Infantry Fighting Vehicles (IFVs), and many countries focused on counterinsurgency operations during the first decade of the 21st century. This meant that Cold War vehicles had to continue service for longer than planned, although several replacement designs have entered production since 2010. The development of IFVs did continue in other countries, particularly in those facing an active conventional threat, such as Israel and South Korea.

▽ **CV90**

| | | | |
|---|---|---|---|
| **Date** 1993 | **Country** Sweden | | |

**Weight** 25.1 tons (22.8 tonnes)

**Engine** Scania DI 14 diesel, 550 hp

**Main armament** 40 mm Bofors L/70 cannon

The CV90 (or Stridsfordon 90) was developed during the late 1980s and had a capacity of 6–8 infantrymen. Its variants include command, antiaircraft, and forward observation and recovery vehicles. The versions armed with 30 mm or 35 mm cannon have been exported, primarily to Nordic countries. Swedish, Norwegian, and Danish vehicles have seen combat in Afghanistan.

40 mm cannon

140228

30 mm cannon

◁ **ASCOD Infantry Fighting Vehicle**

**Date** 1996 **Country** Austria/Spain

**Weight** 33 tons (30 tonnes)

**Engine** MTU 8V-199-TE20 diesel, 720 hp

**Main armament** 30 mm MK30-2 cannon

Named ASCOD, for Austrian Spanish Cooperation Development, the Spanish version is called Pizarro and the Austrian (shown here) is named Ulan. Both have the same main armament, suspension, and a capacity for eight infantry. However, they use different engines, fire control systems, and armor configurations. Almost 400 have been built in total, including variants.

Grousers
on hull

25 mm cannon

▷ **Dardo**

**Date** 2002 **Country** Italy

**Weight** 25.3 tons (23 tonnes)

**Engine** Iveco 8260 diesel, 520 hp

**Main armament** 25 mm Oerlikon KBA cannon

The Italian Army ordered 200 Dardos to replace their M113 derived VCC-1 Armored Personnel Carriers (APCs). The Dardo can be armed with TOW or Spike anti-tank missiles. It can carry six infantry, who have firing ports in the sides and rear ramp. The vehicle has been deployed with Italian forces in Iraq, Afghanistan, and Lebanon.

Smoke grenade launchers

## △ BvS 10 Viking

**Date** 2004 **Country** Sweden

**Weight** 12.4 tons (11.3 tonnes)

**Engine** Cummins ISBe250 30 diesel, 275 hp

**Main armament** 7.62 mm L7 machine gun

Developed for the British Royal Marines, the Viking is a lightly armored vehicle developed from the smaller, unarmored Bv206. It runs on rubber tracks and is steered by hydraulic rams between the two cabs, giving it excellent mobility, even over sand and snow. Operations in Afghanistan saw the vehicle equipped with extra armor.

## ▽ Namer

**Date** 2008 **Country** Israel

**Weight** 68.3 tons (62 tonnes)

**Engine** Continental AVDS-1790 diesel, 1,200 hp

**Main armament** .50 Browning M2 machine gun

Israeli experience of urban warfare demonstrated the vulnerability of the M113 APC, so several replacements based on existing chassis were developed. The Namer uses the highly mobile Merkava 4 chassis, equipped with even heavier armor. To enhance protection against Anti-Tank Guided Missiles (ATGMs), it is now equipped with the Trophy APS (see pp.221).

Remote controlled machine gun

Merkava 4 chassis

Unmanned turret with 30 mm cannon

## ◁ Schützenpanzer Puma

**Date** 2010 **Country** Germany

**Weight** 47.4 tons (43 tonnes)

**Engine** MTU MT 892 Ka-501 diesel, 1,090 hp

**Main armament** 30 mm MK30-2/ABM cannon

The replacement for the venerable Marder, the Puma uses an unmanned turret, keeping all three crew and six infantry together in the hull. Modular armor can be added or removed to match a threat level, or to reduce its weight to 34.2 tons (31 tonnes) for air transportation.

## ▽ Ajax

**Date** 2016 **Country** UK

**Weight** 41.9 tons (38 tonnes)

**Engine** MTU 199 diesel, 800 hp

**Main armament** 40 mm CTAI CT40 cannon

An Intelligence, Surveillance, Target Acquisition, and Reconnaissance (ISTAR) vehicle developed for the British Army, the Ajax adopts its basic design from the ASCOD. The vehicle has a digital electronic architecture that enables it to share information with friendly forces. A number of variants are planned, including specialized personnel carrier, engineer reconnaissance, repair, recovery, and command.

Smoke grenade launchers

Camouflage covering

## △ BMD-4M Airborne Assault Vehicle

**Date** 2014 **Country** Russia

**Weight** 15.5 tons (14 tonnes)

**Engine** UTD-29 multifuel, 500 hp

**Main armament** 1 x 100 mm 2A70 smoothbore gun, 1 x 30 mm 2A72 cannon

Based on the BMD-3 hull, the original BMD-4 entered service with the Russian Airborne Troops (VDV) in 2004, although just 60 were delivered. The improved BMD-4M uses the engine and other automotive components from the BMP-3 to ease costs, logistics, and maintenance. An APC variant, the BMD-MDM, has also been introduced.

# Wheeled Troop Carriers

Wheeled personnel carriers have become popular since the end of the Cold War, especially 8x8 vehicles. Automotive developments have given them cross-country mobility similar to tracked vehicles, and wheels remain more reliable and durable than tracks. The ability of wheeled vehicles to self deploy over long distances, without needing transportation, was demonstrated in Mali in 2013. Wheeled vehicles also have a greater resistance to mines and IEDs—most modern 8x8s can be driven even with multiple destroyed wheels.

## △ ASLAV

| | | | |
|---|---|---|---|
| **Date** 1992 | **Country** Australia | | |
| **Weight** 14.8 tons (13.4 tonnes) | | | |
| **Engine** Detroit Diesel 6V53T diesel, 275 hp | | | |
| **Main armament** 25 mm M242 cannon | | | |

Based on the USMC LAV-25 and the Canadian Bison, a total of 257 ASLAV vehicles were purchased in two configurations. The nonturreted personnel carrier hull can be converted to command, surveillance, or ambulance using removable kits. The ASLAV has seen service in Iraq and Afghanistan.

## ▽ XA-185

| | | | |
|---|---|---|---|
| **Date** 1994 | **Country** Finland | | |
| **Weight** 14.9 tons (13.5 tonnes) | | | |
| **Engine** Valmet 612 DWI diesel, 246 hp | | | |
| **Main armament** 12.7 mm NSV machine gun | | | |

The first XA series vehicle, the XA-180 was introduced in 1984. The XA-185 had a more powerful engine. Further upgrades led to the XA-186, XA-188, and the larger XA-203, which were no longer amphibious. XA vehicles have been sold to Finland, Norway, Sweden, Estonia, and the Netherlands. Besides peacekeeping missions, the XA-185 has been used in Afghanistan.

**Bullet-resistant** front windows

## △ Type 96

| | | | |
|---|---|---|---|
| **Date** 1995 | **Country** Japan | | |
| **Weight** 16 tons (14.5 tonnes) | | | |
| **Engine** Komatsu diesel, 360 hp | | | |
| **Main armament** .50 Browning M2 machine gun | | | |

The Type 96 has a two-man crew and space for eight infantrymen, who get in and out using a rear ramp or five roof hatches. It has two firing ports on each side. Although never exported, the Type 96 was used by the Japanese Iraq Reconstruction and Support Group between 2004 and 2006.

**Propeller** for propulsion in water

## △ Pandur I

| | | | |
|---|---|---|---|
| **Date** 1995 | **Country** Austria | | |
| **Weight** 14.9 tons (13.5 tonnes) | | | |
| **Engine** Steyr WD 612.95 diesel, 260 hp | | | |
| **Main armament** .50 Browning M2 machine gun | | | |

The 6x6 Pandur I is used by Austria, Slovenia, Kuwait, and Belgium. Some were also supplied to the US Special Operations Command. The Belgian vehicles are used for reconnaissance, and some Kuwaiti vehicles are armed with a 90 mm gun. The upgraded Pandur II, in 8x8 configuration, was made available from 2005.

**6x6 drive** capability

## ▷ Piranha III

| | | | |
|---|---|---|---|
| **Date** 1998 | **Country** Switzerland | | |
| **Weight** 24.3 tons (22 tonnes) | | | |
| **Engine** Caterpillar C9 diesel, 400 hp | | | |
| **Main armament** Varies | | | |

The Piranha III has been sold to more than 12 countries, with variants ranging from standard Armored Personnel Carrier (APC) to electronic warfare and assault gun. The Canadian variant, LAV-III, is used by Canada and New Zealand, and forms the basis of the US Army's Stryker family.

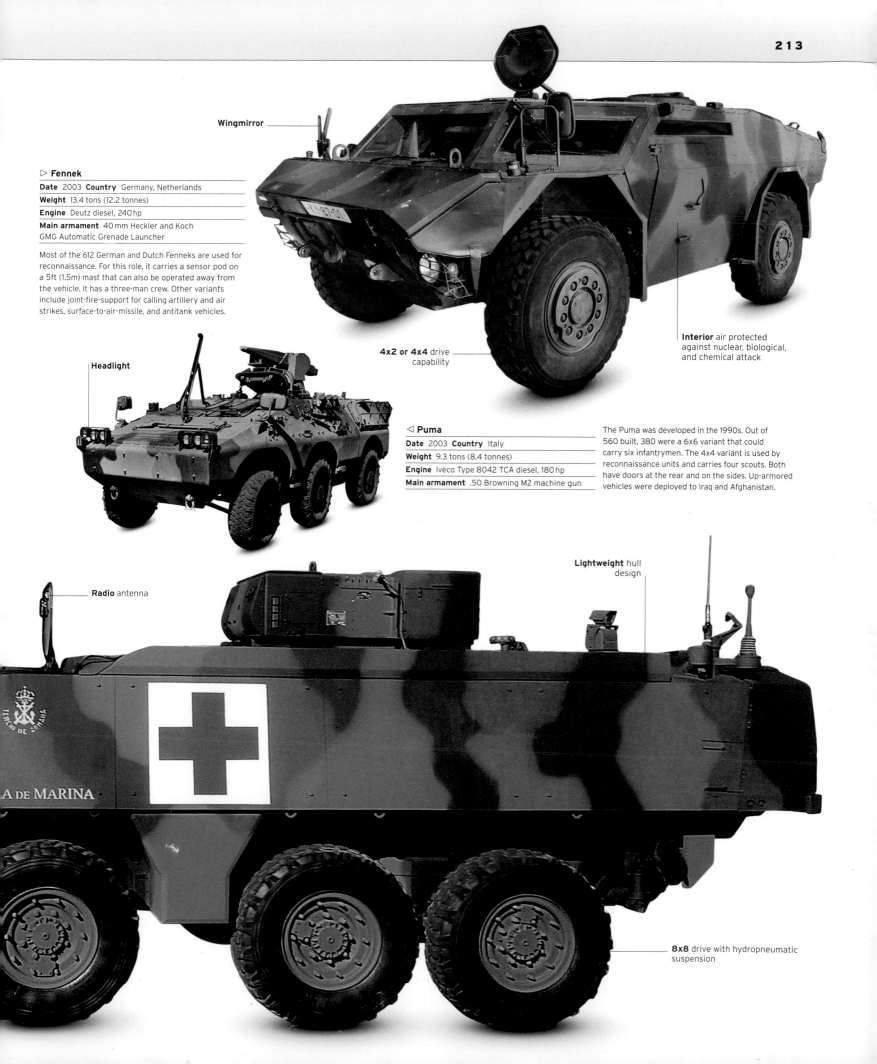

Wingmirror

## ▷ Fennek

**Date** 2003 **Country** Germany, Netherlands

**Weight** 13.4 tons (12.2 tonnes)

**Engine** Deutz diesel, 240 hp

**Main armament** 40 mm Heckler and Koch GMG Automatic Grenade Launcher

Most of the 612 German and Dutch Fenneks are used for reconnaissance. For this role, it carries a sensor pod on a 5 ft (1.5 m) mast that can also be operated away from the vehicle. It has a three-man crew. Other variants include joint-fire-support for calling artillery and air strikes, surface-to-air-missile, and antitank vehicles.

**4x2 or 4x4** drive capability

**Interior** air protected against nuclear, biological, and chemical attack

Headlight

## ◁ Puma

**Date** 2003 **Country** Italy

**Weight** 9.3 tons (8.4 tonnes)

**Engine** Iveco Type 8042 TCA diesel, 180 hp

**Main armament** .50 Browning M2 machine gun

The Puma was developed in the 1990s. Out of 560 built, 380 were a 6x6 variant that could carry six infantrymen. The 4x4 variant is used by reconnaissance units and carries four scouts. Both have doors at the rear and on the sides. Up-armored vehicles were deployed to Iraq and Afghanistan.

**Lightweight** hull design

**Radio** antenna

A DE MARINA

**8x8** drive with hydropneumatic suspension

# Wheeled Troop Carriers (cont.)

Many 21st-century designs can carry a range of different weapons, from machine guns attached to remote weapon stations, to turrets armed with cannon that are usually found on Infantry Fighting Vehicles. Such options have made these wheeled APCs even more popular. However, such improvements in firepower and protection have led to significant increase in their height and weight, with some vehicles approaching 33 tons (30 tonnes). This makes them more prominent targets and harder to move by air.

**Modular design** allows different turrets to be mounted

**Hydraulic suspension** on each wheel

### △ Patria AMV

**Date** 2004 **Country** Finland

**Weight** 24.3 tons (22 tonnes)

**Engine** Scania DC13 diesel, 483 hp

**Main armament** .50 Browning M2 machine gun

The Patria AMV is available with a wide variety of engines, transmissions, weapons stations, and role-specific equipment. Depending on the turret attached, up to 10 infantrymen can be carried. More than 1,500 AMVs have been sold to seven countries. Poland has the largest fleet and has deployed the Rosomak, as they named it, to Afghanistan.

### △ Eagle IV

**Date** 2003 **Country** Switzerland

**Weight** 7.7 tons (7 tonnes)

**Engine** Cummins ISB 6.7 E3 diesel, 245 hp

**Main armament** Varies

The Eagle I, II, and III were based on the HMMWV chassis, whereas the Eagle IV and V use the DURO III truck as its basis, giving it a larger payload. The vehicle is used for reconnaissance, patrol, command, and as an ambulance. More than 750 Eagle IV and Vs have been built for Denmark, Germany, and Switzerland.

**25 mm** GIAT M811 cannon

**Crew** compartment

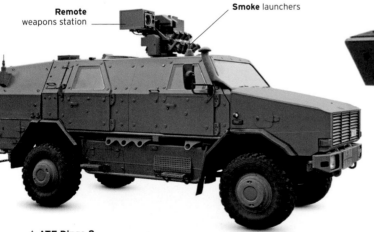

**Remote** weapons station

**Smoke** launchers

### △ ATF Dingo 2

**Date** 2005 **Country** Germany

**Weight** 13.8 tons (12.5 tonnes)

**Engine** Mercedes-Benz OM 924 LA diesel, 222 hp

**Main armament** Varies

The Dingo is based on the Unimog truck chassis, equipped with an armored hull and underbody mine protection. It has an eight-man crew. Six countries operate the Dingo 2 in roles such as NBC reconnaissance, medical evacuation, patrol, and battlefield surveillance. It has been deployed in the Balkans, Lebanon, and Afghanistan.

### ▷ VBCI

**Date** 2008 **Country** France

**Weight** 31.9 tons (29 tonnes)

**Engine** Volvo diesel, 550 hp

**Main armament** 25 mm GIAT M811 cannon

Unusually for a wheeled vehicle, the VBCI was designed for use as an IFV rather than an APC. It has a three-man crew and carries up to nine infantrymen. France operates 630, of which 110 are command posts. The VBCI has been deployed in Lebanon, Afghanistan, and Mali, where its stabilized cannon proved highly effective.

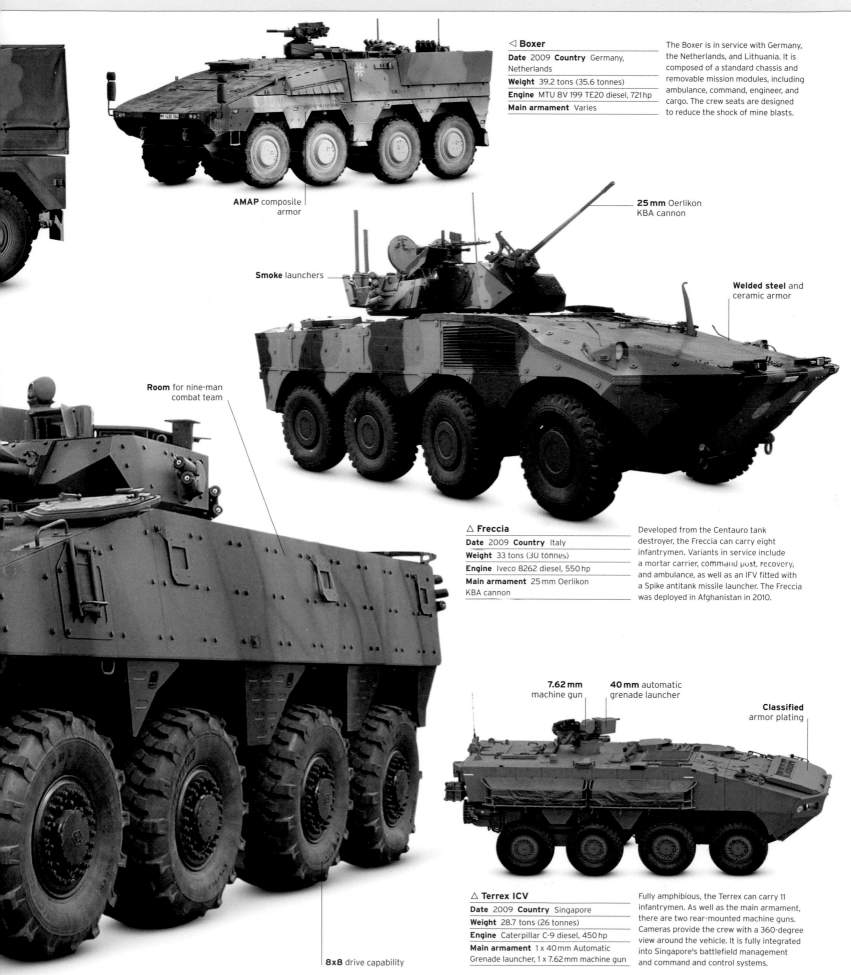

◁ **Boxer**

**Date** 2009 **Country** Germany, Netherlands

**Weight** 39.2 tons (35.6 tonnes)

**Engine** MTU 8V 199 TE20 diesel, 721hp

**Main armament** Varies

The Boxer is in service with Germany, the Netherlands, and Lithuania. It is composed of a standard chassis and removable mission modules, including ambulance, command, engineer, and cargo. The crew seats are designed to reduce the shock of mine blasts.

**AMAP** composite armor

**25 mm** Oerlikon KBA cannon

**Smoke** launchers

**Welded steel** and ceramic armor

**Room** for nine-man combat team

△ **Freccia**

**Date** 2009 **Country** Italy

**Weight** 33 tons (30 tonnes)

**Engine** Iveco 8262 diesel, 550 hp

**Main armament** 25 mm Oerlikon KBA cannon

Developed from the Centauro tank destroyer, the Freccia can carry eight infantrymen. Variants in service include a mortar carrier, command post, recovery, and ambulance, as well as an IFV fitted with a Spike antitank missile launcher. The Freccia was deployed in Afghanistan in 2010.

**7.62 mm** machine gun

**40 mm** automatic grenade launcher

**Classified** armor plating

**8x8** drive capability

△ **Terrex ICV**

**Date** 2009 **Country** Singapore

**Weight** 28.7 tons (26 tonnes)

**Engine** Caterpillar C-9 diesel, 450 hp

**Main armament** 1 x 40mm Automatic Grenade launcher, 1 x 7.62 mm machine gun

Fully amphibious, the Terrex can carry 11 infantrymen. As well as the main armament, there are two rear-mounted machine guns. Cameras provide the crew with a 360-degree view around the vehicle. It is fully integrated into Singapore's battlefield management and command and control systems.

# Tracks on the ground

The movement of US Army M1A2 Abrams tanks such as this to an allied nation such as South Korea is an overt way of one country showing military and political support for another.

## SHOW OF STRENGTH

While the tank has obvious tactical capabilities—as can be seen by the firing of its powerful 120 mm gun—the movement of such tanks is also a classic symbol of power projection in world politics, as well as being a source of reassurance to the allied or friendly nation. Despite the fact that many other more powerful, advanced, or expensive

military assets may have also been deployed for a joint exercise such as this, it is often the tanks that will be photographed and featured in the media coverage of the events. The tank is such a distinctive, large, and powerful weapon—or is seen as such by the general public—that it is often the symbolic piece of military equipment most seen to represent a nation's military supremacy and geopolitical strength.

**An M1A2 Abrams fires on a range** at Pocheon, South Korea, during a joint South Korean and US Army exercise in 2011.

# Post-Cold War Tanks

The end of the Cold War slowed down the development of tanks, but by no means ended it. Former adversaries reduced the size of their militaries, selling or scrapping many vehicles as such large armies were no longer needed. Many vehicles that were under development during the late 1980s were brought into service slowly and in small numbers. On the other hand, some existing tanks continued to receive upgrades, such as the introduction of the L/55 120 mm gun mounted on the German Leopard 2A6.

### △ M1A2 Abrams

| Date | 1992 | Country | USA |
|------|------|---------|-----|

**Weight** 69.4 tons (63 tonnes)

**Engine** Textron Lycoming AGT1500 gas turbine, 1,500 hp

**Main armament** 120 mm M256 L/44 smoothbore gun

Introduced in 1985, the M1A1 had a more effective 120 mm gun than the M1 and an improved suspension and transmission, while the M1A2 added a Commander's Independent Thermal Viewer (CITV), enabling the commander to look in a different direction from the gunner. Experience in the Gulf also led to enhancements, especially to the electronics and computer systems.

**120 mm** L/52 smoothbore gun

### ▽ Type 90

| Date | 1991 | Country | Japan |
|------|------|---------|-------|

**Weight** 55.1 tons (50 tonnes)

**Engine** Mitsubishi 10ZG diesel, 1,500 hp

**Main armament** 120 mm L/44 smoothbore gun

With the exception of the main gun, all the components of the Type 90 were designed and built in Japan. The tank features an autoloader, reducing the crew to three men. Due to Japan's difficult mountainous and urban terrain, most of the 341 Type 90s are deployed in Hokkaido, where their size and weight is less restrictive.

### △ Leclerc

| Date | 1992 | Country | France |
|------|------|---------|--------|

**Weight** 62.3 tons (56.5 tonnes)

**Engine** Wartsila V8X T9 diesel, 1,500 hp

**Main armament** 120 mm CN120-26 L/52 smoothbore gun

The Leclerc replaced the much lighter AMX-30. A total of 406 were built for France and 388 for the United Arab Emirates (UAE). An autoloader has reduced its crew to three. The electronics and armor have been steadily improved across production batches. French Leclercs have been used for peacekeeping in Kosovo and Lebanon, and the UAE's tanks have seen service in Yemen.

**Armored** skirt

**Thermal imaging** and gunnery sight aperture

**120 mm** rifled main gun

### ▷ Challenger 2

| Date | 1994 | Country | UK |
|------|------|---------|-----|

**Weight** 82.5 tons (74.9 tonnes)

**Engine** Perkins CV12 V12 diesel, 1,200 hp

**Main armament** 120 mm L30A1 L/55 rifled gun

Despite the name, only five percent of Challenger 2 parts are compatible with the Challenger 1. The British ordered 386, while Oman uses 38. Equipped with add-on armor, this tank took part in the invasion of Iraq in 2003. It features level 2I Dorchester armor modules on the hull and turret sides, electronic countermeasures, and heat and radar absorbent Solar Shield camouflage.

**Solar Shield** camouflage covers entire tank

**125 mm** main gun

**Aerial** mount

▷ **T-90S**

**Date** 1994 **Country** Russia

**Weight** 53.5 tons (48.6 tonnes)

**Engine** ChTZ V92S2 V12 diesel, 1,000 hp

**Main armament** 125 mm 2A46M5 L/48 smoothbore gun

Originally named the T-72BU, the T-90 was intended to replace earlier Soviet tanks. All of its onboard systems were upgraded, incorporating features from the T-80, and the Shtora Active Protection system (APS) was integrated. Of the seven users, the largest operator is India with 1,250 T-90s, followed by Russia with around 550 tanks. The T-90 has seen combat in Ukraine and Syria.

**Idler** wheel

**7.62 mm** machine gun

**Fume** extractor

▷ **Ariete**

**Date** 1995 **Country** Italy

**Weight** 59.5 tons (54 tonnes)

**Engine** Iveco MTCA V12 diesel, 1,275 hp

**Main armament** 120 mm OTO Melara L/44 smoothbore gun

The Ariete was designed during the Cold War to replace Italy's fleet of M60s and Leopard 1s, and 200 tanks were delivered to Italian forces between 1995 and 2002. It is equipped with a laser warning receiver for protection against missiles. The Ariete was used in Iraq during 2004, where extra armor was added to the turret and hull sides.

**Explosive** Reactive Armor (ERA)

**Smoke grenade** launchers

**125 mm** smoothbore gun

◁ **PT 91 Twardy**

**Date** 1995 **Country** Poland

**Weight** 50.6 tons (45.9 tonnes)

**Engine** PZL-Wola Type S12U multifuel, 850 hp

**Main armament** 125 mm D81TM smoothbore gun

An upgrade of the T-72M, the Twardy has additional Explosive Reactive Armor (ERA), more effective gun stabilization, and a more powerful engine and transmission. Poland bought 233, along with armored recovery and engineering variants. Malaysia ordered 48, and India bought over 550 of the recovery variants.

**Stowage** bin

**Exhaust** under cover

▽ **Type 96**

**Date** 1996 **Country** China

**Weight** 47.2 tons (42.8 tonnes)

**Engine** Norinco diesel, 780 hp

**Main armament** 125 mm L/48 smoothbore gun

Shocked at the effectiveness of M1A1 Abrams and Challengers in the Gulf War of 1991, China began upgrading its tanks to counter them. After a series of development vehicles, the Type 96 was adopted. It was the first Chinese tank to use modular armor that can quickly be replaced. The gun has an autoloader. The more advanced Type 96B was first seen in 2016.

**Drive** sprocket

# Post-Cold War Tanks (cont.)

Conflicts since 1989 have shown that tanks still have a role on the battlefield. Although heavy and difficult to deploy, when needed they offer unmatched protection and all-weather, long-range surveillance, along with accurate firepower. Tanks have been used for peacekeeping operations in the Balkans and Lebanon, as well as for counterinsurgency in Iraq and Afghanistan, and conventional fighting in Syria, Yemen, and Ukraine. During the 21st century, a number of new vehicles have begun to enter service, some with countries that are new to tank design.

### △ Type 99

**Date** 2001 **Country** China

**Weight** 55.1 tons (50 tonnes)

**Engine** WD396 V8 diesel, 1,200 hp

**Main armament** 125 mm ZPT-98 smoothbore gun

Along with the Type 96, the Type 99 forms the backbone of the Chinese Army's tank fleet. Protected by advanced ERA and a laser warning system, it uses more modern thermal sights, gun stabilization, and has hunter-killer capability. The Type 99A and Type 99A2 have recieved further upgrades.

**Smoke grenade** launchers

**Spaced armor** at front of turret

### △ Leopard 2A6

**Date** 2001 **Country** Germany

**Weight** 68.8 tons (62.4 tonnes)

**Engine** MTU MB 873 Ka-501 diesel, 1,500 hp

**Main armament** 120 mm Rheinmetall 120 L/55 smoothbore gun

A significant upgrade to the 2A4 from the Cold War era, the 2A6 incorporates distinctive wedge-shaped spaced armor on the turret and the more powerful L/55 gun. The gunner's sight has moved to the turret roof, and the turret is now electrically powered rather than being hydraulically driven.

**12.7 mm** anti-aircraft machine gun

**Composite** armor

### ▷ Al-Khalid

**Date** 2001 **Country** Pakistan/China

**Weight** 52.9 tons (48 tonnes)

**Engine** KMDB 6TD-2 multifuel, 1,200 hp

**Main armament** 125 mm smoothbore gun

A collaboration between Pakistan and China, the Al-Khalid, or the MBT-2000, was the most advanced part of a Pakistani project to upgrade its tank fleet. It has a three-man crew, ERA, and a laser-warning system. As of 2016, upgrades to this tank are under development.

One of two _____
machine guns

## ▷ Merkava Mark 4

**Date** 2004 **Country** Israel

**Weight** 71.1 tons (65 tonnes)

**Engine** MTU 883 V12 diesel, 1,500 hp

**Main armament** 120 mm IMI MG253
L/44 smoothbore gun

The latest in the Merkava line, the Mark 4
retains the unique front-mounted engine and
rear-access door. Features like automatic fire
protection, Nuclear Biological Chemical (NBC)
system, and Trophy Active Protection System
emphasize crew protection. Electronic systems
such as Automatic Target Tracking and a Battle
Management System make the tank even more
effective. It has seen combat in Lebanon and Gaza.

**Engine** mounted
at front of tank

**Space** for four crew and
six infantry

**120 mm**
main gun

**12.7 mm** machine gun _____

## ▷ Type 10

**Date** 2012 **Country** Japan

**Weight** 48.5 tons (44 tonnes)

**Engine** Mitsubishi V8 diesel, 1,200 hp

**Main armament** 120 mm Japan Steelworks
L/44 smoothbore gun

The latest Japanese tank, the Type 10
features upgradable modular armor as well
as a computerized network for sharing
information, an active suspension that can
raise or lower the height of the vehicle, and
a transmission that enables the same speed
forward and backward.

**Armored skirt**
protects wheels

**Bar armor**
protects engine
and drive sprocket

## ◁ T-14 Armata

**Date** 2015 **Country** Russia

**Weight** Unknown

**Engine** ChTZ 12N360 V12 diesel, 1,500+ hp

**Main armament** 125 mm 2A82-1M smoothbore gun

The T-14 represents a break from the previous Soviet
and Russian tank designs. It is much longer and
taller, and the three-man crew are all seated in the
front of the hull. The unmanned turret contains
the gun and autoloader. The turret also contains the
sights and both a hard-and a soft-kill APS.

**Tracks** with
rubber pads

**Russian**
insignia

**125 mm** smoothbore
main gun

**120 mm** main gun

## ▷ Altay

**Date** 2016 **Country** Turkey

**Weight** 71.7 tons (65 tonnes)

**Engine** MTU MT 883 Ka-501 diesel, 1,500 hp

**Main armament** 120 mm L/55 smoothbore gun

Turkey has upgraded its M60 and Leopard
tanks, but the Altay represents a significant step
forward as a new design. Most components are
being developed by Turkish companies, including
the advanced fire control system and sights.
It has a four-man crew. A total of 1,000
vehicles are planned.

# M1A2 Abrams

The American Abrams has been made in large numbers (some 11,000) and now equips seven national armies. Nevertheless, it has been subject to the West's ambivalent attitude to tanks–the dilemma of potentially needing them and seeing others still developing them versus the pressure on factory capacity amid tightening military budgets.

**THE ABRAMS WAS DESIGNED** as a replacement for the M60 at a time when Soviet Bloc tanks were considered the most likely enemy. The first model was equipped with a version of the L7 105mm gun from the UK, separate ammunition storage in a blow-out compartment to protect the crew, and a gas turbine engine that was small and incredibly powerful but twice as thirsty as an equivalent diesel engine. During a visit to the UK in 1973, an American team was shown the latest developments in Chobham armor, and this led to a redesign of the tank to incorporate the new protection system. Later, a new version of the laminate armor incorporating depleted uranium was fitted to the M1A1 model of the tank, doubling protection levels. The M1A1 was also equipped with the 120mm German smoothbore gun, which gave it a tremendous advantage in the 1991 Gulf War.

Further upgrades, such as a new Fire Control System, Commander's Independent Thermal Viewer, and improved digital systems, led to the M1A2 model. City fighting in the Iraq War led to the development of the Tank Urban Survival Kit (TUSK) in 2006. These were fitted to tanks in theater to improve protection in built-up areas.

Time and again the Abrams has proved itself in battle, and it will undoubtedly continue to be a potent weapon for decades to come.

**REAR VIEW**

## SPECIFICATIONS

| | |
|---|---|
| **Name** | M1A2 Abrams |
| **Date** | 1992 |
| **Origin** | USA |
| **Production** | Approx 1,500 |
| **Engine** | Textron Lycoming AGT1500 gas turbine, 1,500hp |
| **Weight** | 69.4 tons (63 tonnes) |
| **Main armament** | 120mm M256 smoothbore |
| **Secondary armament** | .50 Browning M2HB, 2 x 7.62mm M240 MGs |
| **Crew** | 4 |
| **Armor thickness** | Unknown |

Engine
Commander
Gunner
Loader
Driver

**Engine compartment** at rear

**Commander's cupola**

**Depleted uranium** armor on front of turret

**Armored skirt**

**THREE-QUARTER VIEW**

**Rubber pads** on tracks

JZ08PD

**Tank badge**
The badge of the US Army Maneuver Center of Excellence based at Fort Benning, Georgia. The center unites the Infantry School and Armor School under one command. The full color badge replaces the black with blue, yellow, and red segments, the traditional colors of the US Infantry, Cavalry, and Artillery.

**Mobile powerhouse**
The latest version of the Abrams is the M1A2 SEPv2 (System Enhancement Package). This has added an Auxiliary Power Unit, a Thermal Management System, and upgrades to electronic systems such as communications, display screens, and sights.

## EXTERIOR

The M1A2 is one of the heaviest main battle tanks
in the world—partly due to its formidable composite
armor, which has been further improved by the addition
of depleted uranium mesh at the front of the hull and
turret. This extraordinary armor offers protection against
all known antitank weapons.

**1.** Towing eye   **2.** Road wheel hub   **3.** Road wheels and track
**4.** Track with rubber pads   **5.** Commander's (left) and loader's
hatches   **6.** Commander's cupola   **7.** Loader's 7.62mm M240
machine gun   **8.** Common Remotely Operated Weapons Station
sights   **9.** Nuclear, Biological, and Chemical protection system vent
**10.** Vapor Compression System Unit, part of the Thermal
Management System   **11.** Infantry phone   **12.** Drive sprocket

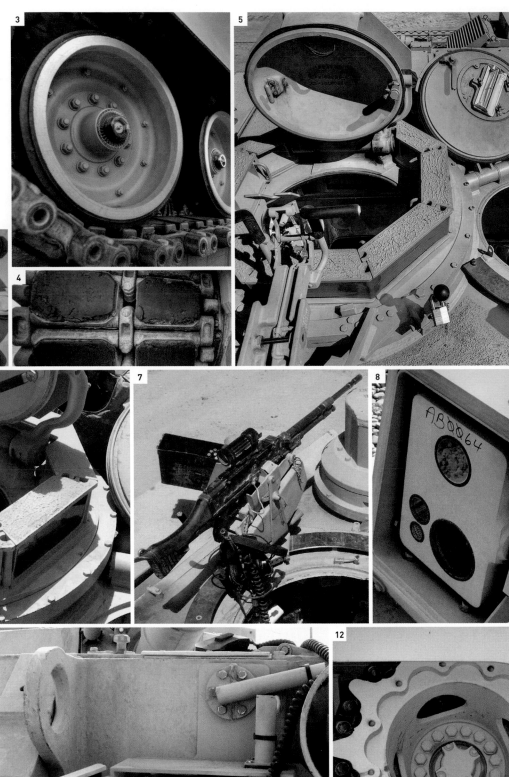

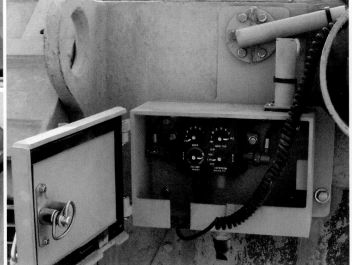

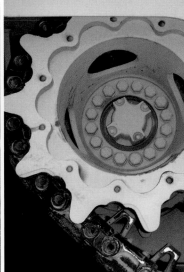

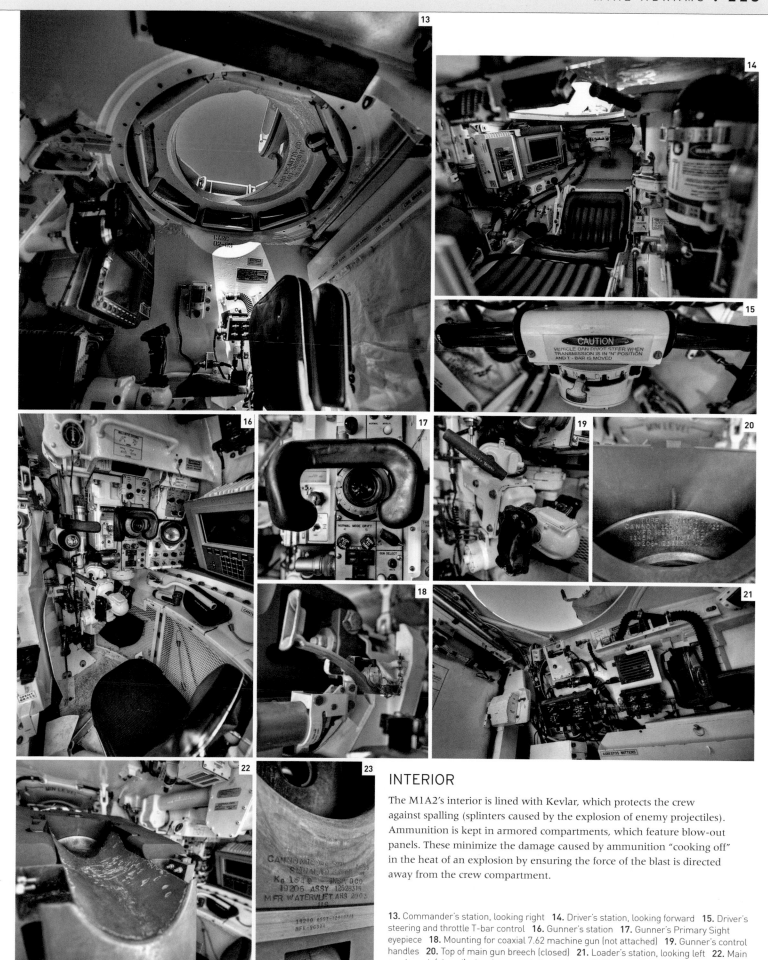

## INTERIOR

The M1A2's interior is lined with Kevlar, which protects the crew against spalling (splinters caused by the explosion of enemy projectiles). Ammunition is kept in armored compartments, which feature blow-out panels. These minimize the damage caused by ammunition "cooking off" in the heat of an explosion by ensuring the force of the blast is directed away from the crew compartment.

**13.** Commander's station, looking right **14.** Driver's station, looking forward **15.** Driver's steering and throttle T-bar control **16.** Gunner's station **17.** Gunner's Primary Sight eyepiece **18.** Mounting for coaxial 7.62 machine gun (not attached) **19.** Gunner's control handles **20.** Top of main gun breech (closed) **21.** Loader's station, looking left **22.** Main gun breech (closed), showing case deflector tray **23.** Bottom of main gun breech (open)

The BAE stand at the
Farnborough International
Airshow, UK, 2010

# Key manufacturers
# BAE Systems

BAE Systems is one of the world's largest defense contractors. It produces virtually everything military, from aircraft carriers and nuclear submarines to rifles and ammunition. One of its core activities is the manufacture of armored vehicles.

**BRITISH AEROSPACE, CREATED IN 1977**, was a government-owned conglomerate of aircraft manufacturers whose component companies had a history stretching back to World War I. Denationalized in 1981, it soon began to expand, acquiring the Royal Ordnance Factories—producers of a wide variety of armaments and munitions, and every Main Battle Tank in service with the British Army since World War II—in 1987. Vehicle manufacturers The Rover Group was acquired in 1988, and finally, after radical restructuring, BA merged with Marconi Electronic Systems in 1999 to form BAE Systems. MES was itself a conglomerate, with naval shipyards as well as a first-rate electronics capability. However, other than ROF, BAE had no interest in military vehicle production. That shortcoming was soon rectified, however, for in 2004 it outbid General Dynamics for Alvis Vickers, by then the UK's most important armored vehicle builder.

Since 1919, Alvis had been a low-volume producer of automobiles. It became involved in building armored cars as early as 1937, and continued down that path after World War II, developing the six-wheeled FV600 series, which included the Saracen APC and Saladin armored car, adopted by the British Army in 1958. Briefly part of The Rover Group, and later British Leyland, the company changed hands again in 1981 to become part of United Scientific Holdings, which

manufactured gunsights. USH adopted the name Alvis in 1995. In 1997 it acquired Swedish competitor Hägglunds, and in the following year GKN Sankey, which was then supplying the British Army with its FV500-series tracked Infantry Fighting Vehicles (the Warrior and variants), which operated alongside Alvis' own lighter, aluminum-hulled FV100 family, the most successful member of which was FV101 Scorpion. In 2002, Alvis became Alvis Vickers on acquiring Vickers Defence Systems, which had a history of tank production stretching back to 1920, and was then producing Challenger 2, the British Army's Main Battle Tank.

Two years later, BAE acquired Alvis Vickers and merged it with ROF to create BAE Land Systems. In one stroke, BAE became the UK's only significant player, and soon strengthened its position in the US by acquiring United Defense Industries in 2005, and Armor Holdings two years later. UDI was an important supplier to the US military, boasting the M2/M3 Bradley Fighting Vehicles, M88 Hercules Armored Recovery Vehicle, and M109 Paladin self-propelled howitzer, as well as arguably the most widely-used Armored Personnel Carrier in the world, the M113. Armor, for its part, had taken over development of the Family of Medium Tactical Vehicles, based on a design by Steyr of Austria, just prior to its acquisition by BAE. The only fully protected member of the family was the Caiman MRAP (Mine-Resistant, Ambush-Protected) APC, which the US Army

**Terrier armored digger**
Weighing in at 33 tons (30 tonnes), the Terrier was much more capable than the British Army's previous Combat Engineer Tractor, and could be operated remotely if needed.

operated alongside the Marine Corps' Cougars, but others were installed with armored cabs. Land Systems Hägglunds AB was to produce the Combat Vehicle 90 (Stridsfordon 90) family of tracked IFVs. As well as the original 40 mm Borfors cannon, versios armed with 30 and 35 mm Bushmaster chain

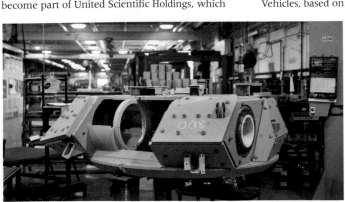

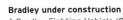

**Bradley under construction**
A Bradley Fighting Vehicle (BFV) turret awaits installation on the assembly line at the BAE Plc Land & Armaments facility in York, Pennsylvania, US.

# "The FIN round rent the air as it tore across the battlefield"

## CAPTAIN TIM PURBRICK, TROOP COMMANDER, QUEEN'S ROYAL IRISH HUSSARS BATTLEGROUP

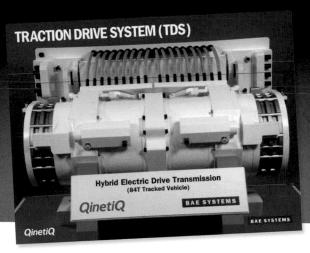

TRACTION DRIVE SYSTEM (TDS)

Hybrid Electric Drive Transmission
(84T Tracked Vehicle)

QinetiQ    BAE SYSTEMS

QinetiQ    BAE SYSTEMS

### Hybrid Electric Drive Transmission

In 2012 BAE unveiled designs for a new Ground Combat Vehicle to replace the Bradley Fighting Vehicle. It featured the first ever hybrid electric tank engine.

gns were sold. Other armament options, including 105 mm rifled and 120 mm smoothbore guns and a turretless APC were also developed. A vehicle installed with BAE's infrared camouflage system, Adaptiv, has been demonstrated. The camouflage is made of individual thermoelectric plates that can combine to replicate the overall heat signature of a variety of everyday objects.

Another Hägglunds product, the BvS10 Armored All-Terrain Vehicle, was adopted by Austria, Britain, France, the Netherlands, and Sweden. Hägglunds

also produced an improved version of the German Leopard 2 MBT, a competitor in international markets for BAE's own Challenger 2, which Vickers demonstrated in 1989 and which entered service with the British Army in 1994. Uniquely among NATO MBTs, Challenger 2 mounted a rifled cannon, the 120 mm, 55-caliber L30A1, which could fire HESH (high-explosive squash head) as well as APFSDS (Armor-Piercing Fin-Stabilizing Discarding-Sabot) rounds. It first saw combat in 2003, during the invasion of Iraq.

Production of Challenger 2 ended in 2002. Since then operational experience has led to the development of add-on armor kits incorporating improved "Dorchester" composite armor, and in the mid-2010s work began on a Life Extension Program to allow

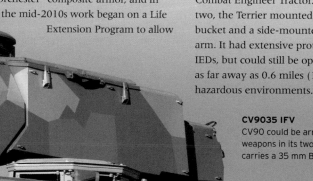

### CV90 Armadillo

BAE offered a range of CV90 Armadillo vehicles. This APC variant carried eight infantrymen and its weapons mount could accommodate machine guns, cannon, or grenade launchers.

it to remain in service beyond 2025. Alongside the MBT, BAE also produced an innovative armored combat engineer vehicle known as the Terrier, which replaced the smaller, less-capable FV180 Combat Engineer Tractor. Manned by a crew of two, the Terrier mounted both a clamshell front bucket and a side-mounted articulated excavator arm. It had extensive protection against mines and IEDs, but could still be operated remotely from as far away as 0.6 miles (1 km) in especially hazardous environments.

### CV9035 IFV

CV90 could be armed with a range of weapons in its two-man turret. This version carries a 35 mm Bushmaster III Chain Gun.

# Army games

The idea of tanks competing against each other started in World War I, with races over a simple course. Feeding the military desire to develop competition and excellence, a number of competitions went on to be established. Beginning in 1963, the Canadian Army Trophy (CAT) saw NATO forces compete to win a small silver trophy of a Centurion tank, which was awarded to the best tank team based on the accuracy of their gunnery. Over the years this competition developed, from tanks simply firing from static positions at static targets, to better reflect likely combat situations. Despite growing rivalry between competitors and high levels of expectation, in 1987 a team from the Royal Hussars in the British Army's new Challenger tank failed miserably. However, ironically, the tank went on to see sterling service in the First Gulf War and still holds the record for the longest range, confirmed tank-on-tank kill—firing an Armor-Piercing Fin Stabilized Discarding Sabot (APFSDS) round a distance of 2.9 miles (4,700 m).

## RUSSIAN TANK BIATHLON

Russia started a biathlon event in 2013, in which tanks fire at targets as they race to complete a route in the fastest time. The route gets progressively harder and penalties are given if targets are missed or the obstacle course is not completed correctly. The value of the event for training or judging equipment may be questionable, but it certainly provides an amazing spectacle.

**A tank crew takes part** in the individual race event of the 2016 Tank Biathlon, held at the Alabino training ground near Moscow.

# Evolution of the Tank

There were surprisingly few truly wrong turns taken along the road to developing the heavy armored fighting vehicle, and it followed a steady progression, incorporating innovations as and when they appeared, such as the rotating turret carrying the main armament. The first vehicle to be equipped in this way was the diminutive Renault FT-17, but from then on the arrangement was virtually ubiquitous—although tanks with multiple turrets appeared, too, like the Vickers A1E1 "Independent," which had no

less than five. There was some uncertainty as to what form the main armament should take—some armies favored light vehicles armed with machine guns—but by the time World War II was underway all had settled on the format we see most commonly today (although some, like the French Char B1 and the American M3 Lee, retained multiple cannon), with a main gun capable of knocking out enemy vehicles, supplemented by machine guns to deal with softer targets.

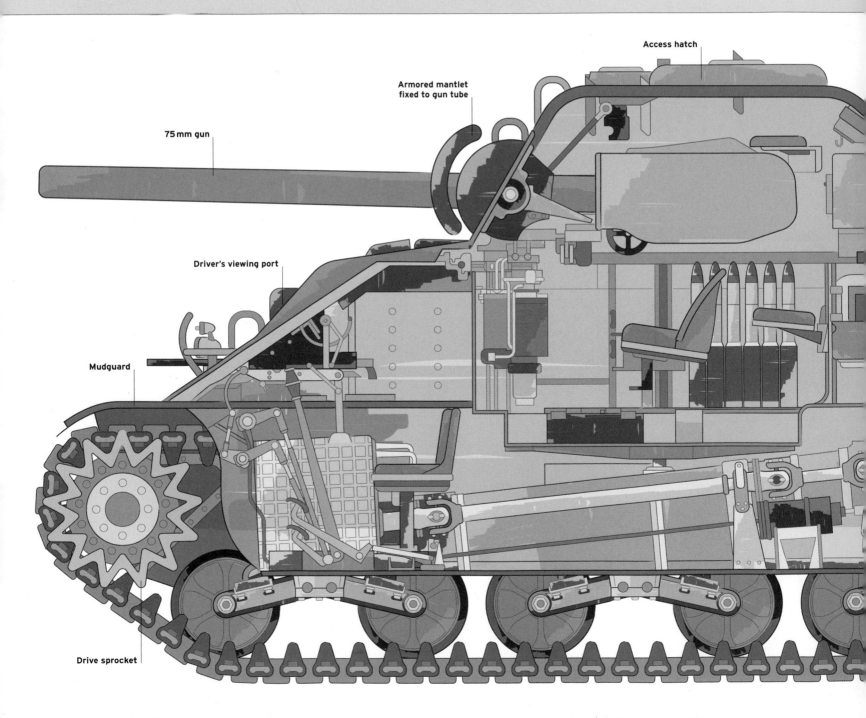

Access hatch

Armored mantlet
fixed to gun tube

75 mm gun

Driver's viewing port

Mudguard

Drive sprocket

## EARLY DESIGN: MARK IV

Early British tanks featured an elongated lozenge shape designed to cross trenches, with the crew, tracks, engine, and armament all contained within the hull. Even as the first British Mark I tanks were going into action during the Somme campaign of 1916, an improved version, to be known as the Mark IV, was taking shape in the mind of Albert Stern, the real driving force behind British tank development. He was unable to change the engine, as he wanted, but specified improved armor and ventilation, exchanged the strip-fed Hotchkiss machine guns for Lewis guns with larger-capacity pan magazines, reduced the size of the gun cupolas, and swapped the guns themselves for models with shorter barrels. He also moved the gas tank outside the vehicle, between the tracks.

Simultaneously, tacticians such as General Elles and Colonel Fuller were working on new ways of employing the tank. The revised vehicle's first outings, on the Ypres salient, were imperfect, but at Cambrai, on November 20, 1917, the attack breached the German frontline across a front 6 miles (9.7 km) wide. Although the attack was ultimately unsuccessful, it established the basic principle of armored warfare.

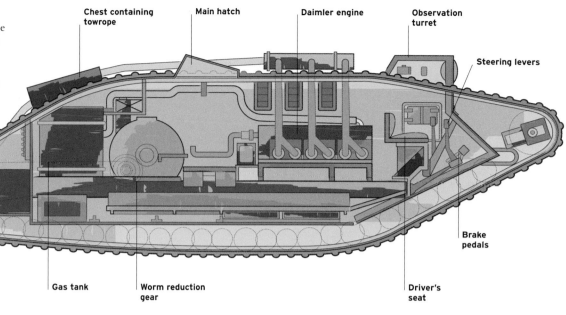

Chest containing towrope — Main hatch — Daimler engine — Observation turret — Steering levers — Brake pedals — Driver's seat — Worm reduction gear — Gas tank

### Manning the Mark IV

In addition to the commander and the driver, two men were required to engage and disengage the gearboxes, and thus steer the vehicle by means of its tracks. Two more manned the 6-pounder guns, and another pair acted as loaders for the 6-pounders and also manned the sponson-mounted machine guns.

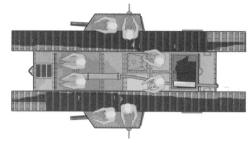

---

Air intakes — Exhaust pipe

## CLASSIC DESIGN: M4A4 SHERMAN

The M4A4 demonstrated the layout that would become the norm for tank design for decades—the main armament in a rotating turret, a rear-mounted engine, and angled hull armor. One of the many subtypes of the M4, the M4A4, known to the British as the Sherman V, was characterized by its Chrysler A57 Multibank engine. A total of 7,499 were produced, and virtually all of them were operated by the British Army, many as Sherman VC Fireflies, with the 17-pounder gun installed in place of the original 75 mm and the machine gunner's position sacrificed to allow more ammunition to be stowed. In all, 49,234 M4 gun tanks weres produced (and many more chassis were completed in other forms, such as engineering vehicles); examples were still in service many years after the end of World War II.

### Manning the M4

As designed, the M4 had a crew of five: the commander, the gunner, and the loader–located in the turret, with the commander directly below the access hatch, behind and raised above the others–and the driver and the machine gunner in the bow of the vehicle, to port and starboard respectively.

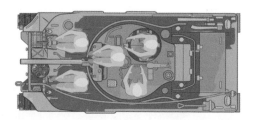

Each track link has a guide — Water pump

# Tank Engines

The earliest tanks to see combat were powered by engines intended for large agricultural tractors (the British Mark I had a 105 hp Daimler-designed sleeve-valve 6-cylinder of 15.9 liters, which unfortunately belched smoke). Several interwar tanks used aircraft engines, such as the American V-12 Liberty, which powered the Mark VIII, BT-2, and BT-5, and early British Cruisers including the A13, Crusader, and Centaur. Other types of aero-engines of various configurations, often down rated, continued to power many Allied tanks throughout World War II, but already there was a move toward purpose-built units. By the 1950s, most tanks were propelled by 12-cylinder gasoline or diesel engines producing at least 750 bhp, many of which were air-cooled, and that de facto standard continued, with power output constantly being increased—even doubled—until well into the last quarter of the 20th century, when gas turbines first appeared, notably in the American M1 Abrams and the Soviet T-80.

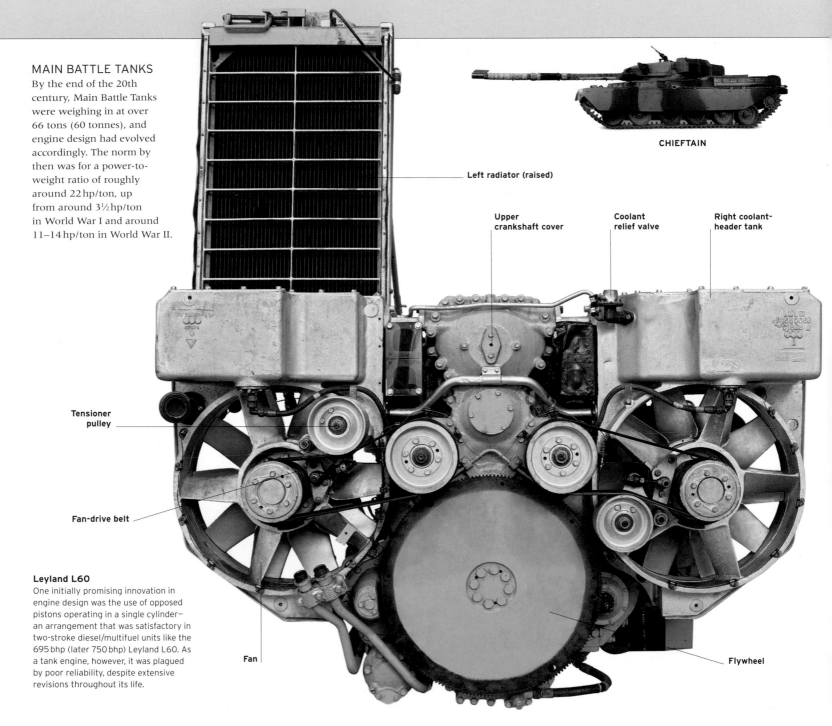

**MAIN BATTLE TANKS**
By the end of the 20th century, Main Battle Tanks were weighing in at over 66 tons (60 tonnes), and engine design had evolved accordingly. The norm by then was for a power-to-weight ratio of roughly around 22 hp/ton, up from around 3½ hp/ton in World War I and around 11–14 hp/ton in World War II.

**CHIEFTAIN**

Left radiator (raised)

Upper crankshaft cover

Coolant relief valve

Right coolant-header tank

Tensioner pulley

Fan-drive belt

**Leyland L60**
One initially promising innovation in engine design was the use of opposed pistons operating in a single cylinder—an arrangement that was satisfactory in two-stroke diesel/multifuel units like the 695 bhp (later 750 bhp) Leyland L60. As a tank engine, however, it was plagued by poor reliability, despite extensive revisions throughout its life.

Fan

Flywheel

## OTHER KEY ENGINES

From the sheer variety of engine types employed in tanks through the years, it is clear that their designers were given a very free reign. Some stuck closely to existing principles and produced inline units, others chose to employ radial power plants originally intended for aircraft—and then there were those who thought laterally, producing units like the Chrysler A57 Multibank, which could reasonably be described as a multiple radial. Despite its unconventional character, it proved to be extremely reliable, although routine maintenance tasks on it, such as changing spark plugs, were rather difficult.

### RICARDO 150HP

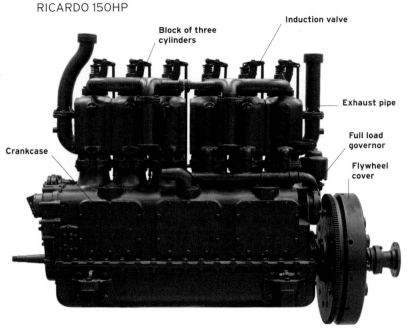

Block of three cylinders

Induction valve

Exhaust pipe

Full load governor

Flywheel cover

Crankcase

Harry Ricardo, an extremely talented independent engine designer, was asked to solve the problem of the telltale smoke produced by the Daimler unit installed in the first generation of British tanks. Instead of adapting the engine, he came up with a new design that produced significantly more power, and which was adopted for the Mark V tank.

**MARK V TANK**

### WRIGHT CONTINENTAL R-975

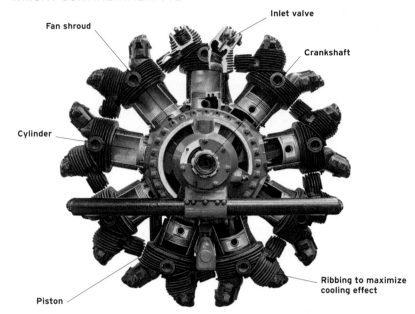

Fan shroud

Inlet valve

Crankshaft

Cylinder

Ribbing to maximize cooling effect

Piston

In 1939, the US Army chose a version of the supercharged, air-cooled Wright R-975 radial engine to power a new generation of tanks, starting with the M2 Medium. Produced by Continental Motors, it later found its way into variants of the M3 Grant/Lee, M4 Shermans, and the M18 Hellcat tank destroyer.

**M18 HELLCAT**

### KHARKIV V-2

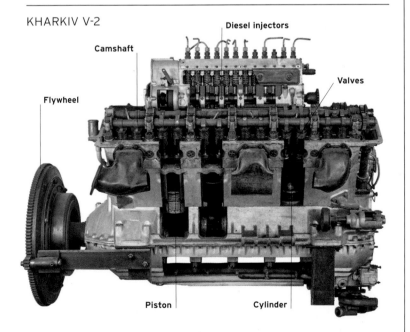

Diesel injectors

Camshaft

Valves

Flywheel

Piston

Cylinder

Until the T-34 appeared, all Soviet tanks had gasoline engines. The designer of the powerplant for the new tank stuck to the V-12 arrangement of the T-28, but switched to diesel fuel, and reduced the size and capacity (from 46.9 liters to 38.8 liters) while achieving the same 500 bhp output.

**T-34**

### CHRYSLER A57 MULTIBANK

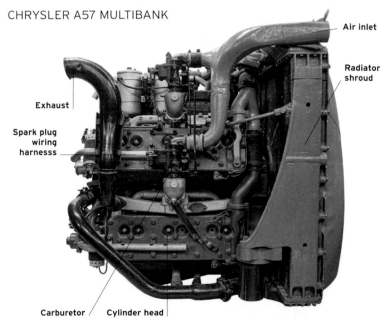

Air inlet

Radiator shroud

Exhaust

Spark plug wiring harnesss

Carburetor

Cylinder head

Engineers at Chrysler's new Detroit Tank Arsenal were instructed to come up with an alternative to the Wright radial engine, and took an innovative approach, using five off-the-shelf 6-cylinder blocks and mating them to a purpose-built crankcase, the 30 pistons driving a single crankshaft. No other changes were needed to produce 425 hp.

**M4A4 SHERMAN**

# Tracks and Suspension

British tanks of World War I had no sprung suspension system at all: the tracks simply ran over fixed rollers. As a result, the ride was nothing short of chaotic, and crew members risked serious injury. The French Schneider and St. Chamond used simple leaf and coiled spring systems, which were only marginally better, although the light FT-17 improved on the basic principle. J. Walter Christie's original hybrid system, as demonstrated in 1919, was a real step forward, as was the leaf-spring system adopted for the Vickers Medium in 1922. However, it was not until Christie unveiled his M1928, with lengthened suspension travel, that top speed increased dramatically—even if it was rejected by the armed forces of his native US, and only adopted by the UK and the Soviet Union. In the meantime, more complex Horstmann and volute-spring systems became popular, but both eventually gave way to much simpler, and cheaper, torsion bars.

## CONTINUOUS TRACK

It was accepted from the outset that the most reliable way of moving a heavy armored vehicle across the battlefield was by way of "continuous" tracks, even though the system had some drawbacks, including high cost, low durability, and the vulnerability of the entire vehicle if a single track segment was damaged. The design of the tracks themselves and the way in which links were joined was a matter of concern, too, as were factors such as whether they should be driven from the rear or from the front—which determined whether the upper, "return," track or the load-bearing lower one should be under tension; each had their pros and cons. Finally, there was the issue of where the tracks should be located and how they should be held in place.

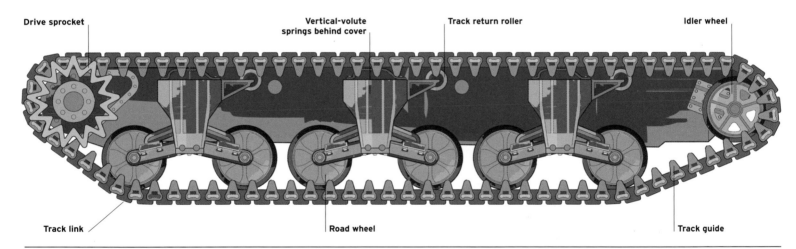

**Drive sprocket**

**Vertical-volute springs behind cover**

**Track return roller**

**Idler wheel**

**Track link**

**Road wheel**

**Track guide**

## TYPES OF TRACK

The earliest continuous tracks were simple strips of metal that were connected by hinges to form a closed loop. They were unable to move sideways, and thus were easily shed, and were prone to slippage. It was more than a decade before designs evolved that enabled lateral movement by means of track guides and grips that provided adequate traction on both hard and soft ground.

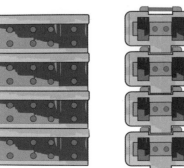

**Tank Mark IV**
The earliest tracks had link-wide hinges and shallow flanges for grip.

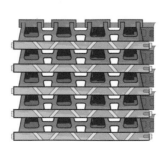

**Vickers Medium**
The Medium had narrow links with short hinges that provided flexibility.

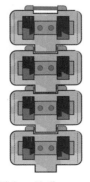

**PzKpfw IV Tiger**
The Tiger had wide, aggressive tracks for combat and narrower ones for transportation.

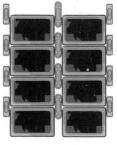

**M1 Abrams**
Like many modern tanks, the Abrams' tracks have removable rubber pads.

### DRIVE SPROCKETS

Although they started out as simple toothed wheels, drive sprockets evolved into much more complex assemblies over the years, incorporating reduction gears and a free-wheeling capability. They are mounted at the rear of most modern tanks, putting the lower track run under tension, which reduces wear on all major components.

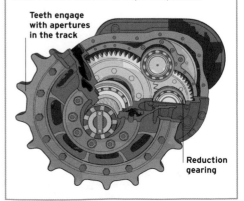

**Teeth engage with apertures in the track**

**Reduction gearing**

## TYPES OF TANK SUSPENSION

There have been six successful suspension systems employed in tracked armored fighting vehicles, and several more that were abandoned. Of the successful ones, five relied on the most significant physical property of spring steel: its determination to return to the form in which it was manufactured at the earliest possible opportunity. The most effective of these "spring" systems is the torsion bar, which is the only one still in widespread use today. The sixth system is the active hydropneumatic arrangement, which was first employed in Citröen passenger cars in the mid-1950s.

### LEAF SPRING

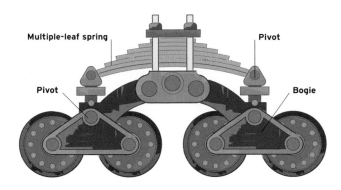

In use since medieval times, leaf springs are the simplest form of sprung suspension. Strips, or "leaves," of arced, highly resistant steel are stacked together and mounted so that they absorb the upward pressure of a wheel, pair of wheels, or pair of wheel bogies (as above), and then return to their original configuration.

### CHRISTIE

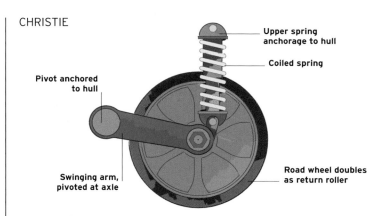

Developed by J. Walter Christie as part of his efforts to improve overall tank design, this simple system incorporated a coiled spring, which he first mounted vertically, although later horizontal versions proved to be more effective. The large-diameter road wheels acted as return rollers and were mounted in pairs with the track guides running between them.

### VOLUTE SPRING

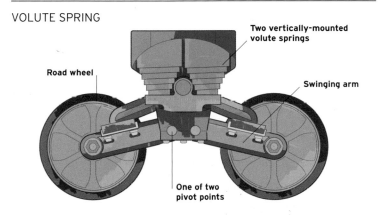

A volute spring is a coil-wound leaf spring, the center of which is then pulled out to form a truncated cone. It acts in compression, the coils sliding over each other, and can be mounted vertically (as above) or horizontally. Volute springs were commonly mounted in tandem pairs on a bogie; road wheels acted on the springs by way of swinging arms.

### HORTSMANN

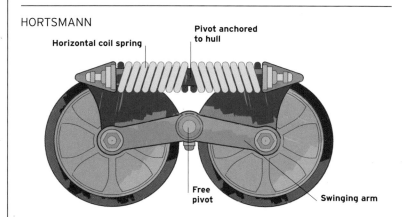

In the Horstmann system, paired road wheels are mounted on swinging arms, the upward motion of which is cushioned by the compression of springs mounted horizontally between them. It is similar to the horizontal volute-spring system, but improves on it: unlike the volute spring, the coiled spring operates in both extension and compression, and so increases wheel travel.

### TORSION BAR

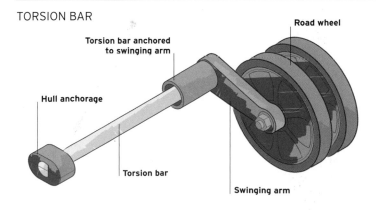

Torsion bar suspension also relies on the "memory" of yield-resistant spring steel to maintain its original configuration—in this case as a rod anchored at one end to the tank's chassis. As its name suggests, the pressure takes the form of a twisting motion imparted by an arm connecting the rod's free end to the road wheel's axle.

### HYDROPNEUMATIC

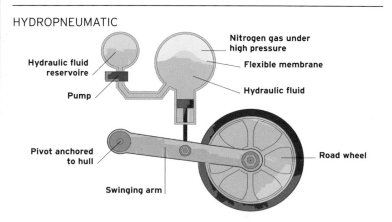

In this system, each road wheel is attached to a sphere containing two chambers—an upper one containing nitrogen gas under high pressure, and a lower one containing hydraulic fluid—with a flexible membrane in between. A pump pressurizes the fluid, to which additional pressure is applied from the road wheel when under load; the gas compresses, thus acting as a spring.

# Firepower

In tank warfare, the shape of things to come was sketched out near Villers-Bretonneux on April 24, 1918, when British and German tanks met for the first time. The British prevailed, thanks to one of their vehicles being a "male," armed with two 6-pounder QF guns. During the interwar period, however, tank-on-tank encounters were not uppermost in the minds of designers or strategists, and it took exposure to a new type of mechanized warfare during World War II to shake the belief that the primary role of the tank was to support infantry. This remained important, but as tank armour grew thicker, guns and ammunition had to grow increasingly specialized in order to reliably penetrate it. In 1945 most tank guns firing AP rounds had muzzle velocities of around 2,800ft/s (850m/s), and could penetrate roughly 6-8in (150-200mm) of armour at 328ft (100m). By 2010 this had increased to over 5,750ft/s (1,750m/s) with APFSDS, giving penetration of over 23.6in (600mm) at 6,560ft (2,000m).

## MACHINE GUNS

Tanks will always be vulnerable at close quarters against determined infantry, with machine guns being the usual defence. Most modern tanks mount at least two—one coaxially (i.e on the same axis) with the main gun, and one mounted on the roof that is aimed independently. Up until the late 1940s, most tanks also had a bow machine gun in the front of the hull. This provided extra firepower, but was difficult to aim. It also created a weak point in the frontal armor. As main-gun ammunition increased in size, the space was instead used to store more of it. Coaxial and bow machine guns are usually of around 7.62mm/0.3in caliber. Roof-mounted guns often fire heavier 12.7mm/0.5in rounds. On some tanks this weapon can be aimed and fired from inside the vehicle.

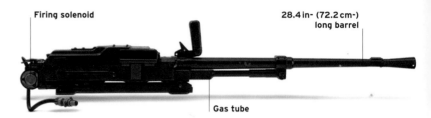

**PKT 7.62mm machine gun**
The PKT was developed by Mikhail Kalashnikov from his AK assault rifle, but chambered for the longer and more powerful 7.62 x 54mm rimmed round. As it was mounted coaxially, the sights, butt, bipod, and trigger were not fitted. Instead, an electrically fired solenoid trigger unit was installed and the tanks' sights were used for aiming.

Labels: Firing solenoid · 28.4in- (72.2cm-) long barrel · Gas tube

**Vickers Mark VI .303in machine gun**
Variants of the Vickers machine gun, including the Mark VI, were used as a secondary armament in a number of British tanks during the interwar period. They were gradually replaced in tanks by Browning and Besa machine guns in the early 1940s, although the Vickers continued to be used elsewhere until the 1960s.

Labels: Cocking lever · Water cooling jacket

**Browning M2 .50-caliber machine gun**
One of a number of highly reliable recoil-operated designs developed by John Moses Browning, the M2 has been used by infantry, on armored and unarmored vehicles, aboard ship, and on aircraft since the 1920s. When fitted to a tank, it is invariably roof-mounted and aimed by the commander.

Labels: 45in (114.3cm)-long heavy barrel · Trigger · Barrel shroud

## MAIN GUNS

The development of the tank's main gun has been largely linear. Size, both in terms of caliber and barrel length, has steadily increased in order to fire more powerful ammunition, but the fundamental principle of a high-velocity, direct-fire weapon remains. Many of the innovations in tank gunnery have been in fire control systems, ensuring that this weapon can hit its target as often as possible. Modern systems integrate stabilizers, laser range finders, high-magnification thermal sights, and ballistic computers to allow highly accurate fire at extreme range under any conditions. Another innovation is the autoloader, which uses a mechanical system rather than a crew member to select and load ammunition. Many recent tanks are armed with smoothbore guns, which fire projectiles stabilized by fins rather than spinning. Smoothbores can also be used to fire guided missiles.

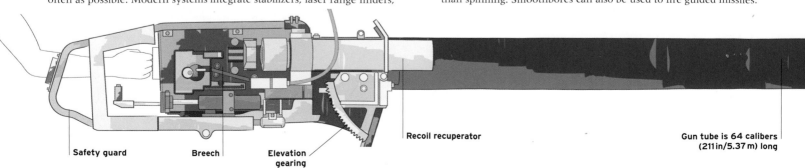

Labels: Safety guard · Breech · Elevation gearing · Recoil recuperator · Gun tube is 64 calibers (211in/5.37 m) long

## HIGH-EXPLOSIVE SQUASH HEAD

Developed in Britain in the late 1940s, HESH rounds have a very short delay in their fuse. This gives them time to expand across the surface of the armor on impact before detonation. Their explosive force causes partial disintegration of the plate, which drives lethal fragments of metal off the inner surface of the armor, potentially killing crewmen inside the tank.

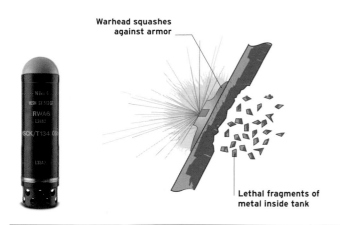

**Warhead squashes against armor**

**Lethal fragments of metal inside tank**

## HIGH-EXPLOSIVE ANTITANK

HEAT rounds utilize a shaped charge to produce a "superplastic" jet of molten metal that punches its way through armor plate. It does not burn through: the effect is caused exclusively by kinetic energy. This Munroe effect, as it is also known, is widely used in antitank grenades. HEAT rounds are less effective against composite armor containing ceramic plates.

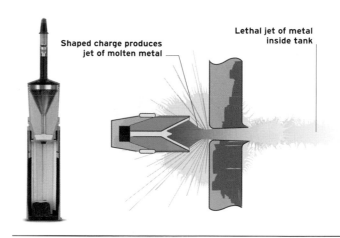

**Shaped charge produces jet of molten metal**

**Lethal jet of metal inside tank**

## ARMOR-PIERCING FIN-STABILIZED DISCARDING SABOT

APFSDS rounds are the most effective antitank weapons on the modern battlefield. The penetrator dart is made from a highly dense material, often tungsten or depleted uranium, as this maximizes its mass and therefore armor penetration. APFSDS rounds do not spin, since this reduces armor penetration, instead relying on their fins for stability in flight.

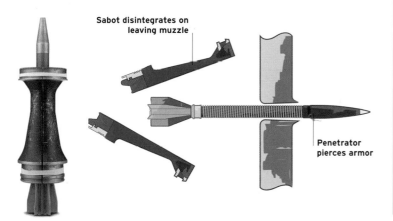

**Sabot disintegrates on leaving muzzle**

**Penetrator pierces armor**

## ARMOR-PIERCING DISCARDING SABOT

APDS rounds were developed during World War II. Unlike earlier Kinetic Energy rounds, it uses a subcaliber (i.e. smaller than the gun barrel) penetrator encased in a sabot. This design allows for the highest possible velocity, which maximizes armor penetration, combined with the best aerodynamic performance, which ensures high accuracy.

**Sabot disintegrates on leaving muzzle**

**Penetrator pierces armor**

**Rifling imparts spin to projectiles to increase accuracy**

**CENTURION MARK 3**

**Muzzle counterweight**

### Ordnance QF 20-pounder
The 20-pounder armed the FV4007 Centurion Mk 3 tank, in service with the British Army (and many others) from 1948. This was a much more powerful weapon than its predecessor, the wartime 17-pounder. It had a caliber of 3,28 in (83.4 mm), and could fire APCBC and APDS antitank rounds, as well as HE, canister, and smoke shells.

**SHELL SIZES**

The effort to produce increasingly powerful main gun ammunition to counter ever-thicker armor had an entirely predictable effect: the projectiles got bigger, the charge needed to launch them increased proportionately, and so did the length of the cartridge case containing it.

**2-pounder**   **75mm**   **85mm**   **88mm**

# Protection

When tanks were conceived, they were imagined to have one sole function: to precede attacking infantry across no-man's-land and give them protection from enemy machine gun fire by supressing it with their own guns and machine guns. They themselves had to be protected, which meant equipping them with 0.47 in (12 mm) of rolled steel armor on their exposed front faces, although that soon increased to 0.55 in (14 mm) to withstand the armor-piercing 7.92 mm K bullet.

However, it was not possible to make armor thick enough to protect against the German 7.7 cm field gun, which was soon in an antitank role. By the 1930s, effective antitank guns had also appeared—and had of course found their way into tanks. Thus a vicious circle was established, with ever more powerful antitank guns being created and put into tanks, and designers piling heavier and heavier armor onto their vehicles in the hope, often forlorn, of staying ahead of the opposition.

## ARMOR

The earliest type of armor consisted of plates of rolled steel, which were made by passing cast billets between rollers until the metal was the desired thickness. This repeated compression had the effect of aligning the molecules in the steel, which toughened the material. The next stage was face hardenening, which saw the plates reheated on a bed of granular carbon, a process known as "carburizing" (the two types were often employed together, to produce what was known as "cemented" armor—a process developed in Germany by Krupp). From then on it was necessary to introduce alloys such as chromium, molybdenum, nickel, and later tungsten to produce a tougher product. Some antitank rounds burn through armor rather than penetrating by kinetic energy and to combat these, layers of ceramic blocks were introduced, giving modern vehicles their distinctive angular appearance. Such armor is often known as "Chobham," after the Surrey town where it was developed, and is invulnerable to AT rounds.

**Light armor**
Small, light tanks such as the British Mark VIB sacrificed armor weight for the sake of speed, maneuverability, and transportablity.

**Heavy armor**
Large, heavy vehicles such as the German Jagtiger sacrificed speed and maneuverability for the sake of protection.

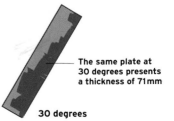

**Composite armor**
Modern vehicles such as the Israeil Merkava Mark 4 are both fast and maneuverable, being protected by composite armor, which is generally lighter than all-metal alternatives.

**PzKpfw VI Tiger armor**
Somewhat surprisingly, the Tiger's designers at Henschel u Söhne chose nearly vertical armor for their heavy tank, relying on thickness rather than geometry to defeat Allied antitank weapons. Only the front glacis was acutely sloped, at 13 degrees to the horizontal, while other sloped faces (the front and sides of the hull and turret) were at just 9 degrees from the vertical.

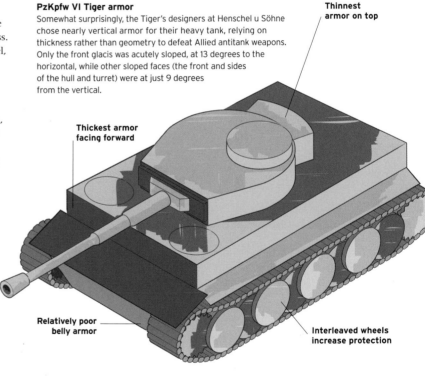

Thinnest armor on top

Thickest armor facing forward

Relatively poor belly armor

Interleaved wheels increase protection

| | 25 mm | | 60 mm | | 80–100 mm | | 100–120 mm |

### SLOPED AND UNSLOPED ARMOR COMPARED

Setting armor at an angle to the vertical offers two advantages. Firstly, the angle increases the thickess of the armor to be penetrated. Secondly, it makes it likelier that an antitank projectile, especially one with an curved profile, will be deflected away from the tank and so expend itself uselessly.

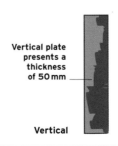

Vertical plate presents a thickness of 50 mm

Vertical

The same plate at 30 degrees presents a thickness of 71 mm

30 degrees

## BAR ARMOR

Fitting light armored vehicles with bar armor is an inexpensive way of improving their overall level of protection by mounting a framework of hardened steel bars (usually horizontally) over vulnerable areas. Such protection is ineffective against kinetic energy rounds such as APFSDS, and of only limited efficacy against HESH rounds, but it can defeat lightweight HEAT rounds such as those delivered by grenade launchers like the RPG-7, which such vehicles will often encounter—by detonating them before they reach the bodywork of the vehicle itself.

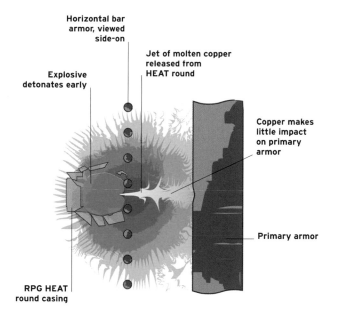

Horizontal bar armor, viewed side-on

Explosive detonates early

Jet of molten copper released from HEAT round

Copper makes little impact on primary armor

Primary armor

RPG HEAT round casing

## EXPLOSIVE REACTIVE ARMOR

An alternative form of supplementary armor, Explosive Reactive Armor (ERA) consists of a layer of relatively thin armor plating with a backing of high explosive. When the exposed armor plate is struck by a HEAT projectile, the jet of molten metal formed in the incoming round's warhead pierces it in the usual way, but then detonates the high explose charge beneath, which reacts by blowing the entire panel off the target vehicle before the HEAT round can penetrate its main defensive armor. It can be defeated by so-called "tandem charge" HEAT rounds, which employ two charges, the second detonating milliseconds after the first, by which time the armor has been exposed.

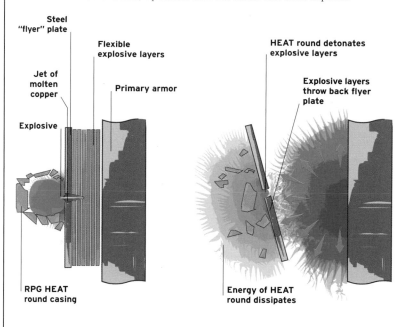

Steel "flyer" plate

Flexible explosive layers

Jet of molten copper

Primary armor

Explosive

RPG HEAT round casing

HEAT round detonates explosive layers

Explosive layers throw back flyer plate

Energy of HEAT round dissipates

## SMOKE GRENADES

Smoke has long been used to screen or obscure targets on the battlefield. Modern smoke grenades work in both the visual and infrared ends of the spectrum, meaning that tanks can also be hidden from thermal imaging systems. Since the 1940s, the method of choice for delivering smoke has been by means of grenades launched from projectors usually located on the vehicle's turret. These can be fired from within the vehicle, and a salvo of grenades will quickly form a large screen.

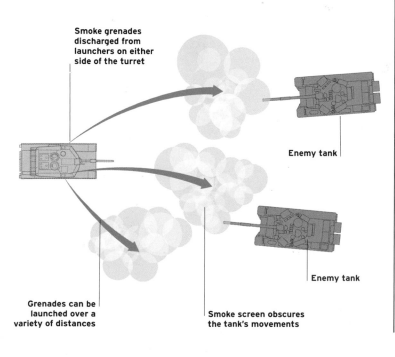

Smoke grenades discharged from launchers on either side of the turret

Enemy tank

Grenades can be launched over a variety of distances

Smoke screen obscures the tank's movements

Enemy tank

## CAMOUFLAGE

The intricate paint scheme on the first tanks was intended to hide them from enemy guns. Ever since, camouflage has become more sophisticated in order to defeat increasingly capable sensors. Methods have included paint, infrared suppressive paint, and thermal cladding.

**Challenger 2 thermal insulation**
The easiest way to detect a large vehicle in poor visibility is by means of its thermal image, or the heat it gives off. A surprising degree of protection can be achieved simply by equipping the vehicle with thermal insulation—such as the Solar Shield system fitted to this Challenger 2.

**PL-01 radiation-absorbent coating**
The experimental Polish PL-01 tank is coated with radiation-absorbent material, which "soaks up" all forms of electromagnetic radiation, including radar. This techonology exists in a variety of types, and is similar to that used in so-called stealth aircraft.

# Antitank Weapons

The first effective antitank weapons were steel-cored rifle bullets for the 7.92 mm Mauser rifle that proved able to pierce the armor of Mark I and Mark II tanks. Mauserwerke was then instructed to develop something more powerful, and responded with the first purpose-built AT weapon—the 13.2 mm Tankgewehr M1918 rifle. However, it was not until 1928 that a true antitank gun, the German PAK36, appeared. It was soon adopted as a tank gun, as were other nations' towed AT guns, such as the British 2- and 6-pounders. From then on, as armor grew thicker, AT guns became more powerful and significantly larger, culminating in the 17-pounder, the PAK43, and the Soviet ZiS-2. Meanwhile, more effective and lighter infantry AT weapons, including mines, grenades, and recoilless guns, were being developed, as were vehicles designed specifically to hunt and kill tanks. Since the 1960s, guided missiles, whether carried by infantry or on vehicles, have also become increasingly common.

**Hawkins No. 75 grenade**
The No. 75 could be used as a grenade or, more effectively, as a mine.

**RKG-3 grenade**
On being released, a parachute deployed from the RKG, ensuring that it struck nose-down.

**Tellermine 35**
Filled with 12 lb (5.5 kg) of TNT, the Tellermine 35 was triggered by 198 lb (90 kg) of pressure.

**Mauser T-Gewehr M1918**
The single-shot, bolt-action T-Gewehr 18 weighed 41 lb (18.5 kg) loaded and with its bipod in place. Its round could pierce .87 in (22 mm) of armor at 330 ft (100 m), but its recoil was fearsome.

**Barrel** incorporates a recoil compensator

**Boys Mk 1 antitank rifle**
Though able to pierce only 0.9 in (23 mm) of armor at 300 ft (90 m), the .55 in-caliber Boys AT Rifle, skillfully used, proved effective against German PzKpfw IIs during the Battle of France in 1940.

**Panzerfaust**
This simple rocket-propelled grenade launcher was very effective at close range. Toward the end of World War II, it was issued to German troops in large numbers.

**Warhead**

**Projector, Infantry, Antitank (PIAT)**
PIAT was actually a spigot mortar that fired a 3 lb (1.36 kg) bomb with a shaped-charge warhead, which could penetrate 3 in (75 mm) of armor at 360 ft (110 m).

**Switch** ignites propellant charge

**RPG-7**
The RPG-7's two-stage propellant charge gives it a range of over 3,300 ft (1,000 m)—at which its HEAT warhead can still penetrate 20 in (500 mm) of armor.

**Gun shield**

**Handles**
used to split trail into firing position

**Vertically-acting**
sliding breech block

**Recoil**
compensator

**ZiS-2**
The 57mm-caliber ZiS-2 went into production in mid-1941. Manufacturing ceased within six months, but restarted again in 1943, when it became clear that its intended upgrade, the 76mm ZiS-3, was inadequate. Semiautomatic, the ZiS-2 could fire 25 rounds per minute.

### Sd.Kfz 302/303 Goliath

A self-propelled, wire-guided mine carrying up to 220 lb (100 kg) of explosive, powered either by batteries or a 2-stroke gas engine, Goliath was an early attempt at introducing unmanned vehicles to the battlefield. It was unsuccessful due to the vulnerability of its guide cables and its low speed.

### Humber Hornet

Introduced in 1958 to deploy the Anglo-Australian Malkara optically-tracked wire-guided missile, the Hornet was air portable and could be dropped by parachute. Malkara was the most powerful missile of its type, with a 60 lb (27 kg) warhead. It could destroy any tank then in service.

### M10 Achilles

A British modification of the American M10, mounting the 17-pounder antitank gun, the Achilles had an excellent combat record, due largely to its ability to pierce 7.6 in (192 mm) of armor at a range of 3,300 ft (1,000 m) with APDS projectiles. It saw service from 1944.

### M56 Scorpion

A short-lived and unsuccessful attempt to produce a lightweight tank destroyer for airborne units, the Scorpion was simply an M54 90 mm AT gun mounted on an unarmored aluminium body. Inside, there was room only for ammunition, the engine, and a driver.

### FV102 Striker

The antitank guided-missile-launcher member of the CVR(T) family, Striker carried five Swingfire wire-guided missiles in a launcher at the rear, with five reloads. The missiles could be launched and guided remotely, allowing the vehicle to remain hidden.

**Observation** ports

**Launcher** holds five missiles

**Smoke grenade** launchers

**Drive sprocket** at front

# Uniforms and Protective Clothing

The ineffective or nonexistent suspension in the first tanks meant that even driving was risky for the crews. They were left to hang on and hope to avoid broken bones and cracked heads as they carried out their roles. Added to that, in combat there was the danger of "splash"—molten metal from bullets and shell fragments entering the tank through the gaps between the sheets of armor plating—and "spalling" (lethal fragments chipped from the tank's own armor) if the tank took a direct hit from a heavier weapon. Some protective clothing was available, but where it was effective it was often too restrictive to be practical. Later generations of vehicles were much easier on the crew, and by the time of World War II, the only protection generally worn was a helmet, and uniforms were often little more than coveralls. Combat experience revealed the dangers of fire, and more recently tank crews have been issued with purpose-designed fireproof clothing.

**Coveralls**
One-piece cotton coveralls were worn over breeches and tunics. They ranged in color from black through blue to grey with matching cloth belts.

**Telogreika**
The winter uniform was made of cotton duck cloth padded with cotton batting.

**Sergeant's stripes**

### T-34 TANK CREWMAN'S KIT
Russian tank crews of World War II were consistently better supplied than their adversaries, especially during the cold weather. Nevertheless, their clothing was strictly utilitarian, displaying none of the decorative elements sometimes found in other armies.

**Helmet and goggles**
After 1941, cowhide helmets were replaced by canvas padded with kapok. Goggles protected against wind and dust only; their glass was not shatterproof.

**PISTOL HOLSTER**

**Spare magazine**

**Tokarev TT Model 1933**
The Tokarev was widely issued to all ranks. Chambered for the 7.62 x 25 mm round, it lacked the firepower of handguns issued in other armies.

**Eight-round magazine**

**Schuba**
In particularly cold conditions, troops were issued with these three-quarter length sheepskin coats.

**Sapogi**
The tankman's *Sapogi*, worn over bandages, not socks, had rubber soles, with no hobnails or heel and toe irons. Only the lower part of the boot was leather, the rest was synthetic rubber or rubberized canvas.

**US 1ST ARMORED DIVISION**

**BRITISH ROYAL TANK REGIMENT**

**GERMAN WORLD WAR II TANK BATTLE BADGE**

**SOVIET WORLD WAR II "EXCELLENT TANKER"**

## TANK INSIGNIA

Since their inception, tank crews have been considered an elite force. As with other elite units they have made use of distinctive badges and insignia to celebrate this.

Some were awarded on completion of crew training, others after taking part in combat. The British Tank Arm Badge was the first to be introduced, during World War I.

## UNIFORMS OF WORLD WAR II

Tank crews during World War II wore a wide variety of uniforms, depending on their environment. Much of it was similar to that of their comrades fighting on foot, especially in extreme conditions such as the desert, but specialized clothing was also developed to meet their needs. As tank crews are usually seated and cannot move around to keep warm, their clothing was often more heavily padded, and featured pockets in places accessible when sitting down, such as the lower leg. Waist-length jackets, to prevent them bunching up while seated, were common, as was the use of smooth-faced material such as leather, and clothing with minimal external features like straps so that crews did not risk getting snagged on their tank as they tried to evacuate in an emergency.

Rank badges (in this case three "pips") worn on epaulet

7.65 mm Modèle 1935A pistol in button-down holster

**CAPT., 3RD KOH, BRITISH ARMY**

**SGT., CHAR DE COMBAT, FRENCH ARMY**

French pattern metal helmet worn over beret

Three-quarter length French pattern leather jacket

**TANKMAN, POLISH ARMY**

Winged eagle, insignia of the Wehrmacht

Bergmütze peaked field cap

Knee-high, lace-up boots were impractical in desert conditions

**GEFREITER, 15TH PANZER DIVISION, GERMAN ARMY**

Pre-1941-pattern helmet in padded cowhide

Large button-down patch pocket

**TANKMAN, RED ARMY**

### HELMETS

Protective steel helmets as issued to infantrymen were of very little use to tank crew, who risked not bullet wounds but cracked skulls as their unsprung vehicles bounced across the battlefield.

**UK World War I**
British crews wore boiled cowhide helmets, some of which had visors and chain-mail masks for the lower face (not shown).

**UK World War II**
Since they often went into battle with open hatches, British tank crews were issued with steel helmets for protection.

**Soviet 1960s**
The Red Army issued helmets with padded ribs well into the 1960s, although by then provision was made for wearing earphones.

**UK contemporary**
As is common today, British crews wear lightweight helmets made of composite materials. Earphones are worn separately.

**US contemporary**
American tankmen wear ergonomically-designed helmets that incorporate earphones and microphones.

# Glossary

**Action**
The method of loading and/or firing a gun.

**Active Protection System (APS)**
A method of defeating antitank weapons that does not rely on armor. Passive systems use jamming and smoke to defeat missile guidance systems. Active systems use projectiles to shoot down the missile.

**Amphibious vehicle**
A vehicle that can swim across water as well as drive on land.

**Antitank Guided Missile (ATGM)**
Also known as ATGW (Antitank Guided Weapon). A term covering weapons intended to destroy tanks that can be controlled in flight by the firer. Guidance can take the form of radio, infrared imaging, laser homing, or even a length of wire connecting the missile to the launcher.

**Appliqué armor**
Add-on armor plates that can be mounted onto the hull or turret of an AFV to increase protection.

**Armored car**
A lightweight wheeled armored fighting vehicle used for reconnaissance and armed escort duties.

**Armored Fighting Vehicle (AFV)**
An armed and well-armored combat vehicle. Combining battlefield mobility, offensive capabilities, and armor protection, AFVs can include tanks, armored cars, troop carriers, amphibious vehicles, air defense vehicles, and self-propelled artillery.

**Armored Personnel Carrier (APC)**
A type of AFV designed to transport infantry to the battlefield, where they are dropped off to fight on their own. APCs are usually lightly armed and armored.

**Armor Piercing (AP)**
A type of ammunition that relies on its kinetic energy rather than explosive power to defeat armor. Types of AP ammunition include APC, APCBC, HVAP, APDS, and APFSDS.

**Armor Piercing Capped (APC)**
An Armor-Piercing round fitted with a softer cap to prevent the round from shattering on impact with armor plate.

**Armor Piercing Capped Ballistic Cap (APCBC)**
An APC round fitted with a thin aerodynamic nose cone to ensure its velocity remains high throughout its flight. The nose does not affect the round's armor penetration ability.

**Armor Piercing Discarding Sabot (APDS)**
A projectile of a caliber smaller than that of the barrel in which it is fired, and so is carried by a casing or "sabot" inside the barrel. Once fired, the sabot falls away. APDS rounds have greater armor penetration than full-caliber projectiles.

**Armor Piercing Fin Stabilized Discarding Sabot (APFSDS)**
An APFSDS round uses the same design principle as APDS. Unlike APDS it does not spin and is stabilized by fins like a dart. APFSDS rounds are longer, travel faster, and can penetrate more armor than APDS. It is the most effective armor-piercing round used by modern tanks.

**Armor Piercing High Explosive (APHE)**
An AP round that contains a small explosive charge. This detonates after the round has penetrated the target's armor, causing much more damage inside the tank than a conventional AP round.

**Autoloader**
A device designed to insert shells into the breech of the main gun of a tank. It replaces the loader, or crewman dedicated to loading the gun.

**Automatic**
A gun that continuously loads and fires while its trigger is pressed.

**Ball mount**
A spherical machine-gun mount usually located on the frontal plate of a tank's hull. Unlike a fixed or coaxial mount, a ball mount moves independently of other weapons, giving the gunner greater flexibility when aiming. Ball mounts fell out of favor after World War II.

**Bar armor**
Also known as slat armor or cage armor, bar armor is a mesh of steel bars that is added to an AFV's hull to protect it against RPGs.

**Battalion**
A military unit consisting of around 700 soldiers or 30–50 tanks. It is made up of companies or squadrons. Battalions can operate independently for limited periods.

**Bogie**
An arrangement of wheels, typically featuring two pairs.

**Bore**
The internal diameter of a gun barrel.

**Bow**
The front end of a tank.

**Breacher vehicle**
An armored vehicle outfitted with equipment such as a plough or dozer blade that is designed to drive through minefields, clearing a path for troops and vehicles.

**Breech**
The closed rear end of a gun's barrel. It is opened to receive ammunition.

**Bridge layer**
Officially known as an Armored Vehicle-Launched Bridge (AVLB), a bridge layer is a combat support vehicle that can deploy and retrieve a removable metal bridge to enable tanks and other AFVs to cross rivers, craters, trenches, and other obstacles.

**Bridging weight**
The weight classification of a vehicle used to calculate what kind of bridge it can cross safely.

**Brigade**
A military unit made up of regiment- or battalion-size units. Its strength is usually around 5,000 soldiers.

**Caliber**
The internal diameter of a gun barrel. Since the 1950s this has almost always been expressed in millimeters (mm).

**Canister shot**
An antipersonnel round intended to give tanks and artillery protection from infantry. Canister rounds contain a large number of small, nonexplosive projectiles. When fired, the canister disintegrates, releasing the projectiles onto the enemy at high velocity.

**Cartridge**
A unit of ammunition consisting of a projectile and a brass or steel case containing its propellant.

**Ceramic plate**
A component of composite armor.

**Chain gun**
A machine gun or cannon that uses a motor-driven chain to power its moving parts, rather than gas or recoil from the fired round.

**Chobham armor**
Chobham armor is the unofficial name for a type of composite armor developed in the 1960s at the British tank research centre on Chobham Common, Surrey. It was designed to be particularly effective against shaped charges. Its elements remain a secret, but they are known to include ceramic tiles encased in metal mesh bonded to a backing plate with several elastic layers. Official names or different variants of Chobham include Burlington and Dorchester armor.

**Breacher vehicle** *(see above)*

**Christie suspension**
A revolutionary type of tank suspension designed by American engineer J. Walter Christie in 1928. Each wheel was given its own suspension spring and an unprecedented freedom of vertical movement, thus enabling the vehicle to move at high speed over rough ground. Early versions had powered road wheels and could be driven without tracks.

**Coaxial machine gun**
A machine gun mounted on the same axis as a vehicle's main gun. It is aimed using the same sights, and can be used if the main gun's force is deemed excessive or inappropriate.

**Column**
A formation of tanks arranged one in front of another.

**Combat engineer vehicle**
An AFV used to transport combat engineers around the battlefield, often equipped with mine-breaching devices such as a bulldozer's blade.

**Combat weight**
The total mass of a tank when fully equipped for the battlefield.

**Command vehicle**
A vehicle containing the facilities a commander needs to lead his unit. This can include multiple radios, map boards, and desk space for aides and staff officers.

**Commander**
The tank crewman responsible for commanding the tank. Depending on his seniority he may also be in command of other tanks and supporting arms.

**Company**
A military unit, normally equivalent in size to the squadron and consisting of around 150 soldiers or 14–18 tanks. "Company" was traditionally an infantry term.

**Composite armor**
A type of vehicle armor composed of different layers of material, such as metals, plastics, and ceramics.

**Corps**
A military unit, usually made up of several divisions, with a strength of 50,000 soldiers or more.

**Counterinsurgency**
Military operations aimed at defeating an enemy that does not operate as a distinct military force. The objective of counterinsurgency is generally political control and securing civilian suport, rather than military victory. Counterinsurgency vehicles are usually armored against mines or IEDs, and are often wheeled to appear less threatening.

**Cruiser tank**
Also called the cavalry tank or fast tank, the cruiser tank was a British concept developed in the interwar period. Light and fast, it was intended to make rapid advances after a breakthrough.

**Cupola**
A mini turret situated atop the main turret, giving the commander a better view of the battlefield.

**Deep battle**
A tactical doctrine developed in the interwar period—notably by Mikhail Tukhachevsky in the Soviet Union—that emphasized attacking the enemy throughout the depth of their positions rather than at the front line only. The intention was to quickly break through and destroy vital support facilities such as command units and supply dumps, preventing front-line forces from continuing to fight.

**Depleted uranium**
An extremely dense material used both in tank armor and in armor-piercing projectiles.

**Depression**
The extent to which a tank's main gun can be lowered beneath the horizontal. This ability is particularly important when the tank is behind the crest of a hill, with its hull pointing upward. Depression is the opposite of elevation.

**Diesel**
A liquid fuel that ignites when compressed.

**Direct fire**
Fire aimed at a target that can be seen by the gunner. Direct fire is the opposite of indirect fire.

**Ditching**
A tank or armored vehicle becoming stuck in a trench or other depression.

**Division**
A military unit, usually made up of a number of brigades. Containing their own logistical units, divisions are generally the smallest units capable of independent operations on the battlefield. Their strength is usually around 20,000 men.

**Driver**
The tank crewman responsible for driving the vehicle.

**Echelon**
A formation of tanks arranged diagonally. Following vehicles are either positioned to the rear and right (right cchelon) or left (left echelon) of the leader.

**Electronic Countermeasures (ECM)**
Electronic devices used to disrupt and deceive enemy detection, communication, or signaling systems. Their functions include making targets invisible to sensors, jamming communications, and preventing the activation of roadside bombs.

**Elevation**
The extent to which a tank's main gun can be raised above the horizontal; the greater the angle, the greater the range. Elevation is the opposite of depression.

**Enfilade**
Gunfire aimed along an enemy position from end to end. In World War I, trenches were vulnerable to such attack, especially from tanks, and so were dug in a zigzag fashion.

**Explosive Reactive Armor (ERA)**
See *Reactive armor*.

**Firing port**
A port on the side of an IFV that enables infantry to bring small arms fire to bear without leaving the vehicle.

**Flame tank**
A type of tank equipped with a flamethrower, usually used in specialized operations, particularly attacks on fortifications.

**Flanking maneuver**
The movement of an armed force around the side, or flank, of an enemy force to gain tactical advantage.

**Fume extractor**
A vent on a gun barrel that prevents poisonous fumes from a fired round from leaking back into the crew compartment. It uses the changes in pressure in the barrel to force the fumes out of the muzzle.

**Gasoline**
Processed oil that is used as a fuel in internal combustion engines.

**Glacis plate**
The sloped, front-most section of the hull of a tank. Its angle helps deflect projectiles, and presents a greater thickness of armor for a projectile striking it horizontally to pass through.

**Gradient**
The degree of slope up which a tank can travel.

**Grousers**
Studded or treaded extensions that are added to a tank's tracks to give it greater traction on loose materials such as soil or snow.

**Guided munition**
Unlike a bullet, which follows a trajectory determined by gravity and its propellant charge only, the flight path of a guided munition can be altered.

**Gunsight**
An optical device used by gunners to aim with greater accuracy. Telescopic sights for tanks were adopted before World War II.

**Gunner**
The tank crewman responsible for aiming (or "laying") and firing the main gun.

**Half-track**
A vehicle with conventional wheels at the front for steering, and a caterpillar track at the rear for propulsion. The design fuses the cross-country capabilities of a tank with the handling of a road vehicle.

**Heavy tank**
A class of slow but heavily armored tanks designed for infantry support. The very first tanks of World War I were of this class, and became known as "heavies" as lighter, faster, more maneuverable tanks were introduced. Heavy tanks were usually more heavily armed and armored, but slower than other vehicles.

**High Explosive (HE)**
A type of ammunition that uses explosive blast to affect the target. Types include HE-Frag, HEAT, HESH, and APHE. Modern HE rounds are less effective against tanks, but can still damage or destroy lighter vehicles and are highly effective against unprotected infantry.

**High Explosive Fragmentation (HE-Frag)**
HE-Frag uses explosive blast and fragmentation to destroy its target. It is most effective against lightly armored targets.

**High Explosive Antitank (HEAT)**
A HEAT round uses a shaped-charge warhead to form a high-speed jet of molten metal that penetrates armor. Because they do not depend on velocity for their effect, HEAT warheads are commonly affixed to slower munitions, such as missiles and mines.

**High Explosive Squash Head (HESH)**
A HESH round is a munition used against armored vehicles and fortifications. On impact, the plastic explosive at the head of the round squashes against the surface of the target before exploding. This transmits a shock wave through the armor, causing fragments of steel to detach from the tank interior at high velocity, potentially killing crew members.

**High Velocity Armor-Piercing (HVAP)**
An armor-piercing round that has a high-density core surrounded by lighter material. The latter reduces weight, enabling higher velocity and greater armor penetration.

**Hobart's Funnies**
A number of tank variants used by the British 79th Armored Division during World War II. These included tanks modified to carry bridges, mine ploughs, flails, a swimming tank, and engineer vehicles that could destroy fortifications or carry fascines to fill obstacles. They took their name from Major General Sir Percy Hobart, the commander of the division.

**Horsepower**
A unit of power equal to 550 ft-lb per second (750 watts) used to measure the output of an engine. The term was adopted in the 18th century by British engineer James Watt to compare the output of steam engines with the amount of work performed by a single draft horse.

**Horstmann suspension**
A type of suspension developed by British engineer Sidney Horstmann in 1922. Featuring coil springs, it was used on the Vickers Light, Centurion, and Chieftain tanks, among others.

**Hull**
The body of the tank beneath the turret.

**Hull-down / Hull-up**
When only the turret of a tank is visible above the crest of a hill or another obstacle it is said to be hull-down; when the entire body is visible it is said to be hull-up.

**Humvee**
The High Mobility Multipurpose Wheeled Vehicle (HMMWV) is a four-wheel drive military light truck that came of age during the First Gulf War.

**Hydropneumatic suspension**
A form of suspension that uses oil and pneumatic pressure to keep a vehicle level.

**Idler**
A nondriven end wheel of a tracked vehicle that serves to adjust track tension.

**Improvised Explosive Device (IED)**
A bomb constructed in an improvised manner rather than being designed for the purpose. IEDs can be made from chemicals such as fertilizer, or make use of adapted mines or artillery shells. They are also known as roadside bombs.

**Indirect fire**
Fire aimed at a target that cannot be seen by the gunner. It usually requires a separate forward observer to correct the aim. Indirect fire is the opposite of direct fire.

**Infantry Fighting Vehicle (IFV)**
A type of AFV used to carry infantry to the battlefield. Unlike APCs, IFVs are able to enter combat, possessing heavier armor and armament, which sometimes includes antitank weaponry, and very often firing ports that allow the infantry to fight from inside the vehicle.

**Infantry tank**
A British and French concept developed in the interwar period. Infantry tanks were slow but well-armored vehicles that were deployed in support of infantry on foot. Once infantry tanks had broken through enemy lines, faster cruiser or light tanks were expected to penetrate deep into enemy territory.

**Infrared**
A type of light radiation that allows the perception of heat signals, among other things. It is useful for night vision and thermal imaging.

**Kinetic-Energy (KE) projectile**
A type of munition that relies on its own mass and motion (i.e. kinetic energy) for its destructive power. KE projectiles do not explode. Armor-piercing rounds are examples of KE projectiles, as are ordinary bullets.

**L/x (Barrel length)**
The length of a gun barrel expressed in multiples of its caliber. For example, the 120mm L/55 gun has a barrel length of 22 ft (6.6 m) or 6,600mm (120 x 55).

**Landships committee**
A British committee established by Winston Churchill, First Lord of the Admiralty, in 1915. Its purpose was to develop armored fighting vehicles, or "landships," to break the stalemate on the Western Front. Its chief outcome was the invention of the tank.

**Laser range finder**
A means of calculating the range to a target by measuring the time taken for a laser pulse to be reflected off the target and return to the range finder. This has replaced previous methods of calculating range on AFVs.

**Leaf-spring suspension**
One of the oldest forms of suspension, leaf springs are still common on military vehicles. They are made of slender arcs of steel that are stacked and bound together, forming a springing mount on which a single axle rests.

**Light reconnaissance car**
A series of vehicles used by the British Reconnaissance Corps during World War II. Lightly armed and armored, they were based on commercial vehicle chassis.

**Light tank**
A thinly armored tank designed for rapid movement rather than aggressive combat power. Today, its role is largely confined to reconnaissance.

**Line**
A formation of tanks arranged side by side.

**Loader**
The tank crewman responsible for loading the main gun.

**Machine gun**
A weapon that uses the gas or recoil from its fired projectile to cycle its action and so give continuous automatic fire.

**Main Battle Tank (MBT)**
Otherwise known as a universal tank. MBTs are the mainstay of modern tank units, combining elements of their medium and heavy predecessors.

**Main gun**
A tank's primary armament. Today, main guns are capable of firing kinetic-energy projectiles, high-explosive rounds, and even guided missiles.

**Mantlet**
A plate of armor that protects the area where a tank's main gun projects from its turret. In order to fire the gun, this section cannot be concealed from the enemy, so it is often the thickest part of a tank's armor.

**Materiel**
All the hardware needed by a military force to complete a specific mission—from ammunition to fighter jets, if needed.

**Medium tank**
A class of tank that is almost as mobile as a light tank and almost as protected as a heavy tank. Medium tanks came of age during World War II, but first saw service in World War I in the form of the British Medium Mark A "Whippet."

**Military logistics**
The art of planning and executing the movement of military forces, from directing men and materiel to battlefields to setting up and maintaining supply chains.

**Mine Resistant Ambush Protected (MRAP)**
A class of vehicle designed as a response to the increasing use of IEDs in Iraq after the invasion of 2003. MRAPs use design features such as V-shaped hulls to protect against IED blasts, and are armored against direct fire attack.

**Molotov cocktail**
Originally an antitank weapon deployed by the Finns against the Soviets during World War II. It was little more than a bottle filled with gasoline with a lighted wick that was dropped into the hatches of Soviet tanks—a "gift" for the Soviet Foreign Minister Vyacheslav Molotov.

**Multibank engine**
An engine with a high number of cylinders arranged in multiple lines or banks.

**Muzzle**
The forward, open end of a gun's barrel.

**Muzzle brake**
A device attached to the end of the barrel of a main gun to vent propellant gases and reduce recoil.

**NATO**
An acronym for the North Atlantic Treaty Organization, an international alliance of countries from North America and Western Europe originally formed in 1949 in opposition to the Soviet Union.

**NBC**
A term used to refer to Nuclear, Chemical, and Biological weaponry (commonly known as Weapons of Mass Destruction). The effects these weapons can have on a target require the use of specialized protection systems if personnel and equipment are to operate in areas where they have been used.

**Optical range finder**
A system that uses the operator's eyesight and trigonometry to determine the distance to a target. Two prisms a known distance apart reflect images of the target into the eyepiece of the operator, who then adjusts the angle of the prisms until the two images appear as one. This angle is used to calculate the distance.

**Ordnance**
Weapons and ammunition, specifically artillery.

**Organic**
An organic military unit is an integral part of a larger formation, rather than being temporarily assigned to it for a specific mission.

**Paraffin**
A combustible hydrocarbon fuel, a derivation of which, JP8, is used to power several NATO tanks.

**Platoon**
A military unit, normally equivalent in size to the troop and consisting of around 30 soldiers or 3–5 tanks.

**Pounder**
The system used to identify British artillery and antitank rounds based on the weight of the projectile in pounds (1 lb = 0.454 kg). It fell out of use after World War II, and was replaced by caliber.

**Radial engine**
An engine configuration in which the cylinders are positioned in a circle, "radiating" out from a central crankcase.

**Rate of fire**
The number of rounds that can be fired by a given weapon, usually expressed in rounds per minute.

**Reactive armor**
A type of appliqué armor that reacts to incoming enemy projectiles to reduce the damage done to the vehicle. The most common type is Explosive Reactive Armor, which explodes when hit by a penetrating weapon, damaging the latter and dissipating its energy.

**Regiment**
A military unit whose nature varies depending on its country of origin. Some nations use the term for an operational unit of brigade or battalion size, others for a ceremonial or administrative unit that does not fight on the battlefield.

**Return rollers**
Small wheels located above a tank's road wheels that keep the top of the caterpillar track running straight between the drive sprocket and the idler.

**Rifling**
An arrangement of spiral grooves within the barrel of a gun that imparts rotary motion to the fired projectile, which then travels through the air with greater accuracy.

**Road wheels**
The main wheels that rotate within the tracks of a tank. They are unpowered and serve only to distribute the tank's weight.

**Rocket-Propelled Grenade (RPG)**
An infantry antitank rocket launcher, originally made by the Soviet Union. A large number of different models of RPG have been manufactured since the late 1940s, the most common being the RPG-7.

**Scout car**
A lightly armed and armored wheeled vehicle generally used for reconnaissance.

**Scouting**
The action of gathering information about an area or the disposition of enemy forces. Also known as reconnaissance.

**Self-propelled gun**
A mobile artillery piece, such as a howitzer, that is mounted on a motorized wheeled or tracked chassis.

**Semiautomatic**
A gun that will only fire one round when the trigger is pulled, but loads the next round automatically.

**Shaped charge**
An explosive charge shaped in order to focus the energy of its explosion in a particular direction, which enhances its effect. Shaped charges are used in HEAT rounds.

**Shrapnel shell**
An antipersonnel artillery munition, shrapnel shells were designed to explode in midair over enemy positions, showering the area with lethal balls of steel or lead. Since the end of World War I, shrapnel has been superseded by high-explosive shells, which produce both explosive blast and fragments on detonation.

**Sloped armor**
Armor that is sloped to give greater protection to a tank's hull or turret. The angled surface helps deflect projectiles,

and presents a greater thickness of armor for a projectile striking it horizontally to pass through.

**Smoke**
A means of hiding the movements of a vehicle or unit. Smoke can be dispensed by injecting fuel into a tank's exhaust, activating a vehicle's smoke grenade launchers, or firing a shell from a tank's main gun. Modern smoke works in both the visible and infrared ends of the spectrum.

**Smoothbore**
A cannon designed to fire fin-stabilized rather than rotating projectiles, and so lacking interior rifling. Because they do not spin, the projectiles travel faster and so have greater armor penetration.

**Spalling**
Flakes broken off armor plate after the impact of a projectile. Some tanks have spall liners as a defense against high-velocity spalling.

**Sponson**
A gun platform projecting from the side of a tank.

**Spotting gun**
A small-caliber rifle or machine gun used as a ranging device for tank guns. They were used as an alternative to optical range finders until the development of the laser range finder.

**Spring**
The part of a suspension system that both absorbs the upward movement of the wheels when on rough terrain and keeps the wheels pressed onto the ground.

**Sprocket**
A cogged wheel that meshes with a tank's track to give the track linear motion. Sprockets are usually the only powered wheels on an AFV.

**Squadron**
A military unit, normally equivalent in size to the company and consisting of around 150 soldiers or 14–18 tanks. "Squadron" was traditionally a cavalry term. In the US Army it is the equivalent of a battalion.

**Stalemate**
A tactical impasse on a battlefield. The stalemate between the Allied and German armies on the Somme during World War I was caused by both sides being dug in and defended by machine guns and artillery. The tank was developed by the British specifically to end this stalemate.

**Strategy**
The overall plan of a campaign. Strategic objectives determine the tactical deployment of troops and materiel.

**Super-heavy tank**
A tank of a size and mass greater than that of a heavy tank.

**Tactics**
The means by which particular military objectives are met, as opposed to strategy, which concerns the overall aim of a campaign.

**Tandem warhead**
A feature of recent ATGMs, intended to defeat ERA. The first warhead detonates and triggers the ERA, the second follows a short period later and is able to penetrate the vehicle's armor, which no longer benefits from the ERA.

**Tank**
An AFV designed for front-line combat, featuring strong armor, heavy firepower, and tracks for battlefield maneuverability. Its name derives from the secrecy under which it was conceived—engineers were told that they were working on a new design of water tank.

**Tank destroyer**
An AFV armed with a direct-fire gun or missile launcher designed specifically to target enemy armored vehicles.

**Tankette**
A tracked AFV resembling a small tank, designed for scouting and light infantry support. Tankettes saw wide use during the interwar years and World War II, particularly in the Imperial Japanese Army, but have since ceased production because they were found to be too lightly armed and armored to survive on the battlefield.

**Thermal sleeve**
An insulating device that is placed around the barrel of a main gun. It ensures that the temperature of the barrel remains even: differences can cause the metal to expand, and so affect accuracy.

**Titanium**
A strong but relatively lightweight metal used in tank armor.

**Top attack**
A method used by modern ATGMs to overcome increasingly capable composite armor. The missile flies over the tank and detonates above it. This directs the warhead at the thinner roof armor.

**Torsion bar**
A suspension system that uses a twisting metal bar to cushion the vehicle's movement.

**Tracer**
A bullet with a pyrotechnic charge in its base. The charge is ignited when the round is fired and shows its trajectory. Tracer helps gunners to direct their fire, especially in circumstances where sights would be less effective, such as in darkness.

**Track**
The continuous belt running through or around the geared sprocket wheel, idler, road wheels, and return rollers of a tank.

**Transmission**
The electrical, hydraulic, or mechanical means by which power from an engine is converted into the rotary motion of a vehicle's wheels or tracks.

**Traverse**
The ability of a gun or turret to rotate from the centerline of its mount. A fully revolving gun or turret is said to have a traverse of 360 degrees.

**Trench**
The field fortification that the tank was designed to overcome. During World War I, strong networks of continuous trenches protected by machine-guns and artillery created a stalemate on the Western Front, and only tanks proved capable of breaking it.

**Trim vane**
A hinged metal screen that can be extended before a vehicle enters a body of water. This reduces the risk of it being swamped by large amounts of water washing over the front.

**Troop**
A military unit, normally equivalent in size to the platoon and consisting of around 30 soldiers or 3–5 tanks. Troop was traditionally a cavalry term. In the US Army it is the equivalent of a company.

**Turret**
The rotating top section of a tank, accommodating the main gun and most of the crew, usually the commander, gunner, and loader. The first turreted tank was the Renault FT of 1917.

**V-shaped hull**
A design feature that angles the underside of a vehicle upward. When viewed from the front or rear the lower hull is shaped like a V. This deflects a mine blast outwards away from the vehicle, rather than upwards into the crew compartment.

**V-twin engine**
An engine design with two banks of cylinders arranged in a "V" formation.

**Volute-spring suspension**
A type of tank suspension featuring a compression spring shaped like a cone, or volute, mounted in a road-wheel bogie for a pair of wheels. Commonly used in US and Italian tanks during World War II, it proved more effective than contemporary spring, leaf-spring, or torsion-bar suspension systems.

**Warhead**
The part of a projectile that contains the explosive. Other parts can include a guidance system or a fuse.

**Warsaw Pact**
A defense treaty between the Soviet Union and the Soviet satellite states of Bulgaria, Czechoslovakia, East Germany, Hungary, Poland, Romania, and Albania. Signed in 1955, the treaty established a counterweight to NATO.

**Wedge**
A formation of tanks arranged in a triangular shape.

# Index

# Acknowledgments

**PICTURE CREDITS**
The publisher would like to thank the following for their kind permission to reproduce their photographs:
(Key: a-above; b-below/bottom; c-centre; f-far; l-left; r-right; t-top)

**12 Alamy Stock Photo:** INTERFOTO. **13 akg images:** arkivi (ca). **Alamy Stock Photo:** Universal Art Archive (br). **14 AF Fotografie. Alamy Stock Photo:** Chronicle (clb); Private Collection / AF Eisenbahn Archiv (cla). **14-15 Bovington Tank Museum. 15 Bovington Tank Museum. Dorling Kindersley:** Gary Ombler / Paul Rackham (c). **16-17 Getty Images:** De Agostini. **18 Bovington Tank Museum. 19 Dorling Kindersley:** Gary Ombler / Board of the Trustees of the Royal Armouries (tl). **22-23 Dorling Kindersley:** The Tank Museum / Gary Ombler (b). **22 Bovington Tank Museum. Olivier Cabaret:** Le Musée des Blindés de Saumur (cl). **23 Bovington Tank Museum. Dorling Kindersley:** The Tank Museum / Gary Ombler (cla). **24 akg-images:** (tl). **28 Alamy Stock Photo:** Chronicle (bl). **Bovington Tank Museum. Richard Pullen:** (cl). **29 Alamy Stock Photo:** AF Fotografie (fcla); Paris Pearce (cla). **Bovington Tank Museum. Richard Pullen. 30-31 Bovington Tank Museum. 32 Bovington Tank Museum. 33 Alamy Stock Photo:** Chronicle (cr). **Bovington Tank Museum. Narayan Sengupta:** (cl). **34 Alamy Stock Photo:** Sunpix travel (br). **Rex by Shutterstock:** Roger Viollet (tr). **35 akg-images:** ullstein bild (crb). **Bovington Tank Museum. 38 Alamy Stock Photo:** World History Archive. **39 Bridgeman Images:** Private Collection / Peter Newark Military Pictures (tc). **Getty Images:** Ullstein Bild (br). **40 AF Fotografie. Alamy Stock Photo:** Universal Art Archive (bl). **Bovington Tank Museum. Gunnar Österlund:** (tr). **41 Alamy Stock Photo:** Uber Bilder (cl). **Paul Appleyard. Massimo Foti. Chris Neel:** (tr). **42-43 Bovington Tank Museum. 44 Paul Appleyard. Dorling Kindersley:** Gary Ombler / The Tank Museum (c). **Militaryfoto. sk:** Andrej Jerguš (tl). **45 Alamy Stock Photo:** PAF (cla). **Arsenalen, The Swedish Tank Museum:** (cra). **Bovington Tank Museum. 46 Bovington Tank Museum. Alex Malev:** (bl). **47 Cody Images:** (cr). **Library of Congress, Washington, D.C.:** Harris & Ewing, Inc. 1955. (tr). **48 Bovington Tank Museum. 52 AF Fotografie. Library of Congress, Washington, D.C.:** Prints and Photographs Division (bl, fcr). **53 AF Fotografie. Alamy**

**Stock Photo:** Lebrecht Music and Arts Photo Library (tl); World History Archive (b). **54-55 Getty Images:** John Phillips / The LIFE Picture Collection. **56 Cody Images. 57 Alamy Stock Photo:** ITAR-TASS Photo Agency (cra); Alexander Perepelitsyn (tl). **Cody Images. Dorling Kindersley:** Gary Ombler / The Tank Museum (br). **58 Bovington Tank Museum. 59 National Army Museum:** (cr). **64 AF Fotografie. 65 akg-images:** Sputnik (br). **Alamy Stock Photo:** Universal Art Archive (c). **66 Dorling Kindersley:** Gary Ombler / The Tank Museum (cl). **Massimo Foti. 66-67 Dorling Kindersley:** Gary Ombler / The Tank Museum (b). **67 Paul Appleyard. Bovington Tank Museum. Massimo Foti. 68-69 Bovington Tank Museum. 70 Dorling Kindersley:** Gary Ombler / The Tank Museum (cl). **Thomas Quine:** (tr). **70-71 Dorling Kindersley:** Gary Ombler / The Tank Museum. **72 Dorling Kindersley:** Gary Ombler / The Tank Museum (cra, cl, br). **Dreamstime.com:** Ryzhov Sergey (cla). **73 Dorling Kindersley:** Steve Lamonby, The War and Peace Show (cb); Gary Ombler / The Tank Museum (ca, br). **74 Alamy Stock Photo:** Michael Cremin (tl). **75 Bovington Tank Museum. 78-79 Getty Images:** Planet News Archive. **80 Bovington Tank Museum. 85 Dorling Kindersley:** Gary Ombler / The Tank Museum (cl). **86 Getty Images:** Paul Popper / Popperfoto (tl). **90-91 Bovington Tank Museum. 92 Bovington Tank Museum. 93 Bovington Tank Museum. Dorling Kindersley:** Gary Ombler / The Tank Museum (ca). **94 Paul Appleyard. Bovington Tank Museum. 95 Dorling Kindersley:** Gary Ombler / The Tank Museum (t, b); Gary Ombler, I. Galliers, The War and Peace Show (cl). **Alf van Beem:** (cr). **96 Dorling Kindersley:** Gary Ombler / The Tank Museum (t). **Dreamstime.com:** Sergey Zavyalov (cl). **97 123RF.com:** Vitali Burlakou (br); Yí Yuán Xînjû (cb). **Alamy Stock Photo:** Alexander Blinov (tr). **Dreamstime.com:** Ryzhov Sergey (cla). **98 Bovington Tank Museum. 102 Bovington Tank Museum:** (c). **Getty Images:** Serge Plantureux (bl); SVF2 (tl); TASS (cr). **103 Alamy Stock Photo:** C. and M. History Pictures (cla); Zoonar GmbH (ca). **Getty Images:** Sovfoto (b). **104-105 Bovington Tank Museum. 106 Alamy Stock Photo:** Martin Bennett (cr). **Massimo Foti. Leo van Midden:** (tl). **107 Dorling Kindersley:** Gary Ombler / The Tank Museum (t). **Massimo Foti. 108 Ryan Keene:** (tr). **Ministerstwo**

**Obrony Narodowej:** (cr). **109 Dorling Kindersley:** Gary Ombler / The Tank Museum (tl, c). **Massimo Foti. 109-109 Dorling Kindersley:** Gary Ombler / The Tank Museum (b). **110 Dorling Kindersley:** Gary Ombler / The Tank Museum (c). **Dreamstime.com:** Sergey Zavyalov (bc). **111 Paul Appleyard. Dorling Kindersley:** Gary Ombler / The Tank Museum (b). **Dreamstime.com:** Viktor Onyshchenko (c). **Landship Photography:** (crb). **112 Bovington Tank Museum. 113 Wikipedia:** Yí Yuán Xînjû **(tc). 116 Bovington Tank Museum. 117 Paul Appleyard. Bovington Tank Museum. Dorling Kindersley:** Gary Ombler / The Tank Museum (cr). **Imperial War Museum. 118 AF Fotografie. Paul Appleyard. Bovington Tank Museum. 119 Paul Appleyard. Narayan Sengupta. 120-121 Getty Images:** Popperfoto. **122 Alamy Stock Photo:** NPC Collectiom (tr). **Dorling Kindersley:** Gary Ombler / The Tank Museum (cl). **122-123 Dorling Kindersley:** Gary Ombler / The Tank Museum (b). **123 Paul Appleyard:** (cb). **Dorling Kindersley:** Ted Bear, The War and Peace Show (tl). **Dreamstime.com:** Sever180 (br). **124 Dorling Kindersley:** Jez Marren, The War and Peace Show (cl). **124-125 Dorling Kindersley:** George Paice, The War and Peace Show. **125 Dorling Kindersley:** Gary Ombler, The War and Peace Show; Gary Ombler, The War and Peace Show (cr). **128 Alamy Stock Photo:** Penrodas Collection. **129 Bridgeman Images:** Private Collection (cl). **Getty Images:** Bettmann (cr). **130 David Busfield:** (tr). **Dreamstime. com:** Sergey Krivoruchko (bl). **131 Paul Appleyard. Dorling Kindersley:** Gary Ombler / The Tank Museum (cl). **Bron Pancema:** (cr). **132 Dorling Kindersley:** Gary Ombler / The Tank Museum (clb). **Dreamstime. com:** Yykkaa (br). **Vitaly Kuzmin:** (cr). **TMA:** (tr). **133 Paul Appleyard. Wikipedia:** Yí Yuán Xînjû **(tc). 134 Bovington Tank Museum. 138-139 AF Fotografie. 140 Image courtesy of General Dynamics Ordnance and Tactical Systems:** (tl). **Getty Images:** Taro Yamasaki (bl). **141 Alamy Stock Photo:** XM Collection (b). **Image courtesy of General Dynamics Ordnance and Tactical Systems. Ministry of Defence Picture Library:** (cla). **142 Bovington Tank Museum. 146 Bovington Tank Museum. iStockphoto. com:** DaveAlan (cl). **146-147 Paul Appleyard. 147 Bovington Tank Museum. Dorling Kindersley:** Gary

Ombler / The Tank Museum (tr); Gary Ombler / The Tank Museum (cl); Gary Ombler / The Tank Museum (b). **148 Ryan Keene. 149 Dorling Kindersley:** Gary Ombler / The Tank Museum (b). **Ryan Keene. 154 Alamy Stock Photo:** Panzermeister (tc). **DM brothers:** (cl). **Massimo Foti. Wikipedia:** PD-Self / Los688 / Japan Ground Self-Defense Force (bl). **155 Alamy Stock Photo:** Panzermeister (tr). **Paul Appleyard. Vinayak Hedge:** (cr). **156 Alamy Stock Photo:** CNP Collection (cla). **Massimo Foti. Wikipedia:** Max Smith (cl). **157 Bovington Tank Museum. TMA. Wikipedia:** Bukvoed (br). **158 Paul Appleyard. Daniel de Cristo:** (tr). **William Morris:** (cr). **158-159 Dorling Kindersley:** Nick Hurt, Tanks, Trucks and Firepower Show. **159 Alamy Stock Photo:** Transcol (cla). **Vitaly Kuzmin. 160 Paul Appleyard. 161 Alamy Stock Photo:** Universal Images Group North America LLC / DeAgostini (cr). **Massimo Foti. Getty Images:** William F. Campbell / The LIFE Images Collection (cl). **166-167 Bridgeman Images:** Everett Collection. **168 Paul Appleyard. Bovington Tank Museum. 169 Alamy Stock Photo:** NPC Collection (tr). **Dorling Kindersley:** Richard Morris, Tanks, Trucks and Firepower Show (cr). **Massimo Foti. 170 Marty4650:** (cla). **Reaxel 270862:** (cl). **Toadman's Tank Pictures:** Chris Hughes (bl). **171 Alamy Stock Photo:** CPC Collection (tl); PAF (c). **Paul Appleyard. 172 Paul Appleyard. Dorling Kindersley:** Gary Ombler / The Combined Military Services Museum (CMSM). **Massimo Foti. 173 Alamy Stock Photo:** CPC Collection (ca). **Jim Maurer:** (t). **Wikipedia:** Chamal Pathirana (br). **174-175 Alamy Stock Photo:** Dino Fracchia. **176 Alamy Stock Photo:** Iuliia Mashkova (br); Zoonar GmbH (c). **177 Alamy Stock Photo:** PAF (tr); pzAxe (br). **Massimo Foti:** (tl). **Nederlands Instituut voor Militaire Historie:** (c). **178 Alamy Stock Photo:** dpa picture alliance archive / Carl Schulze (tr). **Vitaly Kuzmin. 179 Alamy Stock Photo:** Hideo Kurihara (tr); Alexey Zarubin (cl). **Vitaly Kuzmin. 180 Alamy Stock Photo:** Zoonar GmbH (clb). **181 123RF.com:** Mikhail Mandrygin (tl). **Bovington Tank Museum. Dreamstime. com:** Sever180 (br). **RM Sothebys:** (bl). **182 Alamy Stock Photo:** Grobler du Preez (cl). **Jose Luis Bermudez de Castro:** (cr). **Raul Naranjo:** (bc). **Dirk Vorderstrasse:** (cla). **183 Army Recognition Group:** (bl). **Dorling Kindersley:** Bruce Orme, Tanks, Trucks and Firepower Show (cl). **Getty**

Images: Federico Parra / Stringer (crb). **184-185 Getty Images:** Patrick Baz. **186 Paul Appleyard. Massimo Foti. 187 Bovington Tank Museum. Dorling Kindersley:** Gary Ombler, The War and Peace Show (crb). **188 Dorling Kindersley:** Andrew Baker, The War and Peace Show (cla); Brian Piper, Tanks, Trucks and Firepower Show (tr); Gary Ombler, Tanks, Trucks and Firepower Show (cr); Mick Browning, Tanks, Trucks and Firepower Show (clb); Gary Ombler, Tanks Trucks and Firepower Show (bl). **189 Alamy Stock Photo:** Ian Marlow (cra). **Dorling Kindersley:** Andrew Baker, Tanks, Trucks and Firepower Show (cla). **Raul Naranjo. 190-191 Getty Images:** Romeo Gacad. **192 Bovington Tank Museum. 197 Getty Images:** Shane Cuomo / AFP (cr). **198 Alamy Stock Photo:** Stocktrek Images, Inc.. **199 Getty Images:** David Silverman (cl). **200 Bovington Tank Museum. The Dunsfold Collection:** (cl). **Imperial War Museum:** (tr). **201 Alamy Stock Photo:** Grobler du Preez (tr); Grobler du Preez (b). **Witham Specialist Vehicles Ltd:** Ministry of Defence, UK (tl). **202 Alamy Stock Photo:** CPC Collection (br). **Courtesy of U.S. Army:** (tr). **203 Alamy Stock Photo:** Sueddeutsche Zeitung Photo (tl). **Getty Images:** Stocktrek Images (cr). **Ministry of Defence Picture Library: © Crown Copyright 2013 / Photographer: Cpl Si Longworth RLC** (tr, br). **204 akg-images:** Africa Media Online / South Photos / John Liebenberg (tl). **205 Christo R. Wolmarans:** (br). **208-209 Alamy Stock Photo:** epa european pressphoto agency b.v.. **210 Alamy Stock Photo:** Dino Fracchia (br). **Thomas Tutchek:** (clb). **Wikipedia:** Jorchr (c). **211 Alamy Stock Photo:** ITAR-TASS Photo

Agency (clb). **Bovington Tank Museum. Zachi Evenor:** MathKnight (cra). **Katzennase:** (cl). **Ministry of Defence Picture Library: © Crown Copyright / Andrew Linnett (br). 212 Alamy Stock Photo:** Dino Fracchia (clb); Hideo Kurihara (cr). **Michael J Barritt:** (tr). **Kjetil Ree:** (cl). **213 Alamy Stock Photo:** LOU Collection (tr); Universal Images Group North America LLC / DeAgostini (cl). **Wikipedia:** Outisnn (b). **214 Alamy Stock Photo:** Reuters / Morris Mac Matzen (tr); Stocktrek Images, Inc. (bl). **Wikipedia:** Ex13 (cla). **214-215 Wikipedia:** Selvejp (bc). **215 123RF.com:** Jordan Tan (br). **Alamy Stock Photo:** Reuters / Fabian Bimmer (tl). **Wikipedia:** Kaminski (cr). **216-217 Getty Images:** Chung Sung-Jun. **218 Image courtesy of General Dynamics Ordnance and Tactical Systems. Wikipedia:** Megapixie (cl). **219 Dreamstime.com:** Oleg Doroshin (tc). **Vitaly Kuzmin. PIBWL:** (cl). **Wikipedia:** Kaminski (cr). **220 Combat Camera Europe:** (c). **Getty Images:** Aamir Qureshi / Stringer (br). **Wikipedia:** Max Smith (tr). **221 Alamy Stock Photo:** Xinhua (cl). **Zachi Evenor. Otokar:** (br). **Wikipedia:** PD-Self (cr). **222 Alamy Stock Photo:** RGB Ventures / Superstock (tl). **USAASC:** photo by SGT Richard Wrigley, 2nd Armored Brigade Combat Team, 3rd Infantry Division Public Affairs (c). **222-223 USAASC:** (c). **223 Image courtesy of General Dynamics Ordnance and Tactical Systems. 224-225 Fort Benning, GA:** John D. Helms. **226 BAE Systems Land:** (cra). **Getty Images:** Bloomberg (tl); Bloomberg (bl). **227 BAE Systems Land. 228-229 Getty Images:** Sergei Bobylev. **237**

**Bovington Tank Museum. Dorling Kindersley:** Gary Ombler / Courtesy of the Royal Artillery Historical Trust (br); Gary Ombler / The Combined Military Services Museum (CMSM) (tl). **238 Dorling Kindersley:** Gary Ombler / The Tank Museum (clb). **Zachi Evenor:** (bl). **239 OBRUM:** (br). **240 Dorling Kindersley:** Second Guards Rifles Division / Gary Ombler (bc). **241 Bovington Tank Museum. 242 Dorling Kindersley:** Gary Ombler / Stuart Beeny (cla); Gary Ombler / Vietnam Rolling Thunder (crb); Gary Ombler / Pitt Rivers Museum, University of Oxford (clb); Gary Ombler / The Combined Military Services Museum (CMSM) (ca); Gary Ombler / Board of Trustees of the Royal Armouries (cl). **243 Daniel de Cristo:** (cr). **Dorling Kindersley:** Gary Ombler, Tanks, Trucks and Firepower Show (b)

**Wikipedia Creative Commons images:** https://creativecommons.org/licenses/by/4.0/legalcode

All other images © Dorling Kindersley For further information see: **www.dkimages.com**

The publisher would like to thank the following people for their help in making the book:

Additional writing: Roger Ford

Additional fact checking: Bruce Newsome, PhD

Design and photoshoot assistance: Saffron Stocker

Translation and photoshoot assistance: Sonia Charbonnier

Editorial assistance: Kathryn Hennessy, Allie Collins

Index: Margaret McCormack

The publisher would like to thank the following museums, organizations, and inidividuals for their generosity in allowing us to photograph their vehicles:

Andrew Baker
Gordon McKenna
John Sanderson
Chris Till

**Norfolk Tank Museum:**
Stephen MacHaye

**Musée des Blindés, Saumur:**
Lieutenant-colonel Pierre Garnier de Labareyre, Adjudant-chef Arnaud Pompougnac

**Armoured Testing and Development Unit (ATDU), Bovington:** Staff Sergeant Dave Lincoln and team

**The Tank Museum**
The Tank Museum holds the biggest and best collection of tanks and military vehicles from around the world. Located in Bovington, Dorset, the home of British tank training since the First World War, the museum continues to be involved in tank crew training.

The Tank Museum
Bovington
Dorset, UK
BH20 6JG
www.tankmuseum.org
info@tankmuseum.org